Prais  rter®

With its detailed and organized approach, this book is a must read, showcasing all the current options open to you when planning a Disney wedding, bringing originality to your day, and putting you one step ahead of your wedding planner!

— Samantha Byrne, Owner of Disneymooner.com

If I had to sum up PassPorter's Disney Weddings & Honeymoons in two words, they would have to be life saving. This is the only wedding planner tailored exclusively to Disney weddings, and I would recommend it to anyone who is even considering getting married at Disney. The worksheets allowed me to organize all of my information, keep everything important in one place, and prepare me for things that I hadn't even considered! This book was a big factor in keeping the planning process fun and stress-free. Looking back on it, PassPorter's Disney Weddings & Honeymoons helped me so much with tackling all of my pre-wedding, post-wedding, and honeymoon stress that I might have to change my two descriptive words to marriage saving!

— Kendra Swaine in Ontario

The minute I started reading this book, I knew it was exactly what I was looking for. Planning a Disney wedding can be daunting, especially for an Escape bride with only phone planning sessions with Disney. This book told me exactly what my options were and gave me ideas for receptions and enhancements. It made my conversations with Disney much more productive, saved me a good deal of time, and is well worth the small investment.

— Judith Teague in Virginia

This book is priceless. Not only does it help you with Disney guidelines and ideas, but it also helps to convince people that your wedding is not going to be a cheesy affair!

— Rebecca Bennett, New South Wales, Australia

PassPorter's Disney Weddings & Honeymoons is full of information that helped us stay within our budget without sacrificing style as we planned our Disney wedding. We actually came in under budget with the help of this book.

— Sarah Small in Illinois

PassPorter's® Disney Weddings & Honeymoons
by Carrie Hayward

© 2010 by PassPorter Travel Press, an imprint of MediaMarx, Inc.
P.O. Box 3880, Ann Arbor, Michigan 48106 • 877-929-3273
Visit us on the World Wide Web at http://www.passporter.com

PassPorter® is a registered trademark of MediaMarx, Inc.
Photographs © MediaMarx, Inc., unless otherwise noted

PassPorter's® Disney Weddings & Honeymoons is not affiliated with, authorized or endorsed by, or in any way officially connected with The Walt Disney Company, Disney Enterprises, Inc., or any of their affiliates.

While every care has been taken to ensure the accuracy of the information in this book, the passage of time will always bring changes, and consequently, the publisher cannot accept responsibility for errors that may occur. The author and publisher of this book shall not be held liable for any information (valid or invalid) presented here and do not represent The Walt Disney Company.

Walt Disney World® is a registered trademark of The Walt Disney Company. This book makes reference to various Disney copyrighted characters, trademarks, marks, and registered marks owned by The Walt Disney Company, Disney Enterprises, Inc., and other trademark owners. The use in this guide of trademarked names and images is strictly for editorial purposes, and no commercial claim to their use, or suggestion of sponsorship or endorsement, is made by the author or publisher. Those words or terms that the author and publisher have reason to believe are trademarks are designated as such by the use of initial capitalization, where appropriate. However, no attempt has been made to identify or designate all words or terms to which trademark or other proprietary rights may exist. Nothing contained herein is intended to express a judgment on, or affect the validity of legal status of, any word or term as a trademark, service mark, or other proprietary mark.

PassPorter's® Disney Weddings & Honeymoons is edited by Carrie Hayward. The information presented is for entertainment purposes. Any stated opinions are the author's alone, unless otherwise noted, and do not represent The Walt Disney Company or anyone else. Materials submitted and credited by persons other than myself are used here with their permission, and any associated rights belong to them.

Any and all written messages, suggestions, ideas, or other information shared with the author in response to this guide shall be deemed and shall remain the property of PassPorter Travel Press.

Special Sales: PassPorter Travel Press publications are available at special discounts for bulk purchases for sales premiums or promotions. Special editions, including personalized covers and excerpts of existing guides, can be created in large quantities. For information, write to Special Sales, P.O. Box 3880, Ann Arbor, Michigan, 48106.

ISBN-10: 1-58771-088-9
ISBN-13: 978-1-58771-088-9

Version 2.0 (printed in October 2010)

PassPorter's
Disney
Weddings &
Honeymoons

Written & Edited by Carrie Hayward

PassPorter Travel Press

An imprint of MediaMarx, Inc.
P.O. Box 3880, Ann Arbor, MI 48106
877-WAYFARER
http://www.passporter.com

PassPorter Team

About the Author

PassPorter E-Book Editor Carrie Hayward has written and edited for newspapers, magazines, and the web for 15 years, but she's been a fan of Disneyland all her life. She and her husband, Patrick, try to visit the park monthly, and they especially enjoy date nights at Disneyland for swing dancing at Carnation Plaza Gardens. For their wedding, Carrie  and Patrick traveled across the country to Walt Disney World to realize their dream of being married inside a Disney park. Their ceremony was held at Epcot's Morocco Pavilion and followed by a Friendship Boat trip to Disney's BoardWalk Inn for a brunch reception at the Attic. They capped the day with a dessert party in Epcot's UK Pavilion during IllumiNations: Reflections of Earth. Carrie was inspired to write PassPorter's Disney Weddings & Honeymoons by the need for comprehensive, aggregated information on Disney's Fairy Tale Weddings and a desire to share the tips and tricks she accumulated while planning her wedding. She also wanted to create a bridal organizer with worksheets tailored exclusively to the needs of those planning weddings, vow renewals, and commitment ceremonies at Walt Disney World and on the Disney Cruise Line.

Acknowledgments

Thank you to the many people who contributed information and photos to make this book a definitive resource: Rosie Carrabia, Rob Cote, Ben Creighton, Joe DeMatei, Betsy Donahue, Vanessa Ferguson, Sarah Gennaro, Cathy Ingle, bradk, Kenny, Jennifer Kinney, Steven Lane, Lisa Leisher Reese, Cheryl Pendry, Photography By Taz (www.tazfoto.com), Jeff Rawls, Nathan and Jensey Root (www.rootweddings.com), Janet Simonsen, Laura Stickles, Kendra Swaine, and Marnie Urmaza. Thanks also go to the members of all the online communities devoted to discussing Disney's Fairy Tale Weddings for generously sharing their information and experiences in order to help others plan their celebrations. And heartfelt thanks to my friends, family, and especially Patrick for cheering me on as I worked on this, my first honest-to-gosh book, with an ISBN and everything!!

A special thanks to these very important folks behind the scenes at PassPorter Travel Press:

Publishers: Jennifer and Dave Marx
Online Coordinator and Newsletter Editor: Sara Varney

Table of Contents

Introduction
The Basics

Walt Disney World hosts more than 1,500 weddings each year, and it's one of the **most popular honeymoon destinations** in the world. Whether you're looking for a casual vow renewal on the beach, a designer wedding in the shadow of Cinderella Castle, or a honeymoon with a touch of pixie dust, this book is for you!

PassPorter's Disney Weddings & Honeymoons is both a guidebook and a bridal organizer tailored to the unique requirements of planning a wedding, vow renewal, or commitment ceremony at Walt Disney World or on the Disney Cruise Line. It will take you through the entire process, outline your options, offer valuable tips, organize your information, and help you **plan your event down to the last detail**—including what to say when the umpteenth person asks, "Is Mickey going to officiate?" (Answer: "No, that's Goofy's job!")

We've combined **everything you'll want to know** about prices, the contract, locations, food, decor, entertainment, photography, and transportation with worksheets that help you capture essential details, compare choices, and record your inspiration. We've also included a chapter full of ideas for making a Walt Disney World or Disney Cruise Line honeymoon extra special. And you can keep all your wedding and honeymoon information together by inserting pages from this guide in your Deluxe edition of *PassPorter's Walt Disney World* or *PassPorter's Disney Cruise Line and Its Ports of Call*.

We've tried to make the language in the book encompass weddings, vow renewals, and commitment ceremonies, but you'll probably still see the word *wedding* a lot. Don't despair—Disney's Fairy Tale Weddings department treats weddings, vow renewals, and commitment ceremonies interchangeably, so **the resources in this book apply universally**. Simply choose the sections and worksheets that apply to your celebration.

A note about prices: The information is this book is based on Disney's Fairy Tale Weddings' 2011 prices. However, the cost, variety, and availability of options can change at any time—with the exception of the Escape Collection and the Memories Collection, whose package prices are guaranteed through December 31, 2011 and March 31, 2012, respectively. Although we update this book frequently, only your Disney Wedding Consultant, Event Planner, or Coordinator will be able to tell you the exact pricing and availability of the options you want. Also, unless otherwise noted, prices in this book do not include 6.5% sales tax or 21% service fees.

Now let's get started planning your magical day at the **most magical place** on Earth!

A tussy mussy bouquet on display at Franck's Bridal Studio near the Wedding Pavilion

Choose Your Own Adventure

Disney's Fairy Tale Weddings offers **four event categories** at Walt Disney World: the Memories Collection, a pared-down elopement or vow renewal package; the Escape Collection, a ceremony-only package including basic amenities; the Wishes Collection, a completely customizable experience including ceremony and reception; and the Couture Collection, a quartet of luxury wedding decor packages designed by celebrity wedding planner David Tutera. A fifth option, the Cruise Collection, is a Disney Cruise Line package similar to the Escape Collection.

We've devoted a chapter to each collection, but the following pages contain **overviews** to get you started.

The Least Expensive Disney's Fairy Tale Wedding
So what is the cheapest way to have an official Disney wedding, commitment ceremony, or vow renewal? At just $1,991, the **Memories Collection** includes few amenities but is thousands of dollars less expensive than the more traditional Escape Collection. However, dollar for dollar, your best bet may be a **Cruise Collection** event. The least expensive package, a $2,500 onboard ceremony, includes most of the same amenities found in Walt Disney World's Escape wedding package for far less. And although the fee is in addition to the price of your cruise, if you pick the cheapest three-day cruise Disney offers, you'll get an entire wedding and honeymoon—including meals—for less than the price of just the Escape wedding package.

Memories Collection

Number of Guests
Up to 4, plus bride and groom

Cost
- $1,991 (tax & service charge included)

Minimum Expenditure
You are required to book a two-night stay at a Disney resort (not included in price).

Days
Saturday & Sunday

Times
9:00 am, 11:00 am, 1:00 pm, 3:00 pm

Locations
- Conch Key Marina at Disney's Grand Floridian Resort & Spa
- Narcoossee's Landing at Disney's Grand Floridian Resort & Spa
- Luau Beach at Disney's Polynesian Resort

Amenities
- Bride's bouquet
- Violinist for ceremony
- Limousine service for three consecutive hours
- Disney Photography for one hour, plus three 5x7-inch prints
- Services of a Disney Wedding Coordinator
- Personalized Facebook wedding web site

When to Book
All locations can be pencilled in at 18 months and booked between 6 months and 24 hours ahead, subject to availability.

Deposit
A $500 deposit is due within two weeks of booking. A deposit equal to one night's stay is due when you book the required two-night stay at a Disney resort.

© Nathan Root

Narcoossee's Landing (l) and Conch Key (r) at the Grand Floridian Resort & Spa

Escape Collection

Number of Guests
Up to 18, plus bride and groom

Cost
- $4,750 for outdoor locations (tax & service charge included)
- $5,750 for Disney's Wedding Pavilion (tax & service charge included)
- $5,895 for Canada Terrace at Epcot (tax & service charge included)

Minimum Expenditure
You are required to book a four-night stay at a Disney resort (not included in price). Holding a Saturday or Sunday ceremony or adding a private catered event to the package triggers a minimum expenditure of $7,500.

Days
Monday–Sunday

Times
Resort Locations: 10:00 am, 12:00 pm, 2:30 pm, 5:00 pm (on Friday, Saturday, and Sunday, Disney's Wedding Pavilion is only available at 10:00 am and 12:00 pm)

Canada Terrace: 9:00 am

Locations
- Disney's Wedding Pavilion
- Sunset Pointe at Disney's Polynesian Resort (10 people max)
- Wedding Gazebo at Disney's Yacht Club Resort
- Sea Breeze Point at Disney's BoardWalk Inn
- Sunrise Terrace at Disney's Wilderness Lodge (10 people max)
- Canada Terrace at Epcot

Amenities
- Bride's bouquet and groom's boutonniere
- Wedding cake with topper
- One bottle of Fairy Tale Cuvee or two bottles of sparkling cider
- Violinist for ceremony and cake cutting (plus an organist at Disney's Wedding Pavilion)
- Limousine service for four consecutive hours (five at Canada Terrace)
- Disney Photography for two hours, a proof book of all images, and an album of 20 4x6 prints you select
- Telephone consultations with a Disney Wedding Services Coordinator
- Two Walt Disney World annual passes
- Personalized wedding web site
- Mini-motorcoach and event guides (Canada Terrace only)

When to Book
All locations can be tentatively held at 12 months and booked 8 months in advance, subject to availability.

Deposit
A $1,000 deposit is due within two weeks of booking. A deposit equal to one night's stay is due when you book the required four-night stay at a Disney resort.

Wishes Collection

Number of Guests
10+

Minimum Expenditure
$10,000, plus 6.5% sales tax and a 21% service charge on food and beverage

Days
Monday–Sunday

Times
8:00 am, 9:00 am, 10:00 am, 12:00 pm, 2:30 pm, 5:00 pm, 7:30 pm

Ceremony Locations
At the Resorts
- Disney's Wedding Pavilion & Beach
- Sea Breeze Point at Disney's BoardWalk Inn
- Sunrise Terrace at Disney's Wilderness Lodge (10 people max)
- Sunset Pointe at Disney's Polynesian Resort (10 people max)
- Wedding Gazebo at Disney's Yacht Club Resort
- Disney's BoardWalk Inn Ballrooms & Lawns
- Disney's Grand Floridian Resort & Spa Ballrooms
- Disney's Yacht & Beach Club Resorts Ballrooms & Beaches

In the Parks
- **Epcot**
  - American Adventure Rotunda
  - Canada Pavilion
  - China Pavilion
  - Germany Pavilion
  - France Pavilion
  - Italy Pavilion
  - Japan Pavilion
  - Morocco Pavilion
  - The Seas With Nemo & Friends Tank
  - United Kingdom Pavilion

- **Magic Kingdom**
  - Swan Boat Landing

Reception Locations
At the Resorts
- Disney's Beach Club Resort – Ariel's
- Disney's BoardWalk Inn – Atlantic Dance Hall
- Disney's BoardWalk Inn – The Attic
- Disney's BoardWalk Inn Ballrooms & Lawns
- Disney's Grand Floridian Resort & Spa Ballrooms
- Disney's Yacht & Beach Club Resorts Ballrooms & Beaches
- California Grill at Disney's Contemporary Resort
- Cape Town Wine Room at Disney's Animal Kingdom Resort
- Citricos at Disney's Grand Floridian Resort & Spa
- Marina Patio & Terrace at Disney's Grand Floridian Resort & Spa
- Narcoossee's at Disney's Grand Floridian Resort & Spa
- Sago Cay Pointe at Disney's Grand Floridian Resort & Spa
- Summer House at Disney's Grand Floridian Resort & Spa

(Continues on next page)

In the Parks
- **Animal Kingdom**
  - Expedition Everest
  - Festival of the Lion King
  - Flame Tree Gardens
  - Harambe
  - Maharajah Jungle Trek
  - Tamu Tamu Courtyard
  - Tusker House

- **Epcot**
  - American Adventure Dining Room
  - American Adventure Rotunda
  - Bistro de Paris
  - Canada Terrace
  - Terrace des Fleurs (French Island Upper Terrace)
  - Eau de France (French Island Lower Terrace)
  - Rue de Paris (French Island Arm)
  - Germany Pavilion
  - Great Hall of China
  - Italy Isola (Island)
  - Isola West Plaza
  - Living Seas Salon
  - Morocco Oasis
  - Norway VIP Lounge
  - The Odyssey
  - Outpost Overlook (Africa)
  - United Kingdom Courtyard
  - United Kingdom Lochside (Lower Terrace)
  - United Kingdom Terrace (Upper Terrace)

- **Disney's Hollywood Studios**
  - Backstage Prop Shop
  - Chinese Theater Courtyard
  - Disney's Great Movie Ride
  - Fantasmic!
  - Hollywood Brown Derby
  - Hollywood Hideaway
  - Indiana Jones Stunt Show
  - Journey into Narnia: Prince Caspian
  - Lights, Motors, Action!
  - Magic of Disney Animation
  - Muppet Vision 3-D Courtyard
  - Rock 'n' Roller Coaster
  - Theater of the Stars (*Beauty & The Beast*)
  - Tower of Terror Courtyard

When to Book
Theme park locations and non-convention-center venues can be booked 16 months in advance. All other locations can be tentatively held at 16 months and confirmed 12 months before the event, subject to availability. The Wedding Pavilion may be booked at 16 months if the reception will be held in a theme park or non-convention-center venue.

Deposit
A $2,000 deposit is due when you return your signed Letter of Agreement, usually 12 to 16 months prior to the event.

Couture Collection

Number of Guests
10+

Minimum Expenditures
Overall: $65,000, plus 6.5% sales tax and a 21% service charge on food and beverage

Decor: $55,000 plus 6.5% sales tax (counts toward Overall Minimum Expenditure)

Food and Beverage: $175/person food and beverage charge, plus 6.5% tax and 21% service charge

Days
Monday–Sunday

Times
10:00 am, 12:00 pm, 2:30 pm, 5:00 pm, 7:00 pm

Ceremony Venues
Any Wishes Collection ceremony venue

Reception Venue
Disney's Contemporary Resort

Amenities
- Invitations and announcements (postage not included)
- Themed decor, props, and draping
- Custom-designed table linens and place settings
- Chiavari chairs
- Custom-designed beverage bar
- Escort/gift table
- Custom-designed floral centerpieces
- Custom-designed ceiling decor
- Designer lighting package
- DJ and wood dance floor
- Personal wedding web site
- Disney Wedding Planner trained by David Tutera

When to Book
Your locations can be booked as soon as Disney's Fairy Tale Weddings is able to confirm availability.

Deposit
A $10,000 deposit is due when you return your signed Letter of Agreement.

Cruise Collection

Number of Guests
Up to 8, plus bride and groom; additional guests incur additional charges

Cost
- $2,500 for onboard ceremonies (tax & service charge included)
- $3,500 for Castaway Cay ceremonies (tax & service charge included)

Minimum Expenditure
None, but the cost of your cruise is additional

Days
Onboard ceremonies on the Wonder are held on the Nassau day; onboard ceremonies on the Magic are held on a sea day; Castaway Cay weddings are held on a Castaway Cay day

Times
10:00 am on Castaway Cay; 4:00 pm, 4:30 pm, or 5:30 pm onboard

Locations
Onboard ceremonies are held on Deck 7 Aft or at Cadillac Lounge/Sessions; Castaway Cay ceremonies are held on the beach.

Amenities
- Concierge service
- Fresh flower bouquet and boutonniere
- Officiant
- Solo pianist
- Dress and tuxedo steaming
- Two-tier wedding cake and keepsake cake topper
- Disney's Fairy Tale Weddings cake service set
- One bottle of Fairy Tale Cuvee and one bottle of Martinelli's Sparkling Cider
- Wedding Coordinator
- On-site Wedding Coordinator
- Dinner for two at Palo
- Keepsake wedding certificate
- Complimentary 8x10-inch photo
- $100 onboard stateroom credit

When to Book
Package available through the Disney Cruise Line 12 months in advance; you may book the cruise itself more than 12 months in advance. You cannot book the Cruise Collection package until you have booked a cruise.

Deposit
The only deposit required is the one needed to book your cruise; there is no additional deposit for the ceremony package.

Other Ways to Get Married at Walt Disney World

While it is possible to have a Disney's Fairy Tale Wedding for far less than the $28,000 average cost of a wedding in the United States today, Disney's packages are not within everyone's budget. Fortunately, there are several non-Disney-owned hotels on **Disney property** that offer weddings ranging from small and simple to large, completely customized events, either at a lower cost or with more options included in the price. They also give you the flexibility to choose your own vendors for everything from photography to flowers, and some venues may include a night's stay at the hotel in the package. And because they are on-property, these hotels can offer appearances by Disney characters—something you won't find at any other hotel wedding!

© Nathan Root

One avenue we do not suggest is attempting to secretly hold your own ceremony anywhere on Disney property. Although you may hear of couples who had a quickie wedding on an attraction or a small gathering on the grounds of a hotel, Disney's official policy is a total ban on unofficial weddings, and you will be **asked to leave** the property if you are caught.

Garden Gazebo at Shades of Green

Royal Plaza (http://www.royalplaza.com/meetings-social-events/weddings/index.cfm) at Downtown Disney offers ceremony and reception packages, with reception prices based on the menu you choose. The full ceremony package, including rehearsal and altar decor, is $900; smaller packages are available at a lower rate. Reception menu prices start at $65 per person for groups of 50 or more but can be customized for smaller groups. Reception packages include a ballroom venue, a menu tasting, a ballroom for the wedding party to get ready in, votive candles on mirrored tiles for each table, a Champagne toast, white floor-length linens and white chair covers with your choice of colored sash, wedding cake, a 4-hour open bar, a complimentary suite and breakfast for the bride and groom, a dance floor, placement of favors and name cards, discounts on rooms for guests, and suite upgrades for parents of the happy couple. There are additional discounts available depending on time of day, day of the week, and season.

You do not have to be a member of the United States Armed Forces or be related to one to hold your wedding at **Shades of Green** (http://www.shadesofgreen.org/weddings.htm), an Armed Forces Recreation Center located on Disney property near Disney's Polynesian Resort, but you do need a military or government sponsor.

Other Ways to Get Married at Walt Disney World (continued)

Active or retired military personnel and their dependants, active or retired Reserve and National Guard members with current I.D. card and their family members, and Department of Defense civilians are all **qualified sponsors**; the sponsor must attend the event.

© Nathan Root

One of the perks of holding your event at Shades of Green is that you can have **Disney characters** attend your reception. See page 107 for prices.

Gazebo deck at Shades of Green

Shades of Green offers an **Intimate Wedding and Vow Renewal** package at $895 for up to 14 guests. The package includes an officiant, a bridal bouquet and boutonniere, a single-tier cake, a Champagne toast, and photography by in-house service Photo Magic. Couples will receive an album of 20 5x7-inch images plus 40 5x7-inch prints. The package includes one photographer for the ceremony plus one additional hour—either before or after the ceremony, or 30 minutes on either side. An engagement or pre-wedding day bridal portrait session costs $100 and includes a disc of images.

Alternatively, you can pay for the **function space and meal** and then arrange for entertainment, floral, decor, cake, transportation, and the services of a wedding planner on your own. Rental of the Garden Gazebo ranges from $125 to $300, depending on your group's size, while space in the Magnolia Ballroom runs $250 for one-quarter of the room, $500 for half, and $1,000 for the whole ballroom. Other locations include boardrooms, the lobby balcony, the pool, and even a party tent.

Shades of Green's banquet menus are available for **groups of 25 or more**, with prices starting at $9 per person for continental breakfast and topping out at $37 per person for a buffet or a duo-plate sit-down meal. Smaller parties may wish to eat at the resort's restaurant, Mangino's, which offers groups family-style meals for $25–$36/person.

© Nathan Root

Magnolia Ballroom at Shades of Green

© Photography By Taz

Crescent Terrace at the Swan

The **Walt Disney World Swan & Dolphin Resort** (http://www.swandolphin.com/weddings/index.html) offers wedding packages coordinated by local company Just Marry! (http://www.justmarry.com). Package prices start at $2,985 for the ceremony venue, an on-site coordinator, an arch, an officiant, one bottle of Champagne, a two-tier cake, a bouquet and a boutonniere, and a violinist (includes tax). Or you can pay $1,595 for the ceremony venue and the services of a wedding coordinator and then add as many or as few extras as you wish. If you're looking for more than just a ceremony and cake cutting, you have the option of adding a ballroom reception catered by the resort, or you can arrange your own meal at one of the restaurants at the Swan & Dolphin, Downtown Disney, or the Disney resorts—check out the charts in Chapter 2: Escape Collection for details on the most popular private and group dining options at Downtown Disney and the Disney resorts.

The **Hilton** (http://www.hiltonorlandoweddings.com) at Downtown Disney offers weddings and receptions for a minimum of 50 guests. The ceremony package costs $1,500 and includes an outdoor venue (with indoor backup), a choice of several decor packages, and folding chairs. Reception packages are priced per person based on the menu you select and include a four-hour open bar (call brands), a Champagne toast, linens and chair covers, your choice of several centerpiece styles, a wedding cake in one of 16 different styles, valet parking for the wedding party, and a suite for the bridal couple on the wedding night. Plated menu prices start at $121 per person and include cocktail hour food, while a buffet option adds $40-$50 per person to the price of whichever plated menu you choose. Interestingly, one of the two companies the Hilton works with for floral and decor is Disney Floral & Gifts. This means you have access to the same Disney-themed accessories offered for Disney's Fairy Tale Weddings, including Cinderella's Coach centerpieces, the popular Mickey bridal purse, and white chocolate Cinderella Slipper favors.

Notes

Chapter 1
Memories Collection

In September 2010, Disney's Fairy Tale Weddings introduced the Memories Collection in celebration of its 20th anniversary. Designed primarily as a simple **vow renewal** option in honor of the many couples who have wed at Walt Disney World over the last two decades, the Memories Collection will only be offered for 20 months, with dates available until March 31, 2012.

The **Memories Collection** package costs $1,991 (including tax and service charge) for up to 4 guests plus the happy couple. Children under age 3 do not count toward the guest limit. Accommodations and an officiant are not included in the package, and whomever you choose as officiant will not be counted as one of your guests.

You will be required to book **two nights** at any Disney-owned resort, including Disney Vacation Club properties, through Disney or your own travel agent. You may use any applicable discount, including AAA, Annual Passholder, Disney Rewards Visa, and other promotional codes. Although it is not possible to set up a room block as it is with Escape and Wishes Collection events, Memories Collection guests do receive the same ticket discount offered to all guests of Disney's Fairy Tale Weddings—currently $20 off the price of any Park Hopper ticket.

Ceremonies are held on **Saturday and Sunday only**, at 9:00 am, 11:00 am, 1:00 pm, and 3:00 pm. They take place at one of three unique locations open only to Memories Collection events: Narcoossee's Landing at the Grand Floridian Resort & Spa, Conch Key Marina at the Grand Floridian, and Luau Beach at Disney's Polynesian Resort. No rehearsal is available, and no chairs may be set up at any location. Each location has an indoor backup in case of rain.

The **one-hour** event includes a short ceremony preceded and followed by photography—indeed, the focus of these events is on making memories and capturing them on film.

The package includes a bouquet, a violinist, three consecutive hours of limousine transportation, one hour of photography, three 5x7-inch prints, the services of a wedding coordinator, and access to the Disney's Fairy Tale Weddings Facebook app. Almost as important is what the package **doesn't include**: a boutineer, cake, Champagne, or any other food and beverage.

Due to the low cost and streamlined nature of the Memories Collection, there is almost no flexibility with the various components, with the exception of a choice of one of **five standard bouquets**: the Gerbera Daisy Bouquet, the Roses and Lilies Bouquet, the Roses and Hydrangea Bouquet, an Orchid and Maile Lei Set, or the Bright and Bold Bouquet.

Memories Collection (continued)

The **one swap** allowed is an option to forego the three hours of limousine service in exchange for an In-Room Romantic Celebration, a floral and gift package that includes turndown service with rose petals and chocolates, personalized bath towels, a spa basket, a dozen roses, three (artificially lit) candles, Mickey confetti, and a souvenir photo of Mickey & Minnie. Alternatively, you may keep the limousine service but use the three consecutive hours during another part of your vacation.

No other swaps are allowed. Only **floral, photography, and videography** may be added. For example, you may add rose petals or a sand ceremony, request additional hours of photography, or add the services of a videographer. However you may not add any other entertainment, including Disney characters. If you require more elaborate arrangements or options, you may find that Disney's Escape Collection or Wishes Collection is a better match.

If you wish to include a **meal**, you will need to make your own arrangements. The Group Dining Information chart on pages 38–40 of Chapter 2: Escape Collection includes phone numbers, prices, and requirements for making group reservations at some of the most popular restaurants. Another option is to order a meal from Private Dining at your resort to have in your room or another area at the resort. See page 186 of Chapter 8: Honeymoons and Anniversaries at Walt Disney World for complete details.

To add a **cake** to your meal or have one delivered to your Disney resort room, call the Cake Hotline at 407-827-2253 at least 72 hours in advance. Note that your best bet for getting a fancy, fondant-covered cake is to call Private Dining at the Contemporary Resort, the Grand Floridian, the BoardWalk Resort, or the Yacht & Beach Club. For complete details, see page 187 of Chapter 8: Honeymoons and Anniversaries at Walt Disney World.

The Memories Collection can be booked **6 months to 24 hours** in advance, and you can call to get the ball rolling as far out as 18 months ahead.

A nonrefundable **$500 deposit** and signed contract are due within two weeks of booking your date. The deposit will be applied toward your balance, which is due 30 days before your date. The deposit and remaining balance may be paid by credit card, check, money order, or wire transfer. If you book fewer than 60 days in advance, the entire $1,991 package price is due as your deposit. If you need to cancel the event more than 60 days before, you will forfeit the deposit. If you cancel from 60 to 31 days before, you will be charged 50% of the cost of your package and enhancements, including tax and gratuity on enhancements. If you cancel 30 to 0 days before, you will be charged 90% of those costs. Cancellations must be submitted to your Wedding Consultant in writing.

Chapter 2
Escape Collection

The Escape Collection offers small parties an easy and relatively inexpensive way to have a traditional Disney's Fairy Tale Wedding, vow renewal, or commitment ceremony. This ceremony-only package features all the **basic components**—like a location, a cake, transportation, flowers, and photography—for a flat fee that includes tax and service charge. It does not include a reception, so if you wish to have a celebratory meal following the ceremony, you will need to factor in those costs separately.

It is also important to note that, due to the **packaged** nature of the Escape Collection, there is not much flexibility with the various components. However, certain elements can be swapped or upgraded, and you are welcome to add as many extras as you like.

In this chapter we'll examine each of the basic elements of the package and tell you whether and how they can be customized. We'll also look at some of the more popular options for a post-ceremony meal and chart the costs and details so you can compare them. At the end, we'll walk you through the **planning process** and give you a 12-month time line that incorporates general wedding-planning deadlines with those specific to an Escape Collection wedding, vow renewal, or commitment ceremony.

This chapter focuses on services offered by **Disney** because, with the exception of entertainment and videography, they are included in the price of the Escape package. However, you may wish to hire your own vendors for such elements as floral, photography, and videography. Disney does not charge a fee for this, but you are prohibited from using other vendors for entertainment, floral, and decor at outdoor ceremony locations. This includes having a friend or relative perform but excludes such personal floral as bouquets and boutonnieres. Your Wedding Services Coordinator can provide guidance on what is and isn't allowed at your outdoor ceremony site. For more information on selecting outside vendors, see "How to Find Your Own Vendors" on page 122 of Chapter 3: Wishes Collection.

 Disney's Fairy Tale Weddings Online
Disney's Fairy Tale Weddings' web site at http://www.disneyweddings.go.com is a good place to start exploring your options when you are considering a Walt Disney World wedding or waiting to get the ball rolling. Just keep in mind that you will need to speak to your Disney Wedding Services Coordinator for pricing on upgrades and additions.

Escape Collection Basics

The **Deluxe Escape Wedding** package costs $4,750 (including tax and service charge) for up to 18 guests plus the happy couple and includes one of four outdoor locations, a cake, one bottle of Iron Horse Fairy Tale Cuvee or two bottles of sparkling cider, a bouquet and boutonniere, a violinist, a limousine, photography, two Walt Disney World Annual Passes, and access to Disney's planning tool on Facebook.

The Wedding Pavilion package, called the **Premium Escape Wedding**, is $5,750 (including tax and service charge) and features all the same elements plus an organist.

Sea Breeze Point at Disney's BoardWalk

The **Canada Terrace package** costs $5,895 (including tax and service charge) and features everything in the Deluxe Escape Wedding package, plus an extra hour of limousine service, 5 hours of mini-bus service for your guests, and event guides. Ceremonies begin at 9:00 am, and you must depart by 10:30 am. Photographs can be taken in the Canada Pavilion only, and no other Epcot locations are available for Escape ceremonies.

Holding your ceremony on a Saturday or Sunday or adding a catered event to the package triggers a **minimum expenditure requirement** of $7,500, plus tax and service charge. The Escape package counts toward the minimum, and only upgrades and additions receive tax and/or service charges. See page 54 for a list of these.

For all packages, if you have between four and 18 guests, there will be an additional charge for Fairy Tale Cuvee beyond the single bottle the package includes. This is the only other cost required.

Accommodations and an officiant are not included in the Escape package, although Disney offers a list of preferred officiants. If you choose to use one who is not on the list, he or she will be counted as a guest. Children age 3 and older also count toward your guest limit. You will be required to book **four nights** at any Disney-owned resort, including Disney Vacation Club properties, through Disney or your own travel agent. You may use any applicable discount, including AAA, Annual Passholder, Disney Rewards Visa, and other promotional codes.

Canada Terrace at Epcot

If you can guarantee 10 or more room nights will be reserved by you and your guests, you may set up a **room block** at up to four Disney resorts to receive a discount on accommodations.

You will receive one free room night if your guests book 25 nights or more. To learn more about how the process works, check out the "Guest Accommodation Requirement" and "Room Block" sections of Chapter 3: Wishes Collection.

You and your guests will receive a **$20 discount** on any Magic Your Way Ticket that includes the Park Hopper Option.

There are six Escape Collection **ceremony sites** to choose from: Disney's Wedding Pavilion, Sunset Pointe at Disney's Polynesian Resort, the Wedding Gazebo at Disney's Yacht Club Resort, Sea Breeze Point at Disney's BoardWalk Inn, Sunrise Terrace at Disney's Wilderness Lodge, and Canada Terrace at Epcot.

Sunset Pointe at the Polynesian Resort

All locations can be tentatively held up to one year in advance and booked **eight months** in advance. Sunrise Terrace and Sunset Pointe can only accommodate the bride and groom and eight guests. Sunset Pointe is only available from October through March.

Escape ceremonies are held Monday through Sunday at 10:00 am, 12:00 pm, 2:30 pm, and 5:00 pm at all locations except Canada Terrace, which offers only a 9:00 am ceremony. On Friday, Saturday, and Sunday, the Wedding Pavilion is only available at 10:00 am or 12:00 pm. The **one-hour** event includes a 10–15-minute ceremony followed by cake cutting, toasts, ceremonial first dances, and time for photos at

Sunrise Terrace at Wilderness Lodge

the ceremony site. If your ceremony is held at the Wedding Pavilion, the event will last approximately 1½ hours, and the cake cutting will take place at Commander's Terrace at Disney's Grand Floridian Resort & Spa.

A nonrefundable **$1,000 deposit** and signed contract are due within two weeks of booking your date. The deposit will be applied toward your balance, which is due 30 days before your date. The deposit and remaining balance may be paid by credit card, check, money order, or wire transfer. If you book within 60 days of your date, the full package price is due as a deposit. If you need to cancel the event more than 60 days before, you will forfeit the deposit. If you cancel from 60 to 31 days before, you will be charged 50% of the cost of your package and enhancements, including tax and gratuity on enhancements. If you cancel 30 to 0 days before, you will be charged 90% of those costs. Cancellations must be submitted to your Wedding Consultant in writing.

Wedding Gazebo at the Yacht Club

Customizing Your Event

The basics of the Escape Collection package are set, and you will not receive any credit for elements you don't use. However, it is possible to customize your event through **upgrades and additions**.

Floral Options & Enhancements

The Escape package includes your choice of **bridal bouquet** and boutonniere from a small selection of styles. You may change the flower color to any shade in which that type of flower grows. Additional floral options for attendants and family are available for an extra charge. You may also work with Disney Floral & Gifts to create custom arrangements at an additional cost. Speak with your Floral/Photography/Entertainment Event Manager for options.

Bridesmaids' bouquets usually start at around $100. Some **low-cost alternatives** are a rose wand, which requires only a few flowers, or a single presentation rose. Boutonnieres start at $10.50, and crystal Hidden Mickeys are available for $3 each.

Aisle petals

A basket of petals for the flower girl starts at $55. The cost of pre-scattered aisle petals varies depending on the amount of coverage and length of the aisle but starts at around $50. Toss petals start at $3.50 per person for bunches of rose petals in individual organza bags or paper cones.

Disney's flower girl basket

Corsages for mothers of the bride and groom or other members of the family start at $21. Disney Floral & Gifts also offers **presentation roses** that the bride and groom may give to special guests during the ceremony. These cost $20 for a single stem or $30 for a double stem.

If you have allergies or simply want a bouquet you can keep, you may want to investigate artificial flowers. Disney Floral & Gifts can make a **silk bouquet** to your specifications, or you can buy or make your own. A quick Google search will turn up numerous online vendors of artificial flowers and floral arrangements. Some interesting alternatives include flowers made from paper or clay and non-floral bouquets of crystals, beads, or feathers.

Presentation roses honor your special guests

If you've scheduled an in-park bridal portrait session through Disney Event Group Photography within three days of your event, you may request a **floral refresh** to restore your bouquet to its wedding-day glory. Costs vary depending on bouquet size and the type of the flowers used, but the service usually runs about $100. Your bouquet will be collected directly after the ceremony and stored until the day of your photo shoot. Disney Floral & Gifts will replace any wilted flowers and redeliver the bouquet to you that morning. If you'd like to have the bouquet preserved, your Wedding Event Planner can recommend an independent floral preservation service. With prices north of $500, the process isn't cheap, but in the end you'll have the freeze-dried bridal bouquet framed with any other memorabilia you wish to include.

If you plan to have extensive additional floral, you may wish to use an **outside vendor**. However, you will be required to use Disney Floral & Gifts for floral arrangements and decor at all outdoor ceremony locations, with the exception of personal floral like bouquets and boutonnieres. More information can be found in Chapter 3: Wishes Collection under "Floral & Decor," beginning on page 92.

Disney's Fairy Tale Weddings Annual Passes

When you return your signed contract, you will receive two vouchers that can be exchanged at any time for Theme Park Annual Passes. These allow 365 days of admission to all four Walt Disney World parks, including unlimited park hopping. Admission to the water parks and to DisneyQuest is not included in the basic Annual Pass, and upgrading to a Premium Annual Pass will set you back the full price of that pass because the Disney's Fairy Tale Weddings Annual Passes have a $0 value in Disney's ticketing system.

However, your passes entitle you to a number of great benefits, including discounts on merchandise, Disney resort rates, and tickets to special events like Mickey's Not-So-Scary Halloween Party. You will also be eligible to purchase a membership in Tables In Wonderland, a program that gives you 20% off all food and beverage at most of the restaurants on Disney property. For more information about Annual Pass benefits, go to http://disneyworld.disney.go.com/wdw/passholder/learnMore, and for more information on Tables In Wonderland, check out http://allears.net/din/dde.htm.

Cake & Champagne

The two-tier **wedding cake** included in the Escape package serves between 20 and 30 people. It is available in five different designs, all of which come with a Mickey & Minnie cake topper.

Standard cake flavors
- Chocolate
- Yellow
- Marble
- Almond

Standard filling flavors
- Chocolate Mousse
- White Chocolate Mousse
- Strawberry Mousse
- Raspberry Mousse
- Bavarian Cream
- White Buttercream
- Chocolate Buttercream

Requesting half glasses for the toast will make the included bottle of Fairy Tale Cuvee go farther

You may request Wishes Collection cake flavors and fillings, but there may be an additional charge (see the "Food, Beverages, and Cake" section of Chapter 3: Wishes Collection). Certain flavors may not be available at all ceremony locations. You may request a different cake and filling combination for each tier.

Setting up for a cake and Champagne reception on Commander's Terrace at the Grand Floridian

A white chocolate castle cake topper is available for $100. For an additional charge you may add fresh flowers, **upgrade** to one of the Wishes Collection cake designs, or work with the bakery to create a cake of your own design. Upgraded cake costs vary, but the Escape Collection cake usually counts as a $200 credit toward the upgraded design.

Also included in the Escape package is one bottle of Disney's Fairy Tale Cuvee or two bottles of sparkling cider for **toasting**. Each bottle serves between four and eight people. Additional Fairy Tale Cuvee can be purchased for $62 per bottle, while sparkling cider runs $24 per bottle.

Tasting the Cake

The Escape Collection package does not include a cake-tasting session. If you will be traveling to Walt Disney World before your wedding, try ordering a cake from the resort bakery closest to your ceremony site, which will be the bakery that makes your Escape Collection cake. Only BoardWalk Bakery will let you pick up a cake—otherwise you must be planning to stay or dine at the resort you call. The smallest customizable cakes are 6 inches and serve 4–6 people, starting at around $30. To order a cake to be served with a meal, call Walt Disney World's central Cake Hotline at 407-827-2253 at least 48 hours before you plan to dine. Just as your wedding cake will be made by the bakery closest to your ceremony site, this cake will be made by the bakery closest to the restaurant, so choose a restaurant near your ceremony site. Although most restaurants give you the option to order a 6-inch ready-made cake for $21 when you check in for your reservation, these are kept frozen and are not the same cakes served at Disney's Fairy Tale Weddings. To order a cake to be delivered to your room, call your resort's Private Dining number or call the resort bakery directly. Here is the contact information for the bakeries that make Escape Collection cakes.

BoardWalk Bakery (via the resort):	407-939-5100
Grand Floridian Bakery (via Private Dining):	407-824-1951
Polynesian Bakery (via Private Dining):	407-824-2165
Wilderness Lodge Bakery:	407-824-2090
Yacht Club Bakery (via Private Dining):	407-939-3160

Music & Entertainment

The Escape package includes a **violinist** to play during the ceremony and at the cake cutting. If your event is held at the Wedding Pavilion, an organist is provided for the ceremony, and the violinist plays at both the ceremony and the cake cutting. Other types of musicians, from harpist to jazz guitarist, are available at an extra charge.

• Flute	$575
• Classical/Jazz Guitarist	$575
• Key West–Style Guitarist	$745
• Harpist	$800
• Pianist (includes piano rental)	$820
• Violinist	$575
• Vocalist (ceremony)	$650
• Bagpiper	$575
• Violin/Flute Duo	$1,030
• Harp/Flute Duo	$1,200
• Jazz Trio	$1,515
• Classical String Trio	$1,515
• String Quartet	$1,980
• Calypso Trio with Steel Drum	$1,710

Disney Violinist

Music and Entertainment (continued)

You may request **specific songs** from a standard repertoire that includes Disney songs, or you may provide your own sheet music. Non-Disney musicians are not allowed at functions held at outdoor locations. This also prohibits you from having any of your guests perform at these locations.

If you prefer to play **recorded music**, you may either rent a sound system from Disney (about $800, including a sound tech) or bring a portable stereo and ask one of your guests to run it. There are no electrical outlets at the outdoor locations, so be sure your sound system is battery-operated. Disney can provide an iPod setup including two speakers, an audio mixer, and the appropriate cables, starting at $250 (without sound tech).

This being Walt Disney World, you have the option of adding a visit by a Disney character or themed entertainer to your cake-cutting reception. Just about any costumed or face **character** is available, with the exception of licensed characters like Winnie the Pooh & Friends. Some of the Disney characters even have a variety of outfits to choose from, including formalwear.

For up to 30 minutes of character interaction, prices are $900 for one character, $1,350 for two, and $1,800 for three. The clock starts ticking as soon as the characters leave their dressing room, though, so you may not end up seeing them for an entire half-hour. Also, **not all characters** may be available at all locations, due to licensing restrictions. Characters may only appear at the cake cutting, not at the ceremony, and alcoholic beverage service must be stopped during their visit. Considering that the cake cutting usually only lasts about 20 minutes, you might want to instead book a character meal following the ceremony. If you dine at a resort restaurant, you will be able to pose for pictures with the characters in your formal attire for just the cost of the meal.

Disney's themed **entertainers** include Herald Trumpeters, a Major Domo in full regalia, an English Butler, and various faux wedding crashers. In addition to announcing the names of the wedding party and interacting with your guests, these characters may be integrated into the ceremony. For example, many couples enlist the Major Domo as part of a practical joke on

The Major Domo carries the rings to the altar, often as part of a practical joke on the Best Man

the best man involving "misplaced" wedding rings. The cost of an appearance by the Major Domo begins at $675, one Herald Trumpeter starts at $700, and a Trumpet Duo costs $1,100 and up. More information can be found in the "Music and Entertainment" section, beginning on page 104 of Chapter 3: Wishes Collection.

Transportation

Disney provides four consecutive hours of **limousine** service in the Escape package, which can be used in any combination of trips before and after the ceremony. If

you are staying at the resort where your event will be held or have other transportation, you may arrange to use your four hours of limo service during another part of your stay. For example, you could use it for a trip to the courthouse to get your license or to transport a small group to the rehearsal dinner. The limo seats up to eight people, and it can make multiple trips within the four-hour period.

A limo is included in the Escape package

Disney also offers **specialty transportation** upgrades. These options are more for show than for actual transportation, and you may still need to use the limo to get to the site where you will meet the specialty transportation. You can arrive at the ceremony in a Model A Ford for $600 or a vintage Rolls Royce for $800, or choose a Horse-Drawn Landau Coach for $1,700. For the ultimate wedding-day transportation, Cinderella's Glass Coach is available for $2,700. Coaches are only available for ceremonies at the Wedding Pavilion, Sea Breeze Point, and the Wedding Gazebo at the Yacht Club.

One thing to keep in mind when considering specialty transportation such as Cinderella's Glass Coach is the **limited** amount of time you actually spend in it. For example, if you are being married at the Wedding Pavilion and are not staying at the Grand Floridian, you must ride in the limo to the Grand Floridian to meet the coach. From there, the bride will get a short ride to the Wedding Pavilion with up to three guests (depending on the size of the wedding gown!). After the ceremony, the bride and groom make a staged exit in the coach for photographs, then circle back to the Wedding Pavilion for pictures with family and friends. Finally, the coach carries the bride and groom back to the Grand Floridian for the cake cutting.

Horse-Drawn Landau Coach

Photography

The Escape package includes the services of one **Disney photographer** for two hours, enough time for him or her to meet you 30 minutes before the ceremony, capture the ceremony and cake cutting, and take family portraits afterward. You will receive 20 4x6-inch prints of your choice in an album and a spiral-bound proof book with thumbnail versions of every image. The images are also posted online for you to review. For $155 you can get 40 prints instead of 20, and $305 will get you 60 prints. For $125 you can swap the included album for a 5x7-inch album of 20 prints. Additional hours of photography cost $200. You may view samples of Disney Event Group photography online at http://www.disneyeventphotography.com.

The **Photojournalistic package** add-on includes a second photographer at the event and an expanded album that replaces the one in the standard package. The cost is $400 if you choose the 30-print Jasmine album, which measures 9x9 inches and features 5x7-inch images. The cost is $700 if you choose the 36-print Digital Montage 36 album, which measures 6x9 inches and features multi-photo layouts on each page. Each additional spread (two-sided page) costs $30.

Disney Event Group Photography also offers four upgraded photography packages to replace the basic services included with the Escape Collection package. These each **include a disc of high-resolution** images, as well as the proof book and images posted online. Note that couples who reside outside North America receive a disc of high-resolution images at no charge with the standard Escape package, but the images in the albums are selected by the photographer. The disc, album, and any prints are delivered before the couple leaves Florida.

Cinderella's Collection A costs $1,225 and includes your choice of 40 8x10-inch prints in a white or black Disney-themed album, one 11x14-inch portrait, a 4x6-inch print of every image, and the disc of images. **Cinderella's Collection B** includes everything in Collection A but gives you just 24 prints in the album for a price of $900. **Cinderella's Collection C** costs $825 and includes 40 5x7-inch prints in a white or black Disney-themed album, one 11x14-inch portrait, a 4x6-inch print of every image, and the images on disc. **Cinderella's Collection D** includes everything in Collection C but gives you just 24 prints in the album for a price of $750.

If you are willing to forgo the 20-print album, online posting of images, and proof book included in the Escape package, you may **purchase all your high-resolution images** on disc for $395. The images from any additional portrait sessions, including the Magic Kingdom Portrait Session and dessert party photography, are included at no additional charge if you give up the albums that come with those sessions. If you still wish to receive the albums, there is a $100 charge for each.

You are not required to use the Disney photographer included in the Escape Collection package, but there are **no substitutions** if you hire your own photographer. For example, you can't use the two hours of Disney photography at a dessert party instead of at the ceremony. However, Disney no longer charges an escort fee if you hire your own photographer. Disney may also offer to send the included photographer along anyway, but you should check your contract with the photographer you hire to see if this is permitted.

If you are planning a Wishes, IllumiNations, or Fantasmic! **dessert party**, Disney offers a $350 photo package that includes two hours of photography, a proof book, and 4x6-inch prints of every image. Note that only Disney photographers are allowed at in-park events.

One of the most popular photographic enhancements to the Escape Collection package is the **Magic Kingdom Portrait Session** because it is most couples' only opportunity to wear formal attire in the park. The session is open only to the bridal couple, who are picked up from the lobby of their Walt Disney World resort hotel at either 5:00 am or 6:00 am to be photographed before the Magic Kingdom opens. The one-hour session takes place at Cinderella Castle and Prince Charming Regal Carrousel. Other locations may be available on request. The cost is $1,100 and includes a white or black Disney-themed album of 12 5x7-inch prints and loose 4x6-inch prints of every image from the photo shoot.

A similar package is available for **Epcot, Disney's Hollywood Studios, or Disney's Animal Kingdom** at a cost of $650 for a white or black Disney-themed album of 12 5x7-inch prints and loose 4x6-inch prints of every image from the photo shoot. The same package, under the name **Trash the Dress**, is available at either of Disney's water parks.

For $1,400 couples may schedule portrait sessions at the **Magic Kingdom and one additional park** on the same day. This package includes a 30-print black or white Disney-themed album of 5x7-inch prints that can be customized with your names and wedding date.

Also offered is a Walt Disney World **Resort Portrait Session** in formal attire at the resort of your choice for $450. Like the in-park sessions, it is for the bridal couple only; however, the pickup time is flexible. You will receive 24 prints in a 6x6-inch photo book and a 4x6-inch print of every image. For $125 you can upgrade to an album of 12 5x7-inch prints, and $180 gets you the same album with 20 prints.

The $310 **Honeymoon or Engagement Portrait Session** is available at Epcot during regular operating hours. Bridal attire is not permitted, and park admission is not included. Couples will receive a 6x6-inch, soft-cover photo book with 24 images, one 4x6-inch print of every image, and online posting of the images. For $65 you can upgrade to an 8x8-inch, hard-cover photo book. For $400 you can upgrade to the 7x9-inch black leather Digital Montage 24 album, which includes 10 pages and 24 images laid out by a graphic artist. Each additional 2-sided page costs $30. And for $300 you can purchase all the high-resolution images on disc (note that if you use Disney for your wedding photography and purchase that on disc, the portrait session photos can be added at no charge).

A similar **Family Portrait Session** can be arranged at Epcot or a resort. The package includes a 6x6-inch, soft-cover photo book with 25 images, one 4x6-inch print of every image, and online posting of the images. The price is $275 for up to 8 people and $325 for 9–15 people, and bridal attire is not permitted.

In-park photography sessions may be arranged through your Wedding Services Coordinator or your Floral/Photography/Entertainment Event Manager, or by calling Disney Event Group Photography directly at 407-827-5099.

Videography

Videography is one of the few services **not included** in the Escape package, but you can arrange it for an additional fee or hire your own videographer. If your ceremony will take place in the Wedding Pavilion, Disney can shoot it with three stationary cameras installed inside the Pavilion.

The $1,400 **Escape Package** begins with a 2-minute montage of highlights set to Disney music or the song of your choice. The rest of the video covers the entire ceremony and cake-cutting reception. Three cameras are included for the ceremony, along with microphones for the groom and officiant, and one manned camera is included for the cake cutting. The edited DVD includes menus and wedding-party credits. Additional DVD copies cost $100 each.

The $1,200 **Celebration Package** captures the ceremony only, from the couple's arrival at the site to their post-ceremony walk back down the aisle. It includes one-camera coverage of the arrival and departure, which are edited to music. The ceremony is covered by three cameras and includes original audio. Additional DVD copies cost $100.

For $750 you can purchase **Ceremony Documentation** only. This gets you raw footage shot by the three cameras and burned directly to DVD with no editing. You will receive the DVD at the end of the ceremony. Additional DVD copies cost $100.

Among the enhancements is the $400 **Ceremony Web Download**, which allows up to 10 downloads of your ceremony for family and friends (note that these are after the fact; the ceremony will not be webcast live). The $500 **Through the Years Montage** sets 40 of your family photos to music and can be shown at any pre-wedding or wedding-day event. It is also added as a special feature on your wedding DVD.

The $500 **Dessert Party** package is a 2-minute montage of your dessert party, including guest testimonials, that can be added as a special feature to your wedding DVD. It includes one-camera coverage and is edited to the song of your choice. The $800 **Love Story Interview** allows the bride and groom to share the story of their journey to the altar and can be added to the wedding DVD.

The **Bridal Spotlight** is the video equivalent of a Theme Park Portrait Session—a music video of you in the theme park before it opens, set to the song of your choice. The price is $1,000 for the Magic Kingdom, $800 for any of the other Disney parks, $1,400 for the Magic Kingdom plus another park, or $1,000 for two of the other parks. A 15% discount is available if you use Disney videography for your wedding.

Disney no longer charges an escort fee if you hire your own videographer, but you must use Disney's videography services for **in-park events** like dessert parties. For more information about finding and hiring outside vendors, check out "How to Find Your Own Vendors" on page 122 of Chapter 3: Wishes Collection.

Reception

Because Escape Collection events do not include a formal reception, many couples choose to hold an informal reception at one of the many Walt Disney World resort **restaurants**. This can be anything from a casual character meal to an entire restaurant buyout.

The most popular option is to make a large-party dining reservation through a Disney's Fairy Tale Wedding Services Coordinator or by calling Disney's Group Dining Hotline at 407-939-7700. However, some restaurants also offer **private rooms** that can be reserved by calling the restaurant directly. The exceptions are the private rooms at California Grill and Jiko, which are booked through Disney's Fairy Tale Weddings.

Yachtsman Steakhouse's semi-private section

You can also work with your Wedding Services Coordinator to book a **private event** at one of the smaller convention center venues—like the Grand Floridian's Key West Room or the BoardWalk Inn's St. James Room—or at a Disney-owned restaurant before it opens for dinner. Prices and availability vary according to your group's size, the time of day of your reception, and the time of year. There are no venue rental fees, and food and beverage minimums start at $500. Events are limited to two hours. You will be required to meet a $7,500 minimum expenditure for your entire wedding day (including the Escape package you select).

If you choose to book your own restaurant meal, you may be able to work directly with the restaurant manager to add **special touches** like personalized menus, and your Disney Floral/Photography/Entertainment Event Manager or an outside vendor can help with centerpieces and other decor.

Citricos' private room, Chef's Domain

After the cake-cutting reception at your ceremony site, your cake will be **boxed up** and placed in the limo so you can take it to the restaurant. Some restaurants charge a per-person cake-cutting fee, but it is often waived if you cut the cake yourself.

Wedding attire is permitted at all resort restaurants, but you will have to change clothes if you plan to dine in any of the parks. Each member of your party will need **park admission**.

Reception (continued)

Detailed information about every Walt Disney World restaurant is available in *PassPorter's Walt Disney World*, so this section will focus on those that offer private rooms, buyout options, or special accommodation for large parties.

© Patrick Johnson

Private room at bluezoo

The **Private Rooms/Restaurant Buyouts chart** on pages 35–37 will help you compare the prices and amenities of the restaurants that offer private rooms or the option to buy out the entire restaurant. Although this may be more expensive than simply making a reservation, you will have the advantage of flexible seating times, greater capacity, and privacy and still spend less than you would on a Wishes Collection reception.

If a private room is not in your budget, you may want to consider the restaurants in the **Group Dining Information chart** on pages 38-40. Some of them will seat your party in a separate section of the restaurant, and most do not charge a cake-cutting fee. However, with the exception of those at Downtown Disney, these restaurants require large parties to book the first or last seating time. This means you may have to juggle a 5:30 pm or 9:00 pm meal with a 10:00 am, 12:00 pm, 2:30 pm, or 5:00 pm ceremony.

© Photography By Taz

Fulton's Crab House at Downtown Disney

If you have a **small group** and your accommodations include a kitchen, you may want to celebrate there. The cabins at Fort Wilderness Resort & Campground and the Disney Vacation Club villas provide full kitchens, while Disney Vacation Club studios contain a kitchenette.

If it's just the two of you, consider a romantic dinner on a balcony or in the privacy of your hotel room courtesy of Disney's Private Dining at the Grand Floridian (407-824-2474) or at your resort. For more information about a catered dinner for two outdoors or in another public area at a Deluxe resort, check out the "Romantic Dining" section on page 180 of Chapter 8: Honeymoons and Anniversaries at Walt Disney World.

Private Rooms/Restaurant Buyouts

Name	Location	Seats	Meals Served	Food & Beverage Minimum	Tax & Gratuity	Cake Cutting	Phone	Additional Info
California Grill	Contemporary Resort	240	Lunch (end by 3 pm)	$3,000	6.5% tax, 21% gratuity	$2.50/person	407-828-3200	Order off banquet menu only— no customization; no menu-tasting; no outside wine
California Grill: Napa Room	Contemporary Resort (view of the Magic Kingdom)	50	Lunch, Dinner	• $1,000 for events ending before 4 pm • $4,000 for events ending between 4 pm and 6 pm • $3,000 for events starting after 6 pm				
California Grill: Sonoma Room	Contemporary Resort (view of Bay Lake)	40	Lunch, Dinner	• $1,000 for events ending before 4 pm • $3,000 for events ending between 4 pm and 6 pm • $2,000 for events starting after 6 pm				
California Grill: The Wine Room	Contemporary Resort (view of Bay Lake)	32	Dinner	$4,000				

Private Rooms/Restaurant Buyouts (cont'd)

Name	Location	Seats	Meals Served	Food & Beverage Minimum	Tax & Gratuity	Cake Cutting	Phone	Additional Info
Citricos: Chef's Domain	Grand Floridian Resort & Spa	12	Dinner 6 pm or 8 pm	$650	6.5% tax, 18% gratuity	no fee	407-824-2989	$20 corkage fee, plus tax and gratuity
Fulton's Crab House	Downtown Disney	40 or 80	Brunch, Lunch, Dinner	$2,500–$3,500 depending on the room you select; rates are seasonally negotiable	6.5% tax, 20% gratuity	$2.00/ person	407-828-8996	$300 deposit; $15 corkage fee, plus tax and gratuity
Gardenview Tea Room	Grand Floridian Resort & Spa	50	Lunch, Dinner	• $500: 11 am–1 pm, Tuesdays and Saturdays • $1,000: 7 pm–9 pm daily	6.5% tax, 18% gratuity	no fee	407-824-2351	Large-party menu; contract required; no games, speeches, opening gifts
Jiko	Animal Kingdom Lodge	125	Brunch, Lunch (end by 3:30 pm)	$1,500	6.5% tax, 21% gratuity	$2.50/ person	407-828-3200	Buffet only; certain decorations prohibited to protect animals
Jiko: Cape Town Wine Room	Animal Kingdom Lodge	Half: 20 Entire room: 40	Brunch, Lunch, Dinner	• Half room: $2,500 • Entire room: $4,000	6.5% tax, 21% gratuity	$2.50/ person	407-828-3200	Large-party menu; certain decorations prohibited to protect animals

Private Rooms/Restaurant Buyouts (cont'd)

Name	Location	Seats	Meals Served	Food & Beverage Minimum	Tax & Gratuity	Cake Cutting	Phone	Additional Info
Narcoossee's	Grand Floridian Resort & Spa	125	Brunch, Lunch (end by 3 pm)	$1,500	6.5% tax, 21% gratuity	no fee	407-828-3200	Buffet only; $20 corkage fee, plus tax and gratuity
Shula's Steak House	Swan & Dolphin Resort	10-65	Dinner	• Sideline Room (seats 10-14) $1,000 • Ribeye Room (seats 20-28) $2,200 • Porterhouse Room (seats 30-42) $3,200 (Larger rooms available)	6.5% tax, 21% gratuity	$25 plus tax and gratuity	407-934-4000	Group dining menus range from $78-$95/person; audio-visual equipment capabilities
Todd English's bluezoo	Swan & Dolphin Resort	50	Dinner	• Up to 15 people: $1,200 • 16-30 people: $2,400 • 31-50 people: $3,600	6.5% tax, 21% gratuity	$25 plus tax and gratuity	407-934-4556	$25 corkage fee, plus tax and gratuity
The Wave	Contemporary Resort	Half: 35 Entire room: 50	Brunch, Lunch, Dinner	• 1-35 people: $200 for brunch, $400 for lunch, $1,500 for dinner • 36-50 people: $400 for brunch, $800 for lunch, $2,000 for dinner	6.5% tax, 21% gratuity	$25 plus tax and gratuity	407-824-3800	Group dining menu required for parties of 20+

Group Dining Information

Name	Location	Seating	Meals Served	Phone	Additional Info
1900 Park Fare	Grand Floridian Resort & Spa	Open	Breakfast, Dinner Large parties advised to book first or last seating	Up to 12 guests: 407-939-3463 13 or more: 407-939-7700	Character buffet
Chef Mickey's	Contemporary Resort	Open	Breakfast, Dinner Large parties advised to book first or last seating	Up to 12 guests: 407-939-3463 13 or more: 407-939-7700	Character buffet
Fresh Mediterranean Market	Swan & Dolphin Resort	Open	Breakfast, Lunch	Up to 14 guests: 407-939-3463 15 or more: 407-934-1603	Buffet; Large parties not required to order off banquet menu; $15 corkage fee and $15 cake-cutting fee, plus tax and gratuity
Fulton's Crab House	Downtown Disney	Open	Lunch, Dinner	Up to 20 guests: 407-939-3463 20 or more: 407-828-8996	$15 corkage fee, plus tax and gratuity
Gardenview Tea Room	Grand Floridian Resort & Spa	Open	Afternoon Tea Parties of 15 or more are booked at 2:00 pm or 4:40 pm	Up to 14 guests: 407-939-3463 15-25 guests: 407-824-2351	Credit card required for parties of 15+; order off large-party menu; no-shows charged cost of large-party menu; 48-hour cancellation policy; no speeches, games, gift opening

Group Dining Information (cont'd)

Name	Location	Seating	Meals Served	Phone	Additional Info
Narcoossee's	Grand Floridian Resort & Spa	Open	Dinner Large parties advised to book first or last seating	Up to 12 guests: 407-939-3463 Direct: 407-824-1400	Order off regular menu or the fixed-price banquet menu; $20 corkage fee, plus tax and gratuity; personalized menus available
Ohana	Polynesian Resort	Open	Dinner Large parties advised to book first or last seating	Up to 12 guests: 407-939-3463 13 or more: 407-939-7700	Large groups may be split up
Portobello	Downtown Disney	Semi-private sections	Lunch, Dinner	Up to 20 guests: 407-939-3463 20 or more: 407-828-8996	$300 deposit to guarantee space for your party; banquet menus starting at $25/person for lunch and $40/person for dinner; $2.00/person cake-cutting fee; $15 corkage fee, plus tax and gratuity
Raglan Road	Downtown Disney	Semi-private "Snug" section seats 23	Lunch, Dinner	Up to 12 guests: 407-939-3463 13 or more: 407-938-0300	Parties of 25+ must order off banquet menu, starting at $37/person; no outside wine; flowers, candles OK

Group Dining Information (cont'd)

Name	Location	Seating	Meals Served	Phone	Additional Info
Victoria & Albert's: Chef's Table	Grand Floridian Resort & Spa	Semi-private section seats 10	Dinner; not available Wednesday or Friday	407-939-3463	$200/person, food only; $295/person with wine pairings; Dress code; seasonal menu, can be tailored
Wolfgang Puck Grand Cafe and Dining Room	Downtown Disney	Open	Lunch, Dinner	Up to 20 guests: 407-939-3463 20 or more: 407-828-8996	Parties of 20+ must order off banquet menu, starting at $43/person in the Cafe and $50/person in the Dining Room; $2/person cake-cutting fee and $15 corkage fee, plus tax and gratuity
Yachtsman Steakhouse	Yacht Club Resort	Semi-private section seats 16	Dinner Large parties advised to book first or last seating	Up to 12 guests: 407-939-3463 13 or more: 407-938-0300 Direct: 407-934-3818	Parties of 21+ must order off large-party menu, starting at $70/person; children charged at lower rate; $20 corkage fee, plus tax and gratuity, one bottle max; personalized menus available

Getting the Ball Rolling

The first time you call Disney's Fairy Tale Weddings (321-939-4610) a Sales Lead Associate will take down your name, the event date and venue, and your preferred time. You will have **three business days** to call back with the reservation number for a four-night stay at any Disney resort, but you may wish to make the reservation before you call Disney's Fairy Tale Weddings.

The Sales Lead Associate will pass you on to a Wedding Consultant, who will supply you with basic information, answer questions, and collect your deposit. After your first call, your Wedding Consultant will mail or e-mail you a **contract**. You will have two weeks to return the signed contract with your $1,000 deposit, which can be paid by credit card, check, money order, or wire transfer.

Within two weeks of receiving your deposit, Disney will assign a Wedding Services Coordinator to guide you through the rest of the process. He or she will send you a **planning kit** that confirms the details of your event and outlines the options and add-ons. After you mark any changes or additions, you will return the planning kit to your coordinator. The Floral/Photography/Entertainment Event Manager will work with you on the bouquet and boutonniere included in the Escape package, as well as on any floral arrangements and favors you wish to add. Changes and additions to your photography package, including the Magic Kingdom Portrait Session, can be made through the Floral/Photography/Entertainment Event Manager or your Wedding Services Coordinator.

The Wedding Services Coordinator is also your contact for adding a **dessert party** and may be able to book your post-wedding meal, rehearsal dinner, or farewell brunch (with the exception of events at restaurants that require a credit card guarantee).

The last thing you'll receive is the **Banquet Event Order**, a document that outlines your big day down to the tiniest detail. If it isn't in the BEO, it won't be part of the event, so be sure that spellings, dates, and times are correct and that every selection you and your Wedding Services Coordinator discussed is included. The remaining balance on your Escape Collection package is due 30 days before the event.

It can be a good idea to take a **relaxed** approach to your Disney's Fairy Tale Wedding planning. Escape Collection couples do not get a lot of hand-holding from their Wedding Services Coordinators because their events are so simple for Disney to arrange. If you have a year until your event, don't be surprised if you go months without hearing from your coordinator. This is not because he or she doesn't care, it's just that there really isn't much that needs to be done in advance. If all your requests are reflected in your BEO, you can be assured that they will be met. So if you are the super-organized type who likes to take advantage of every spare moment, channel that energy into planning the details you control, like making favors or finding a videographer.

Escape Collection Time Line

This 12-month **check list** will show you one way to structure your time, but don't worry if you have less than a year or don't plan to do everything on the list. Escape Collection events are designed to be easily arranged in a short amount of time. Because Escape events cannot be booked until 8 months out, months 9–12 may be best spent gathering ideas and working on creative projects like favors.

10 to 12 Months

❑ Contact Disney's Fairy Tale Weddings to tentatively hold space at your chosen ceremony site.

❑ Discuss who pays for what and start a **budget**.

❑ Begin compiling a **guest list** with complete names and addresses.

❑ Use *PassPorter's Disney Weddings & Honeymoons* to track your plans and keep all your inspiration pictures and ideas in one place.

❑ Choose your **attendants** and ask them to be in the wedding party.

❑ Begin gathering **ideas**, pictures, and samples to share with your Wedding Services Coordinator and Floral Specialist.

9 Months

❑ If you will be using them, interview and get prices from such **outside vendors** as photographers, videographers, and florists.

❑ If you plan to use frequent flyer miles to travel to Walt Disney World and/or your honeymoon destination, book your **flight** now.

❑ Start shopping for a **bridal gown**.

❑ Decide on and contact your **officiant** to discuss ceremony structure and religious requirements like counseling.

❑ **Finalize** the guest list.

8 Months

❑ Contact Disney's Fairy Tale Weddings to **book** your Escape event.

❑ If you haven't already, reserve a Disney **resort stay** of four nights or longer within three business days of booking your event.

❑ Return your Disney's Fairy Tale Weddings contract with a $1,000 **deposit.**

❑ You will be assigned a **Wedding Services Coordinator** within two weeks of returning your contract.

❑ Schedule an in-park **portrait session**, if desired.

❑ Send your engagement **photo and announcement** to the local paper.

❑ If you will be honeymooning somewhere other than Walt Disney World, make your **honeymoon reservations**.

7 Months

❑ Begin looking over the **planning kit** and filling in as much information as you can.

❑ Order the bridal gown. Be sure it is scheduled to arrive at least **one month** before you leave so there is time to have it altered.

6 Months

❑ Disney's Fairy Tale Weddings confirms **pricing** for extra elements such as floral and Fairy Tale Cuvee.

Additional Tasks
❑
❑
❑
❑
❑
❑

4 to 6 Months

- ❑ Shop for and order **bridesmaids' dresses**.
- ❑ Finalize **contracts** with outside vendors.
- ❑ **Register** for wedding gifts. The rule of thumb is at least three stores with a variety of locations and price ranges.
- ❑ Narrow down selections and details for extra **floral, decor,** and **food** or an upgraded **cake**.
- ❑ Line up **cosmetology** services for the wedding day or in-park portrait session. Schedule a cosmetology trial if you will be visiting Walt Disney World before the wedding.
- ❑ Purchase **rings** and send for engraving.
- ❑ If you will be making **welcome bags** for guests, start collecting items.
- ❑ Make or buy **favors**, if necessary.
- ❑ Book your **flights**.
- ❑ Order or make your invitations, announcements, and other **stationery**.
- ❑ Work with mothers to select their **dresses**.
- ❑ Sign up for **dance lessons**, if desired.
- ❑ Make necessary Walt Disney World **dining reservations**.

Additional Tasks
❑
❑
❑
❑
❑
❑

2 to 4 Months

❏ Buy or make a guest book and such **accessories** as a cake topper, cake knife and server, ring pillow, toasting flutes, garter, candles, etc.

❏ **Finalize** details with outside vendors.

❏ If it is not being handled by your Wedding Services Coordinator, **book** the rehearsal dinner or welcome party.

❏ Send your **invitations**, with an RSVP date of at least one month before the event.

❏ Prepare **maps** and directions or transportation schedules for the ceremony and any other wedding-day activities.

❏ Get anything you need for an **international** honeymoon (passport, birth certificate, visas, vaccinations, etc.).

❏ Pick out or design a **ketubah** or other marriage contract required by your religion.

❏ Have the groomsmen's measurements taken and **order their attire**.

❏ Confirm delivery date for bridal gown and **schedule fittings**.

❏ Talk to people you'd want to do special **performances or readings** as part of the ceremony.

❏ Select **songs** for the ceremony and work with your Wedding Services Coordinator to see if the violinist needs the sheet music.

1 to 2 Months

❏ Confirm that formalwear has been ordered for groom and groomsmen. Schedule **formalwear fittings**.

❏ As you receive presents, be sure to **update** or add items to your registries and track the gifts you get.

❏ Have your first bridal **gown fitting**.

❏ If you will be obtaining your marriage **license by mail**, contact the Brevard County Courthouse to order the paperwork. The license must be used within 60 days.

❏ Submit your wedding **announcement** to newspapers, if desired.

❏ Plan the **seating** for the reception and start writing place cards.

❏ Make sure all bridesmaids' attire has been **fitted**.

30 Days

❏ Your Wedding Service Coordinator will provide a detailed **final budget**.

❏ Full **balance** of Estimated Budget is due, along with signed copies of the BEO.

3 to 4 Weeks

❏ Finalize your **vows**.

❏ Attend **final** gown fitting.

❏ Schedule wedding-related **grooming appointments**.

❏ Finish and print ceremony **programs**, if desired.

❏ Pick up rings and check the **inscriptions** before you leave the store.

❏ Have a follow-up meeting or phone call with the officiant to go over **ceremony** timing and details.

❏ Confirm wedding and honeymoon **reservations**, and give loved ones your itinerary in case of emergency.

❏ Contact bridal party with **critical information** related to the rehearsal and ceremony (dates, times, directions, duties).

❏ Create a **wedding box** to gather your ceremony accessories (candles, ring pillow, petal basket, etc.) and your reception accessories (favors, cake topper, guest book, place cards, cake knife and server, etc.).

1 to 2 Weeks

❏ Pick up your bridal gown and make sure all of your **accessories** are together. Ship the gown to a formalwear dealer for storage, steaming, and delivery to your resort, if desired.

❏ **Ship** wedding box to your hotel if you will not be bringing it yourself. Disney's Fairy Tale Weddings cannot store these items.

❏ Finalize your wedding-day **schedule** and share it with attendants, parents, and outside vendors. Distribute wedding-day directions, schedule, and contact list, unless these will be placed in welcome bags.

❏ Confirm all **final payment** amounts and wedding-day schedule with your outside vendors. Make sure they all have directions and access to the site.

❏ Call guests who haven't sent in their reply cards for the reception or rehearsal dinner to get a final **head count**.

❏ Check in with your **officiant** and give him/her rehearsal details and wedding-day schedule.

❏ Prepare your **toasts** or thanks to friends and family.

❏ **Assemble** welcome bags.

❏ Put cash **tips** in marked envelopes and give them to a designated family member or a friend to distribute on the wedding day.

One Week

❏ Schedule time to go pick up your **marriage license** at the courthouse, if necessary. The three-day waiting period applies only to Florida residents, not out-of-state and international residents.

❏ Pick up **formalwear** and try it on or have it delivered for a fitting.

❏ Finalize your **rehearsal dinner** arrangements or other plans. If you are having a private event arranged by your Wedding Services Coordinator, the final guest count is due four days before the dinner by 12:00 pm.

❏ **Distribute** welcome bags to guests' resorts.

One Day

❏ Hand out **assignment** lists and checklists to ensure everyone knows their tasks, including the person responsible for transporting ceremony and reception accessories.

❏ Assign someone to mail your **wedding announcements**.

Wedding Day

❏ Don't forget the **rings and marriage license**.

❏ Make sure two witnesses **sign** the marriage license.

❏ Be sure to **eat** properly.

❏ Don't let the day pass by in a blur—take time to stop and **enjoy** it!

Additional Tasks
❏
❏
❏
❏
❏
❏

Notes

Chapter 3
Wishes Collection

While the Memories and Escape Collections are cost-effective package deals, the Wishes Collection offers a **completely customizable** event—the only limits are your imagination and your bank account!

Choosing the Wishes Collection opens up a world of possibilities, including dozens of ceremony and reception venues, customized menus and cake designs, and elaborate decor options. Along with this comes **personalized service** throughout the planning stages and during your event, including an in-person planning session and a team of assistants on the big day.

The **requirements** for a Wishes Collection event are that you spend a minimum amount of money, depending on date and venue, and that you guarantee your guests will reserve a certain number of hotel nights.

Choosing a Walt Disney World wedding, vow renewal, or commitment ceremony can greatly simplify the planning process by eliminating the need to deal with numerous vendors and infinite details, but the process is not without its complexities. In this chapter we'll start with the **basics** of reserving your date, including what happens if someone else wants the same venue on the same date, and discuss the contract and the deposit.

© Nathan Root

View from the Wedding Pavilion

We'll also cover the **minimum expenditures** required for a Wishes Collection event and what counts toward them. Then we'll explain the sometimes daunting process of blocking hotel rooms for your guests and talk about the planning session, site visit, and menu tasting.

After that comes the **fun part**: choosing venues for the ceremony and reception, setting your menu and designing your cake, picking out flowers and decor, and selecting music and entertainment.

We'll also cover transportation, photography, and videography and talk about how to find **outside vendors** for certain elements of the event.

And once you have an idea what you'd like to do, we'll give you tips on ways to **save money** and a time line that incorporates the traditional wedding-planning checklist with tasks specific to Walt Disney World events.

Wishes Collection Basics

Before you call Disney's Fairy Tale Weddings to book, you'll need to pick an event **date**. Perhaps you've always dreamed of a Christmas wedding or you want to honor your parents by marrying on their anniversary. Or maybe you are only able to hold your vow renewal during school holidays, or you want a memorable commitment ceremony date like 11/11/11.

There are many important factors to consider when choosing your date, but one of the biggest for a Wishes Collection event is **price**. Disney requires you to spend a certain amount of money on that day based on day of the week, time of day, reception venue, and your date's proximity to major holidays.

Minimum Expenditures

Wishes Collection events are subject to **several sets** of minimum expenditures. There's an overall minimum expenditure for the day of your event—a total amount you must spend with Disney to have your event at Walt Disney World. Then there's a per-person food and beverage minimum expenditure—the amount you must spend on each of your guests for food, beverages, and cake over the course of the day. And many sites also have a venue-specific food and beverage minimum expenditure—a total amount that must be spent on food and beverages at that venue.

Sales tax and Disney's 21% service charge **do not count** toward these minimums.

Overall Minimum Expenditure

The overall minimum expenditure can be met by any service provided by Disney's Fairy Tale Weddings on your wedding day, including venue rental, food and beverage, floral, decor, music, entertainment, photography, videography, and transportation. Only services rendered **on that day** count toward your minimum—rehearsal dinners, farewell breakfasts, and the like will not count. The only exception to this is bridal portrait sessions shot inside the parks before they open: If Disney Event Group Photography is also shooting your wedding, these do not have to be held on the day of your event to count toward your overall minimum expenditure.

Favors provided by Disney Floral & Gifts count toward the overall minimum expenditure

Like hotel rates, the overall minimum expenditure required for a Wishes Collection event varies by the **day of the week** you select. Saturday night is traditionally the most expensive time to be married anywhere, including Walt Disney World. Choosing a weekday wedding can significantly reduce your overall minimum expenditure requirement. Listed below are the 2011 overall minimum expenditures for Wishes Collection events, exclusive of tax and service charge.

Monday-Thursday: $12,000
Friday-Sunday: $15,000
Sunday-Saturday: $10,000 for 4-hour receptions starting before 2 pm

Note: Higher minimums may apply during certain seasons and on holidays.

In 2010 Disney introduced a lower, **$10,000 overall minimum expenditure** for receptions starting before 2 pm and lasting a maximum of 4 hours. The rate is available any day of the week and requires a ceremony time of 9 am, 10 am, or 12 pm.

Per-Person Food and Beverage Minimum Expenditure
Disney also requires you to spend a certain amount **per person** on food and beverages for your Wishes Collection event. The amount varies by ceremony start time. The per-person cost of your wedding cake will count toward this minimum, as will any food and beverages served at other events catered by Disney on that day. This includes the pre-reception, dessert parties, and private events like a bridesmaid's tea. Note that you will not have to meet per-person minimums for guests under age 21, but you will be charged for their food and beverages.

Below are the per-person food and beverage **minimum expenditures**, exclusive of tax and service charge.

Meal	Ceremony Time	Price Per Person
Breakfast/Brunch	8:00 am, 9:00 am, 10:00 am	$75
Lunch	12:00 pm	$100
Dinner	2:30 pm, 5:00 pm, 7:30 pm	$125

All food and drinks served on the day of your event count toward the per-person food and beverage minimum expenditure, including the cocktail hour and dessert party

The cake usually doesn't count toward venue-specific minimums

Venue-Specific Food and Beverage Minimum Expenditure

With the exception of ballrooms and certain theme park locations, all reception venues have an **overall** food and beverage minimum that must be met. This varies by venue and can depend on day of the week and time of day. The cost of the wedding cake only counts toward this minimum at Grand Floridian locations. Specific food and beverage minimums will be listed in the description of each venue later in this chapter.

As an **example**, for a reception at the Living Seas Salon in Epcot after 4 pm, there is a overall minimum expenditure of $3,500 for just the reception food and beverage, as well as Disney's food and beverage minimum expenditure of $125/person for the entire wedding day. This means that, while you aren't required to spend a total of $125/person on just reception food and beverage, what you do spend must add up to at least $3,500.

Guest Accommodation Requirement

The other minimum requirement of Wishes Collection events is a guarantee that you and your guests will reserve a certain number of **room nights** at Disney resorts during your event. The minimum number required to set up a room block is 10 nights, but you may forego the room block entirely if you have a very small number of guests or if most of your guests will not require hotel rooms.

Remember that the guarantee is based on room **nights**, not number of rooms, and your own wedding and honeymoon stay counts toward the minimum.

If your guests reserve 25 nights or more at any of Disney's on-site resorts, including Disney Vacation Club properties, you will receive one **complimentary night** in a standard room at the Disney resort of your choice.

Often this is a Concierge-level room, but it is never a suite. If having a suite or being guaranteed a room on the Concierge level is important to you, you should book and pay for that room. Then you will need to **move to the complimentary room** on the night that you choose to use it.

The Grand Floridian is popular with wedding groups

Disney Vacation Club members staying on **points** receive no alternative compensation, so you may wish to use the free night as a getting-ready room for the bride or groom. Alternatively, you can shorten your stay on points at the Disney Vacation Club resort by one day and make a separate reservation there with the free night.

Your guests will receive a discount for booking their rooms through the Wedding Group Reservation center (see page 58 for more information). If they book their rooms **any other way**—by calling a travel agent or the Walt Disney Travel Company, or by using Disney Vacation Club points, a Disney

Three-bedroom Grand Villas at Disney Vacation Club's BoardWalk Villas are great for large groups

cast member discount, a PIN, or promotions like the free Disney Dining Plan—their reservations will need to be added to your room block manually to count toward your minimum guarantee.

Service Charges & Tax

One of the trickiest aspects of budgeting for your Disney's Fairy Tale Wedding is figuring out which elements incur Disney's 21% service charge and which incur 6.5% Orange County sales tax. Even trickier is that you have to calculate tax on some of the service charges! These numbers are important to know because they do not count toward your minimum expenditure requirements and can add a **substantial amount** to your final bill.

The **rule of thumb** about service charges being applied exclusively to food and beverages doesn't quite apply here. You will also be charged a service fee on any audiovisual elements of your entertainment package that require a technician to set them up, such as iPods, microphones, speakers, and lighting packages. However, AV service charges are not **taxed** like food and beverage service charges are.

Certain elements that do not incur a service charge may instead incur taxable **fees** for handling, set-up, and delivery. Depending on your situation, these may include dessert party set-up and items provided by Disney Floral & Gifts. Wedding cakes incur a taxable service charge, and those that are served at venues other than the Grand Floridian have a taxable delivery fee.

Disney transportation, entertainment, and photography and videography packages are about the only things that **don't** incur service fees or tax, although there is one exception: Tax is assessed on photography and videography if you live in the state of Florida or have your proofs or video delivered to you before you leave Florida.

Service Charges and Tax (continued)

And while **entertainers** like characters, DJs, and bands don't have service charges, there may be fees for setting up lighting packages or other audiovisual elements required for them.

We have included a budget worksheet in Chapter 10: Planning Pages that will help you calculate taxes and service charges on the standard components of a Disney wedding, but the chart below will give you a **general idea** about which elements incur these charges.

© Jennifer Marx

No tax or service fees on these!

Item	Taxed?	Service Charge	Taxed?
Audio/Visual Elements	Yes	Service charge for anything that requires setup by a technician	No
Cake	Yes	Handling fee at all but Grand Floridian venues	Yes
Ceremony Venue Rental Fee	Yes	None	n/a
Dessert Party Viewing Fee	Yes	None	n/a
Entertainment	N	oNone, but there may be service charges on AV elements required with DJs/bands	No
Event Guides	No	None	n/a
Floral & Decor	Yes	Move/set/delivery fees	Yes
Food & Beverage	Yes	21%	Yes
Photography & Videography Packages	No*	None	n/a
Reception/ Dessert Party Venue Rental Fee	Yes	Setup charge for some venues	Yes
Transportation	No	None	n/a

* Unless you are a Florida resident or you receive your photos/video while still in Florida

Discounts

Discounts on the cost of Disney's Fairy Tale Wedding events are rare, and you can't use gift cards or Disney's Honeymoon Registry funds to pay your bill. However, Disney has begun to offer limited-time promotions like additional free hotel nights, so keep checking for the **Special Offers tab** that occasionally appears under "Wedding Specialist" on the official web site.

There may also be cast member or Florida resident discounts available on **certain elements** of the wedding on certain days of the week. Talk to your Wedding Event Planner if you think you might be eligible for these.

 Is It Possible To Have a Wishes Collection Event for the Lowest Minimum Expenditure?

The short answer is yes! The long answer is that keeping the cost of your wedding to Disney's lowest overall minimum expenditure requires creativity and a willingness to scale down or sacrifice some of the trappings of the typical magazine wedding.

For example, instead of a Saturday-night wedding at Christmastime with a duo-plate meal, full bar, and a band, consider a weekday-morning wedding in early December with a brunch buffet, no bar, and an iPod. Food, beverages, floral, and decor usually eat up the biggest chunk of the wedding budget. At Walt Disney World, transportation and entertainment can also be significant expenses.

Think about the three most important elements of your wedding and consider those the areas to spend on. For example, you might choose floral, photography, and gourmet food. Then you can find ways to cut costs on elements that are less important to you. The "Money-Saving Tips" section at the end of this chapter suggests numerous large and small ways to save money on your Wishes Collection event.

It is important to remember that tax and service charge are assessed on top of the overall minimum expenditure—they do not count toward it. For a minimum expenditure of $10,000, these charges could add up to $2,000 or more, depending on which of the elements you've selected incur tax and service charges.

And although Disney's Fairy Tale Weddings can provide nearly every item or service for your wedding day, there are numerous other wedding expenses to budget for, like wedding attire, rings, transportation to Walt Disney World, accommodations, officiant fees, the license, cosmetology, and the honeymoon. Using outside vendors for wedding-day services further increases your expenses beyond Disney's overall minimum expenditure.

But if the extras on your Escape wedding are starting to add up, you might want to consider making the leap to a Wishes wedding knowing that it is possible to have one without going much over the minimum. And you may find that the added level of service and flexibility makes up for any difference in price.

The Planning Process

You can call Disney's Fairy Tale Weddings (321-939-4610) to start the planning process up to **24 months** before the date you've chosen for your event, but your ability to reserve a date or sign a contract depends on the venues you plan to use—many cannot be confirmed until 12 months before.

Booking

On that first call, a Sales Lead Associate will take your contact information and ask **basic questions** about the date, time, and ceremony and reception venues you want. Don't worry if you aren't sure which venues you want before you call. You can work with Disney's Fairy Tale Weddings to determine the ones that best suit your event and even arrange a site visit to see them in person. More information on the site visit can be found on page 62.

After the first call, you will be contacted by a Wedding Consultant, who can **pencil you in** for your desired date, time, and venues at 16 months out. This means that your request has been noted but availability is not guaranteed.

If your reception will be held in a theme park or in venues that are not part of a convention center, both the ceremony and the reception location can be confirmed immediately; all other venues can't be confirmed until **12 months** out. Even if only one of your venues falls under the 12-month rule, you will need to wait until that time to confirm all your venues.

Wishes Collection events are usually held at 10:00 am, 12:00 pm, 2:30 pm, 5:00 pm, or 7:30 pm. In-park events must be held at 8:00 am or 9:00 am (depending on when the park opens) or two hours after the park closes in the evening.

The Lottery
If more than one couple wants the same date, time, and venue for their ceremony or reception, a lottery is held at the **16-month mark**. Usually only the Wedding Pavilion is in enough demand to require a lottery, although other locations may inspire one on popular dates like Valentine's Day or 11/11/11. Requesting a Friday or a Saturday will also increase the likelihood that you'll end up in a lottery.

Initially, the lottery is based on **ceremony time**. Although there may be only two couples who want the same time slot at one venue, every couple holding a wedding there that day must be entered into the lottery because the couples who lose that coveted time slot will need to be scheduled at their second- or third-choice times.

The Wedding Pavilion can be booked 16 months out if your reception won't be at a convention center.

Even if a couple gets their first-choice ceremony site, there may then be competition for their **reception venue**, meaning the times could shift again depending on which is more important to them—the ceremony time or the reception venue. If you will be entered into a lottery, you'll need to consider your priorities. It's a good idea to give your Wedding Consultant a few alternative combinations of date, time, and venue.

The lottery is held 16 months, to the day, before the event date or on the first **business day** following the date if it falls on a weekend. Your Wedding Consultant will notify you of the outcome on the following business day.

After the 16-month mark, no lottery is required. If the site you want is not being used by another group, Disney's Fairy Tale Weddings will **request it** from the central scheduling office and receive confirmation within 48 hours.

Estimated Proposal

Once you begin working with a Wedding Consultant, you may request an **estimate of the costs** for the event you envision. He or she will customize an estimated proposal based on the locations you want, your projected guest count, and the options you select. Proposals produced more than six months before the wedding do not contain guaranteed pricing, but they will give you a general idea of what you can expect to pay.

Disney's Fairy Tale Weddings Web Site

The Disney's Fairy Tale Weddings web site at http://disneyweddings.disney.go.com/ is a good place to **start exploring** your options when you are considering a Walt Disney World wedding or waiting until the 24-month mark to get the ball rolling. You'll find basic information on ceremony and reception sites, floral and decor, food and beverage, photography and videography, transportation, and entertainment.

Probably the most helpful area of the site is the **Design Studio**, which features lots of photos of the floral and decor elements Disney offers, along with dozens of shots of wedding cakes.

Another great resource is the **Special Offer page**, which may occasionally appear under the "Wedding Specialist" tab when promotions or discounts are available.

What you won't find on Disney's official web site are any **prices** other than the minimum expenditure requirements. If you're trying to determine whether a Disney's Fairy Tale Wedding is within your budget, use *PassPorter's Disney Weddings & Honeymoons* to look up the prices for the various elements you want and plug them into the Wishes/Couture Collection Budget worksheet on pages 223-227. In the e-book version of *PassPorter's Disney Weddings & Honeymoons*, the worksheet will automatically calculate tax and service charge on exactly the elements and guest count you input to give you a realistic sample budget.

Room Block

If you can guarantee 10 or more room nights, Disney will reserve a block of rooms for your wedding guests at **up to four** hotels of your choice. This ensures that your guests will be able to book rooms at those resorts until the cut-off date one month before the wedding.

It also gives them a **discounted room rate** at those resorts, usually about 30% off at the Deluxe Resorts that have convention facilities, 15% off at other Deluxe Resorts, a little less than 15% off at Moderate Resorts, and less than 10% off at Value Resorts.

Your guests do not have to book at these resorts for their reservations to count toward your guest accommodation requirement, but they will only receive your event discount at the resorts in your block. If a resort in the block **sells out**, guests will be offered comparable accommodation at the discounted rate. If your guests wait until after the cut-off date to book and rooms are still available at the resorts that were in your room block, they will be able to reserve rooms at the discounted rate. But if those resorts have sold out, guests will not be eligible for your event discount elsewhere.

You determine which resorts to include and **how many nights** should be set aside at each—a difficult task if you have no idea how many of those you invited are coming and where they will want to stay. Here are some things to consider when setting up your room block:

- **Price Level**—Disney suggests that you reserve resorts in each of the three price categories: Deluxe, Moderate, and Value. However couples sometimes find that their guests all gravitate toward just one category—and not necessarily the cheapest! You may already have a good idea which type of accommodation most of your guests will choose based on how far they have to travel, how long you think they will stay, and how often they have been to Walt Disney World.

- **Number of Resorts**—You may reserve rooms at as many as four resorts and as few as one. One of the advantages of reserving the maximum number of resorts is the wide range of choice your guests will have. You may also want to include a resort or two where you plan to stay on your honeymoon so you can take advantage of your wedding discount. However, if you will be providing transportation for your guests, you may want to consider offering them fewer resorts in order to save time and money. For example, if you have guests at four different hotels, you will be required to charter a motor coach for a minimum of five hours, and those who are picked up first may be sitting on the coach for more than an hour before everyone is delivered to your ceremony venue.

- **Locations**—Consider the distance between the resorts you select and the ceremony and reception sites. This will be another factor in the amount of time your guests spend getting to and from your event. You may be able to skip chartered transportation altogether if all your guests are staying at the resort where your ceremony and reception will be held.

Once you've selected the resorts, you decide how to divide up the total number of room nights among them. You are only **required to fill 80%** of the number of rooms you set aside in a block. For example, if you want to make 30 room nights available to your guests, you are only required to fill 25 of them. If you have trouble filling the rooms set aside in your block, adjustments can be made to the guarantee or to the number of rooms in the block before 90 days out from the wedding day.

© Jennifer Marx

If you're still unsure about your resort choices and number of nights, don't worry—the room block is a work in progress and can be **updated** as you learn more about your guests' plans.

The Polynesian Resort is eligible for a 15% discount on room rates

Letter of Agreement

Once you have confirmed your venues and set up the room block, your Wedding Consultant will send you a **contract**, which Disney refers to as a Letter of Agreement. This contains all the basic information about your wedding:

- Your contact information
- Event date, locations, and times
- Room block details and requirements
- Payment amounts and due dates
- Schedule and venue details for the day of the event
- Information about marriage licenses, weather, smoking and alcohol policies, etc.
- General information on service charges
- Optional services provided by Disney
- Deadlines for guest count
- Cancellation policy
- Legal and liability information

After you have reviewed the Letter of Agreement, you will initial each page and have everyone responsible for the wedding sign the last page. This includes the couple and anyone else who is authorized to **make decisions** about the wedding, like a parent.

Your signed Letter of Agreement and deposit must be returned to Disney's Fairy Tale Weddings by the date listed—usually about two weeks after the contract was drawn up—or the hold on venues, date, and times will be released. Your Wedding Consultant will then mail you a copy of the signed contract, along with two complimentary vouchers for Walt Disney World Theme Park **Annual Passes**. Check out the "Disney's Fairy Tale Weddings Annual Passes" sidebar on page 25 of Chapter 2: Escape Collection for more information.

Deposit

Your signed Letter of Agreement must be sent back with a deposit of **$2,000**, which can be made by credit card, check, money order, or wire transfer. If the Letter of Agreement is signed within 90 days of the wedding, the deposit amount will be equal to the full overall minimum expenditure required for your date and venue.

For all others, the full overall minimum expenditure amount must be paid **90 days** before the wedding date.

Save-the-Date E-mail

Disney will send your guests a save-the-date e-mail about two weeks after your signed Letter of Agreement and deposit are received. The e-mail contains everything your guests need to **begin planning** to attend your event: basic details about the day, along with information about booking rooms and the special rate on park tickets.

You will need to provide your Wedding Consultant with a list of your **guests' e-mail addresses** around the time that you submit your signed contract and deposit. Disney will mail printed copies of the save-the-date information to any of your guests who don't have e-mail access.

The save-the-date e-mails are not recommended as a replacement for formal invitations, which are usually sent **two or three months** before a destination wedding, but they help give guests enough notice to begin planning a trip to Walt Disney World. Invitations are not included in the Wishes Collection amenities, although Disney can provide you with a list of stationery vendors.

 Who's Who at Disney's Fairy Tale Weddings

When you make your first call to Disney's Fairy Tale Weddings, you'll speak with a **Sales Lead Associate**, who will take down your contact information and answer basic questions. You will then be assigned a **Wedding Consultant**. He or she acts as a sales manager, overseeing the contract and all related details, including availability of locations and site visits, the room block, and the deposit. Although your Wedding Consultant will be responsible for these details throughout the planning process, after the contract is finalized (but no more than 12 months out) you will be assigned a **Wedding Event Planner**, who will become your main contact at Disney's Fairy Tale Weddings. The Wedding Event Planner handles the details of the wedding day itself, including schedules, menus, entertainment—basically everything except floral. For that, you will be assigned a **Floral Specialist** through Disney Floral & Gifts. In addition to flowers, your Floral Specialist can handle all decor items, including linens, chairs, and any accessories or favors ordered through Disney.

My Disney's Fairy Tale Weddings Facebook Application

In 2010 Disney introduced the My Disney's Fairy Tale Weddings Facebook application, which allows couples to build a **personalized web site** and includes several helpful planning tools.

A user-friendly interface allows couples to customize their site using one of 26 themes with multiple color palettes and makes it easy to post information about themselves, the wedding party, their guests, and the event. Social networking features include the ability to upload and share photos, manage the guest list, track RSVPs, and conduct polls. And guests can use the site to **buy tickets and book rooms** using the couple's wedding discount.

Guests who do not have Facebook accounts can still access the site through a **special link** provided by the bride and groom. They will be able to see all the basic information but not participate in the social-networking aspect of the site.

Couples have access to the app as soon as they begin planning, but certain features need to be **unlocked** by the sales consultant as they move through the planning process.

Planning Kit & Questionnaire

Soon after you return your Letter of Agreement, your Wedding Consultant will send you a planning kit and questionnaire. The kit contains a planning time line; guidelines on such **basics** as minimum expenditures and room-night minimums; venue rental rates and descriptions; information on Disney's photo and video packages; optional lists of officiants, cosmetologists, and formalwear retailers; and details on Florida marriage license requirements.

© Nathan Root

The questionnaire is designed to capture the basic information your Wedding Event Planner will need to begin visualizing your celebration. It **walks you through** each aspect of the day, from where you will get ready to how you will make your getaway, and it includes questions about additional events like the rehearsal dinner and farewell brunch. The questionnaire should be returned about two weeks before your planning session so your Wedding Event Planner can use it when you meet. Don't worry if you don't have all the answers yet—your planner will help you

No floral or decor choices need to be made just yet!

fill in the rest at your planning session.

In-Person Planning

Thanks to technology and the services of your Wedding Event Planner, it is possible to plan an entire Wishes Collection event without setting foot on Disney property before the big day. However, there are several aspects of the planning process that can be more easily accomplished in person. If you are able to make a trip to Walt Disney World before your wedding, you can **meet** with your Wedding Event Planner

Franck's Bridal Studio

in person at Disney's Fairy Tale Weddings' "show" office, Franck's Bridal Studio. (The real office is in the nearby town of Celebration.) Located next to the Wedding Pavilion and a short walk from the Grand Floridian Resort & Spa, Franck's is a replica of the wedding studio in the 1991 remake of *Father of the Bride*.

Site Visit

A site visit allows you to **tour** the ceremony and reception locations you are considering and see firsthand whether they are right for your event. You can arrange a site visit up to 24 months before your wedding by contacting a Wedding Consultant. Usually you will meet him or her at Franck's, although it is sometimes possible to be picked up at your Disney resort. The Wedding Consultant will drive you to the locations you've arranged to view. Alternatively, you may meet the Wedding Consultant at one of the sites if it does not require traveling backstage at any of the parks. Site visits are available Monday-Thursday, usually at 9:00 am, 11:00 am, or 1:00 pm.

We've included a Site Visit Worksheet among the planning pages to help you organize your questions and give you a place to take notes during your site visit.

Menu Tasting

Most reception venues offer menu tastings to help you decide **what to serve** at your buffet or plated meal. If your reception will be held in a theme park, you will have your tasting in the central kitchen. If you choose a conference center

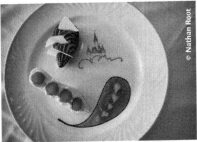

venue, the tasting will probably be held in a ballroom. Menu tastings are not available for some restaurant reception venues, including California Grill. Up to four people can attend the menu tasting, and all must be at least 18 years old.

You must **request** a tasting 2-4 weeks ahead—it is not automatically included in your planning session.

The White Chocolate Cinderella Slipper Dessert is popular at menu tastings

Your Wedding Event Planner will send you a **tasting checklist** so you can request to try items from the menus offered by your reception venue. You can select two or three items for each course—appetizer, salad, entrée, and dessert. One approach is to select only those foods that you are unsure about or have never tasted, since most people know what things like steak or waffles taste like. Whatever you choose, be sure to arrive at the tasting with an empty stomach—you will be served meal-sized portions of everything, and it is a lot of food!

Choose from a selection of napkin folds

The menu tasting is attended by your Wedding Event Planner and one of the venue's chefs, who will make notes about your preferences and your reactions to each dish. He or she can also answer your questions about special **dietary requirements**, substitutions, or re-creating recipes that aren't on the standard menus. Additionally, you will get to choose the style of napkin fold you want at the reception from a variety set out on the tasting table.

Planning Session

A planning session allows you to meet with your Wedding Event Planner and Floral Specialist in person to map out every detail of your day, from the schedule to the cake flavors to the reception centerpieces. This is a great chance to share your ideas and inspiration pictures so that Disney can help you design the day you've imagined. Depending on the complexity of your event and the amount of research you have done beforehand, the planning session can run from a couple of hours to four or more. The sessions are available Monday–Friday from either 9:00 am to 1:00 pm or 1:00 pm to 5:00 pm. Because prices are not guaranteed until six months before the wedding date, planning sessions are usually not scheduled more than **six months out**.

Your Wedding Event Planner will use your answers to the **planning questionnaire** as a starting point for your planning session. You'll set the wedding-day schedule, including the order of the ceremony, the length of your reception, and transportation methods and itineraries. A block of time will be set aside for you to meet with the Floral Specialist to design personal floral and ceremony and reception decor. This includes unity candles and sand ceremonies, chairs and chair covers, tables and linens, and any favors you plan to purchase through Disney Floral & Gifts.

Inside Franck's Bridal Studio

Planning Session (continued)

One thing you won't necessarily discuss is the **price** of everything you're choosing. Sometimes this is because your Wedding Event Planner or Floral Specialist must research certain requests or elements, especially floral, before her or she can give you a price. Also, some couples prefer to think of the planning session as a blue-sky idea session where any and all options are available, regardless of price. But if you're trying to stick to a budget or

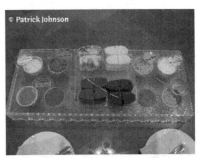
© Patrick Johnson

Samples of cake and fillings

you get the feeling that you may be racking up the expenses, you should feel free to ask how much each element is going to cost. Just keep in mind that you won't get an Estimated Budget until 3-6 weeks after the planning session.

Last, you'll have a chance to try **cake flavors** and fillings. Usually Disney provides samples of four cake flavors and six to eight fillings. If there are specific flavors you wish to try, be sure to let your Wedding Event Planner know at least a week before your planning session. A list of standard flavors can be found in the "Food, Beverages, and Cake" section of this chapter.

When you finish, you will have planned your entire event! And don't worry if you **change your mind** about something later—you can always make changes, especially after you get the Estimated Budget!

The BEO & Estimated Budget

Except for the marriage license, the Banquet Event Order is the single **most important document** related to your event. It lists what is happening and when for every moment of your day, down to the very last detail. This includes locations, the order of events, detailed itineraries, entertainment schedules, the layout of the ceremony site, descriptions of decor, cake flavors and decorations, transportation schedules, menus, seating charts—it's all in there!

The BEO is used by all the people working on your wedding—from your Wedding Event Planner to the cake baker to the bus driver—to make sure things run **according to plan**. It covers big things, like where the reception will take place and what time it will start, and small things, like whether you want half glasses or whole glasses for the Champagne toast. The BEO may also include details of events on other days, such as a rehearsal dinner (if it was arranged through Disney's Fairy Tale Weddings) or a Magic Kingdom Portrait Session.

The thing to remember is, if it isn't in the BEO, it won't happen. So make sure yours includes all the details that are **important to you**—even if it's something as small as requesting that a piece of furniture be repositioned.

Although the BEO includes individual item pricing, you will receive a second document, the Estimated Budget, which lists **all the charges** and tallies them up. A third document, the Wedding Floral Proposal, lists the details and charges for every item handled by Disney Floral & Gifts, including such decor items as altarpieces, centerpieces, chair covers, and table linens, as well as place cards and favors if they will be provided by Disney. The Wedding Floral Proposal is sent separately from the BEO—many weeks later, in some cases—so items and prices from the Wedding Floral Proposal are incorporated into the BEO and Estimated Budget later in the planning process.

You will receive many drafts of the BEO as you plan your wedding. Each time you make a change to any aspect of the day, the BEO must be revised. When you

receive your first draft, be sure that all the basic information, including dates, times, and the spelling of your names, is correct. If you are unsure about anything you see in the BEO, ask your Wedding Event Planner about it. The details of your BEO will determine the amount of the **final payment** you make one month before the wedding, so be sure that they are correct.

Chair sashes and other decor at Franck's

Overall Minimum Expenditure & Final Payment

Disney requires you to pay your full overall minimum expenditure amount 90 days before your wedding date. Your final payment of any remaining amount is due 30 days before the wedding date. That amount is based on the Estimated Budget and guest count at that time. However, **changes** can be made to almost every aspect of the wedding as few as 10 or 15 business days before the date, and the final guest count upon which food and beverage charges are based is not due until three business days before.

Of the $2,000 deposit, $1,000 is applied to the balance due on your wedding at the time of final payment. Disney returns the remaining $1,000 of your deposit to you **after the event**, minus any overages incurred after the final payment was made. If you end up spending less than the amount of the final payment, you will be refunded the difference along with that $1,000 portion of your deposit. You should receive a final invoice from the Walt Disney World Credit Department about two weeks after your wedding. Any refund will be made based on the form of payment used for your final payment, so it may be credited to a card rather than issued as a check.

Deadlines

The 90 days before your event are filled with deadlines and **cut-off dates**. The chart below will help you keep track.

Overall Minimum Expenditure Payment	90 business days
Full Balance Payment	30 business days
Room Block Cut-Off Date	30 business days
Entertainment Changes	30 business days
Wedding Cake Style	30 business days
Floral Changes	15 business days
Wedding Cake Guest Count	15 business days
Table Assignments	10 business days
Food & Beverage Guest Count/Meal Selections	3 business days

Cancellation Policy

If you need to cancel your event, you will be charged some **hefty fees** that get steeper the closer you are to the event date. If you notify Disney 181 or more days beforehand, you will only forfeit your $2,000 deposit. If you cancel between 180 and 60 days before, you will forfeit either the deposit plus the amount of room charges Disney would have been paid if you'd fulfilled your minimum room-night requirement (plus tax and gratuity) or 50% of the overall minimum expenditure required for your date plus the room charges for your room-night requirement (plus tax and gratuity)—whichever is greater. If, for example your room-night minimum was 50 nights, regardless of how many rooms you actually blocked, Disney would charge you the nightly rate at the cheapest hotel in your block multiplied by 50 nights plus either the $2,000 deposit or half the overall minimum expenditure for your date.

Cancellations between 59 and 31 days out incur a charge equal to either the deposit plus the amount of room charges Disney would have been paid if you'd fulfilled your minimum room-night requirement (plus tax and gratuity) or 75% of the overall minimum expenditure required for your date plus the room charges for your room-night requirement (plus tax and gratuity)—whichever is greater. And cancellations made 30 to 0 days beforehand incur a charge of 90% of the food and beverage, room, and entertainment fees, along with all other charges (plus tax and gratuity) that Disney would have been entitled to for your event.

The only **exceptions** to this are cancellations more than 31 days before the wedding due to the death of an immediate family member or because the bride or groom is called to duty as an active member of the U.S. military. For these exceptions, cancellation must be made by registered mail. All other cancellations may be submitted to your Wedding Consultant in writing via e-mail, fax, or mail.

Ceremony Venues

There are **three types** of ceremony venue at Walt Disney World: Disney's Wedding Pavilion, resort venues, and theme park venues. Which one you choose will depend on a number of factors, from the size of your guest list to the time of day you wish to be married and, of course, personal taste. Ceremonies at the Wedding Pavilion have a $3,000 venue rental fee. All other locations cost $2,000, with two exceptions: The scuba wedding in the tank at The Seas With Nemo & Friends comes in a $3,500 package, while the Magic Kingdom venue is part of a $28,000 ceremony-only package that includes transportation, entertainment, floral, photography, and videography.

None of the ceremony sites have dressing rooms, and the Bride's Vestibule and Groom's Vestibule at the Wedding Pavilion are not available more than a few minutes before the ceremony. If you need **more space** to get ready than your hotel room provides, you can arrange to use a resort meeting room or banquet room. These cannot be confirmed until two weeks before the wedding and have a food and beverage minimum of $500. A potentially cheaper alternative might be booking an additional room or a Disney Vacation Club villa at a nearby resort.

To see photos, floor plans and basic information on each venue, check out Disney's Virtual Venue Tour at http://disneyweddings.disney.go.com/weddings/florida/vsi. Click on the "Ceremony" tab, then click "Search" to see all available venues.

Disney's Wedding Pavilion

Located on Seven Seas Lagoon between the Polynesian Resort and the Grand Floridian Resort & Spa, the nondenominational Wedding Pavilion is one of the most expensive ceremony venues but also the **best equipped** for a wedding. Among its custom features are separate waiting rooms for the bride and groom, built-in video

Interior of the Wedding Pavilion

cameras, and a magnifying window that provides a view of Cinderella Castle at the Magic Kingdom. The Wedding Pavilion can accommodate up to 300 guests, and its venue rental fee includes a sound system and an organist for the versatile electric organ.

It is also possible to have your ceremony on the **beach** adjacent to the Wedding Pavilion for the same venue rental fee. The location has views of Space Mountain rather than Cinderella Castle, and the rain backup location is the Wedding Pavilion.

Resort Ceremony Venues

There are several ceremony venues at Walt Disney World's resort hotels. Four of these sites were built **specifically for weddings**: Sea Breeze Point, near BoardWalk Inn; Sunrise Terrace, at Wilderness Lodge; Sunset Pointe, at the Polynesian Resort; and the Wedding Gazebo at the Yacht Club. Ceremonies may also be held in the ballrooms at the Grand Floridian, BoardWalk Inn, and Yacht & Beach Club.

Only Disney floral, decor, and entertainment may be used at outdoor venues; no outside vendors or wedding guests may provide these services. Also, Disney recommends renting a sound system for **outdoor weddings** with more than 25 guests.

View from Sea Breeze Point

The **rain backup** location for outdoor sites is usually a ballroom at the resort, although occasionally the Wedding Pavilion is used as a backup for Sunset Pointe. The backup location depends on availability and the number of guests, and it cannot be confirmed until one month before the wedding.

Sea Breeze Point is an open-air pavilion located along the winding path that connects BoardWalk Inn and the Yacht & Beach Club and circles Crescent Lake. It is the only outdoor ceremony venue that is completely covered, although ceremonies are usually moved to a backup location when it rains. The site offers views across to the Swan & Dolphin resort, and it is a 5- to 7-minute walk from the lobby of BoardWalk Inn.

Sunrise Terrace, located off the fourth floor of Wilderness Lodge, overlooks Bay Lake and the resort's theme pool. The small, uncovered patio accommodates the couple and eight guests, and there is an indoor alcove that can be used in case of rain. Specialty transportation such as Cinderella's Glass Coach is not available at this venue.

The **Wedding Gazebo** is tucked into a courtyard at the Yacht Club Resort, surrounded on three sides by hotel rooms and facing Crescent Lake. The gazebo accommodates only the couple and the officiant, so guests are seated in chairs on the lawn. The rain backup location is a ballroom at the Yacht & Beach Club Convention Center.

Wedding Gazebo at Yacht Club

Sunset Pointe is a palm-lined knoll overlooking Seven Seas Lagoon, with Cinderella Castle visible in the distance. The site accommodates the couple and eight guests and, due to the heat, may only be booked from October through March. The rain backup location for Sunset Pointe is either the King Kamehameha suite at the Polynesian Resort or the Wedding Pavilion, depending on availability.

There are also numerous **ballrooms** available for ceremonies at the conference centers of the Grand Floridian, BoardWalk Inn, and Yacht & Beach Club. These range from the Grand Floridian's intimate Whitehall Room, with its patio beneath the monorail track, to the BoardWalk Inn's spacious Marvin Gardens Room, which can be divided into three separate rooms.

And if none of these choices appeal to you, ask your Wedding Consultant about **additional resort locations**. These might include the Croquet Lawn and the Quiet Pool area at BoardWalk Inn or Shipwreck Beach at the Yacht & Beach Club. Your Wedding Consultant will be able to make recommendations based on factors like your party's size, your reception venue, and the time of year.

© Photography By Taz

Croquet Lawn at BoardWalk Inn

Theme Park Ceremony Venues

In-park ceremonies are the ultimate Disney experience—where else can you be married beneath the spires of a castle or in the shadow of Morocco's gate at Bab Boujeloud, then have your formal portraits taken on Main Street, U.S.A. or in the jungles of India?

The trade-off for these unique locations is a number of **restrictions** not found at resort locations or the Wedding Pavilion. Ceremonies in Epcot's World Showcase must start by 9 am. Magic Kingdom ceremonies begin at 8 am, while those at Animal Kingdom and Disney's Hollywood Studios start 2 hours after park closing. Transportation is included in the price of the Magic Kingdom wedding package. All other theme park weddings require you to charter one or more motor coaches through Disney for a minimum of 5 hours at $98 per hour. Each motor coach holds up to 50 people.

Only Disney photographers and videographers are allowed at any in-park event. You are also required to use Disney's floral and decor services, although you may bring in **personal floral** such as bouquets and boutonnieres. If you want to bring in your own rose petals for tossing or for lining the aisle, you must designate someone in your party to pass them out or arrange them. All entertainment and audiovisual services must be provided by Disney. A sound system is recommended for weddings with more than 25 guests.

The **rain backup** locations for theme park ceremonies vary depending on your party's size and the ceremony venue you pick, but they are always inside the park. The rain backup for a Magic Kingdom ceremony is the Wedding Pavilion.

Theme Park Ceremony Venues (continued)

Perhaps the most unusual place to be married at Walt Disney World is inside the 5.7 million-gallon **tank at The Seas with Nemo & Friends Pavilion**. Open-water-certified scuba divers may say their vows in a 25-minute ceremony inside the aquarium. Up to four divers are allowed in the tank, but only two will have microphones. As many as 100 guests may view the ceremony from the observation deck, although the event will also be visible to park guests. No entertainment, additional decor, or food and beverage are permitted at the hour-long event, and there is no seating. Participants must sign a waiver and wear approved dive attire. The package includes diving equipment, two-way communication, and a two-hour dive rehearsal for the bride and groom. Rehearsal will take place on a different day, before the park opens. The venue requires approval from Epcot, and certain water conditions or sea life activity may require the ceremony to be moved to another location. Ceremonies must be scheduled around the Epcot DiveQuest backstage tour.

Epcot's **World Showcase** offers numerous picturesque ceremony locations. Among the most popular are the UK's Rose Garden, Italy's island on World Showcase Lagoon, Japan's bridge and waterfall, and the American Adventure Rotunda. Many pavilions have more than one venue suitable for a wedding, so you may want to ask your Wedding Consultant for alternatives or arrange a visit to scout them out yourself.

Hollywood Studios and Animal Kingdom are more popular for receptions than for ceremonies, but the information found on pages 81–82 of the Reception Venues section of this book will give you an idea of the capacities and costs.

United Kingdom Pavilion

Morocco Pavilion

Japan Pavilion

American Adventure Rotunda

France Pavilion

Italy Pavilion

Germany Pavilion

China Pavilion

Magic Kingdom ceremonies take place at the Swan Boat Landing at the foot of Cinderella Castle. The venue is part of a $28,000 ceremony-only package for the couple and up to 50 guests; the standard Wishes Collection per-person food and beverage minimum expenditure and room-night requirements apply in addition to the ceremony package. Transportation to the ceremony and reception for you and your guests is included. Guests ride down Main Street, U.S.A. in motor cars to the ceremony site, while the bride arrives in a horse-drawn landau coach.

The package includes a string quartet, a Fanfare Trumpeter and Major Domo to announce the bride, ceremony floral and decor, and a photography and videography package for the ceremony. These elements are available for the reception at an additional charge.

The Swan Boat Landing as seen from Tomorrowland (l) and ceremony set-up (r)

Reception Venues

Disney offers a range of reception venues, from traditional ballrooms to the inside of a theme park ride! These fall into **four categories**: ballrooms, resort restaurants, special venues, and theme park venues. With the exception of ballrooms and a few of the theme park venues, each venue has its own food and beverage minimum expenditure that must be met, exclusive of service charges and tax. The wedding cake only counts toward the venue-specific food and beverage minimums at Grand Floridian venues, but it counts toward the per-person food and beverage minimum expenditure at all venues. Most theme park reception venues have an additional fee for venue rental. However, if you hold contiguous events at two different venues in the park, like a reception followed by a dessert party, the lesser of the two venue rental fees will be waived (ceremony venues excluded). There is a $50 small-party fee for groups of fewer than 20 people.

As with ceremony sites, the reception site you choose will depend on a number of factors, including location, time of day, number of guests, whether you want a buffet or a plated meal, and whether you need space for dancing. We'll cover the **most popular** venues here, but you should feel free to ask your Wedding Consultant about additional reception sites.

To see floor plans and photos of nearly all the available sites, check out Disney's Virtual Venue Tour at http://disneyweddings.disney.go.com/weddings/florida/vsi. Click on the "Reception" tab.

Ballrooms

Walt Disney World's conference centers boast ballrooms of every shape and size, from the Grand Floridian's intimate Whitehall Room & Patio to the Yacht & Beach Club's 5,000-capacity Grand Harbor Ballroom. There are **no venue rental fees** for these venues, and there are no venue-specific food and beverage minimum expenditures, just the standard Wishes Collection per-person food and beverage minimums. The trade-off is that ballrooms may require more decoration than other venues.

The **Grand Floridian Convention Center** features two large ballrooms that can be subdivided into smaller rooms. The Grand Floridian Ballroom can be divided into three large salons of 4,232 square feet that accommodate 440 people each, two 1,380-square-foot salons that can hold 140, and four 690-square-foot salons that seat 70. St. Augustine

Whitehall Room and Patio

Hall can be divided into three 1,334-square-foot halls that seat 130 and a fourth, 1,856-square-foot hall that seats 220. The smaller Whitehall Room includes a patio and seats 40–60, depending on entertainment choices.

Salon IV portion of the Grand Floridian Ballroom

The **Contemporary Resort Convention Center** offers four ballrooms with numerous configurations. The Nutcracker Ballroom includes a private patio and can be divided into three sections to accommodate 100–450 people. The Fantasia Ballroom can accommodate 30–3,000 people in up to 15 sections, while the more intimate Pastoral rooms each accommodate 20–30 guests.

The **Yacht & Beach Club Convention Center's** largest room is the 38,000-square-foot Grand Harbor Ballroom, which can be divided into north and south ballrooms of 1,120 square feet and eight salons, ranging from 1,617 to 1,715 square feet, that seat 250 apiece. Asbury Hall subdivides into four rooms of about 2,000 square feet that hold 365 apiece, while Cape Cod Hall's four 864-square-foot subdivisions seat 144 each. The more intimate Hampton and Saybrook rooms seat 75 in 1,269 square feet.

The **BoardWalk Conference Center's** Promenade Ballroom can be subdivided to form East and West Promenades of 2,509 square feet that accommodate 300 people, as well as six 736-square-foot salons that accommodate 20–40 people each. At 1,860 square feet, Marvin Gardens seats 80 guests and can be divided into three 620-square-foot sections that accommodate 30–40 people each. The 1,216-square-foot St. James Room seats 100 and includes a patio. It can be subdivided into two 680-square-foot rooms that seat 40 and both open to the patio.

St. James Room at the BoardWalk Conference Center

Resort Restaurants

Some of Walt Disney World's finest restaurants are available as reception venues. Whether you want an intimate gourmet dinner or a traditional wedding reception with all the trimmings, Disney's restaurant venues offer **top-notch food** and service without venue rental fees or the need for much decoration. The trade-off is that some of them do not offer menu tastings. One alternative is to make a dining reservation to try the food during regular business hours, but you may not be able to order all the items offered on the banquet menu that would be served at your reception.

Perched atop the Contemporary Resort, **California Grill** affords sweeping views of the Magic Kingdom, Seven Seas Lagoon, and Bay Lake. There are two private spaces, along with the option to use the main dining room. The food and beverage minimum for California Grill Dining Room events ending before 3:00 pm is $3,000 (to use the room after 3:00 pm would require a full restaurant buyout). Events must

© Patrick Johnson

California Grill's main dining

begin after 10:30 am. The price of the wedding cake does not count toward the venue-specific food and beverage minimum. The restaurant seats 240 and can accommodate a dance floor, which is available for an extra charge. Existing seating and California Grill menus must be used. Menus may not be modified, and menu tastings are not available.

The **Napa Room** seats 50 and looks out over the Magic Kingdom. The food and beverage minimum is $1,000 for events ending before 4:00 pm and $3,000 for events that start after 6:00 pm. If you will use the room between

© Patrick Johnson

California Grill's Napa Room

4:00 pm and 6:00 pm, the food and beverage minimum is $4,000. The price of the wedding cake does not count toward the minimum. A dance floor is available for an extra charge, but it will decrease the room's capacity. Restrooms are located outside the room and are shared with restaurant guests.

The **Sonoma Room** seats 40 and looks out over Bay Lake. Although the Magic Kingdom is not visible from this room, you and your guests may walk out to California Grill's viewing platform to see the fireworks. The food and beverage minimum is $1,000 for events ending before 4:00 pm and $2,000 for events that start after 6:00 pm. If you will use the room between 4:00 pm and 6:00 pm, the food and beverage minimum is $3,000. A dance floor is available for an extra charge, but it will decrease the room's capacity. Restrooms are located outside the room and are shared with restaurant guests.

Wedding reception at Citricos

The Grand Floridian's **Citricos** is a light-filled space overlooking the resort's Courtyard Pool (the Magic Kingdom fireworks cannot be seen from the restaurant). Breakfast, brunch, and lunch events have a food and beverage minimum of $2,500, including the price of the wedding cake. Events must conclude by 3:00 pm. Citricos can accommodate up to 200 people with existing seating only, and the pre-reception and reception are held in the same space. The existing seating configuration may not be rearranged. There is no dance floor, and use of entertainment will decrease capacity. Restrooms are located outside the restaurant and are shared with resort guests. Because events at Citricos are catered by Disney's Catered Events team and not the restaurant itself, menu tastings are available.

Animal Kingdom Lodge's award-winning restaurant **Jiko: The Cooking Place** offers private events in its main dining room and the Cape Town Wine Room. The glass walls of the semicircular wine room display the restaurant's elegantly arranged wine collection, with an interior beaded curtain to provide privacy. The space can be divided into Wine Room A and Wine Room B, each accommodating a maximum of 20 people, with a food and beverage minimum of $2,500. The entire room seats 40 and has a food and beverage minimum of $4,000. The main dining room is available for breakfast and lunch events between the hours of 7:00 am and 3:30 pm, with a food and beverage minimum of $1,500. Service is buffet only, and events must be approved by the resort's Food & Beverage Manager. Existing seating must be used, and tables cannot be moved. Your wedding cake will not count toward the food and beverage minimum at Jiko. There is no dance floor. Also, certain decorations may be prohibited to protect the resort's animals.

Located at the Grand Floridian, the octagonal **Narcoossee's** sits over Seven Seas Lagoon directly across from the Magic Kingdom. The restaurant is only available for buffet breakfast, brunch, and lunch events ending before 3:00 pm. The food and beverage minimum is $1,500, including the price of the wedding cake. Narcoossee's accommodates up to 80 people with existing seating only, and the pre-reception and reception are held in the same space.

Narcoossee's at the Grand Floridian

Seating may not be rearranged. There is room for a dance floor; use of entertainment will decrease capacity. Because events at Narcoossee's are catered by Disney's Catered Events team and not the restaurant itself, menu tastings are available.

Theme Park Venues

In-park receptions let you carry the magic of a Disney park visit into your event and share it with your nearest and dearest. As with theme park ceremony venues, the trade-off for this unique experience is a number of requirements and restrictions. All venues require you to **charter transportation** for a minimum of five hours. Unless your party is very small, this means hiring a motor coach, which seats up to 50 guests, at $98 per hour. If your event takes place during park hours, you and your guests may be allowed to meet an event guide at a park gate and walk in instead of chartering transportation. However this can vary widely depending on such factors as your ceremony and reception venues and the potential for inclement weather, so check with your Wedding Consultant.

Guests do not require theme park admission to attend in-park receptions, but there is a $12.95/person **viewing fee** for Epcot's IllumiNations: Reflections of Earth and Disney's Hollywood Studios' Fantasmic! This fee is waived for those guests who have park admission.

Only Disney photographers and videographers are allowed at in-park events. Except for personal floral like bouquets, boutonnieres, and corsages, all floral and decor must be provided by Disney Floral & Gifts. Any talent or entertainment must be secured through your Wedding Event Planner, and characters and amplified entertainment are not allowed at outdoor venues (existing background music stays on).

Note that holiday decor may be visible at your venue during certain times of the year, and Christmas decor is usually installed beginning November 1.

Most theme park reception locations have a **venue rental fee**. However, if you hold contiguous events at two different venues in the park, the lesser of the two venue rental fees will be waived (ceremony venues excluded).

Food and beverage minimums are lower for dessert parties and receptions that don't include a full meal. If you plan to serve breakfast, lunch, or dinner, a higher minimum will apply. Wedding cake doesn't count toward the food and beverage minimum at theme park venues.

You may be able to arrange for your guests to **ride one of the attractions** or experience one of the shows at some point before or during the reception. Taking your guests on a ride can be a great surprise and makes a unique substitute for a cocktail hour.

The cost of **buying out** the entire ride or show after park hours ranges from $700 for Turtle Talk with Crush to $14,750 for the Indiana Jones Epic Stunt Spectacular, with most rides in the range of $3,500–$8,000.

A cheaper option is the **ride mix-in**, available during the last 45 minutes of the attraction's hours. An event guide leads your guests backstage to the ride and holds back day guests momentarily so that your group can ride together. Availability depends on estimated park attendance on that day, and brides are not allowed to ride in their wedding gowns. The cost is $15/person. Among the attractions and shows previously used by Disney's Fairy Tale Weddings are The Twilight Zone Tower of Terror, Rockin' Roller Coaster, Soarin', Kilimanjaro Safari, Expedition Everest, It's Tough to Be a Bug, and Festival of the Lion King—ask your Wedding Consultant for more options.

Epcot Reception Venues

The American Adventure Pavilion offers two reception venues. The **American Adventure Dining Room**, located on the third floor of the building, also features a living room seating area. The dining room holds 60 guests seated at rounds of 10, but changes in seating options and the addition of entertainment will change capacity. With dancing,

American Adventure Dining Room

the capacity is reduced to 30 people. The venue rental fee is $250. The food and beverage minimums are $1,225 for breakfast, $1,500 for lunch, and $3,000 for dinner.

American Adventure Rotunda

Parties of 100–230 can dine and dance under the giant dome of the **American Adventure Rotunda**. The venue rental fee is $2,075, and there is no site-specific food and beverage minimum. Events must begin after 7:00 pm. The lower level seats 150 guests with room for dancing, while the upper level seats 80 guests and requires the purchase of an $800 greens package. Restrooms are located outside the American Adventure attraction and are shared with theme park guests.

Canada Terrace is the upper level of the Canada Pavilion. The food and beverage minimums are $1,750 for breakfast, $2,450 for lunch, and $3,000 for dinner. Disney does not recommend the venue for dessert parties due to limited visibility of IllumiNations. A minimum of 10 guests is required, and the maximum is 85. The venue rental fee is $335. Restrooms are located outside the venue and are shared with day guests.

The France Pavilion offers one indoor venue and several outdoor venues with views of World Showcase Lagoon and Epcot's IllumiNations: Reflections of Earth fireworks show. **Bistro de Paris** features classic French cuisine in an elegant space above the Chefs de France restaurant and overlooking the lagoon. The food and beverage minimum is $5,000 for events ending before 4:00 pm

Canada Terrace has a waterfall at the back

and $8,000 for events ending after 4:00 pm. The venue rental fee is $250. The restaurant seats 120, subject to the addition of entertainment or a dance floor, and existing seating must be used. Menus are based on Bistro de Paris' regular menu.

Epcot Reception Venues (continued)

The France Pavilion's IllumiNations-viewing terraces may be reserved singly or in combination to accommodate the size of your party. They are most often used for private dessert parties, but they also make a spectacular location for an al fresco evening reception capped by fireworks. Due to the distance from Epcot's kitchens, plated meals are unavailable at these venues. Buffet service features cold items and a limited selection of hot items. The restrictions on displaying and serving wedding cakes vary and should be discussed with your Wedding Event Planner. Restrooms are located outside the venues and are shared with theme park guests.

The **Terrace des Fleurs** (formerly known as French Island Upper) is available for receptions and dessert parties of 50 or more guests for a $22/person food and beverage minimum. For a full meal, the site capacity is a minimum of

Terrace des Fleurs

50 guests and a maximum of 60 guests, and the food and beverage minimum is $3,750. The venue rental fee is $335. The staircase adjacent to the site may be used by guests of separate functions held at the lower terrace.

Eau de France

Eau de France (formerly French Island Lower) also has a $22/person food and beverage minimum for receptions and dessert parties of 50 or more guests. For a full meal, the food and beverage minimum is $3,750 for a minimum of 50 guests and a maximum of 80 guests. The venue rental fee is $335. Eau de France is not wheelchair accessible.

Rue de Paris (formerly French Island Arm), is available to groups of 50–100 guests for a $335 venue rental fee and a $22/person food and beverage minimum. For a full meal, the food and beverage minimum is $2,255 and capacity decreases to 30–40 guests.

Rue de Paris, looking toward Morocco

Modeled on Beijing's Hall of Prayer for Good Harvest, the **Great Hall of China** is a distinctive reception venue for a minimum of 60 guests. The maximum is 120 guests, and the use of entertainment will decrease capacity. The venue rental fee is $2,000, and the food and beverage minimum is $4,500. Events must begin after 7:00 pm. Restrooms are located outside the hall and are shared with theme park guests.

Italy Isola

At the **Italy Pavilion** you can dine along the shores of World Showcase Lagoon during IllumiNations. The pavilion's two reception venues offer buffet service only, which is limited to cold items and a small selection of hot items. There are restrictions on displaying and serving wedding cakes that should be discussed with your Wedding Event Planner. Restrooms are located outside the venues and are shared with theme park guests.

Linked to the main walkway by two stone bridges, **Italy Isola** sits on the waters of World Showcase Lagoon and offers prime fireworks viewing. The food and beverage minimums are $1,650 for a reception or a dessert party and $3,750 for a full meal. A minimum of 100 guests is required to use this venue for a reception or dessert party, and the maximum is 150. Dinner has a minimum of 50 guests and a maximum of 60. The venue rental fee is $585.

Isola West Plaza is a small terrace adjacent to Italy Isola's larger bridge. A wall of plants must be rented to separate the area from the main walkway during private events. There is a food and beverage minimum of $440 for a dessert party and $1,500 for a full meal. A minimum of 50 guests is required for a dessert party, and

Isola West Plaza

125 is the maximum. Capacity for a full meal is 30–60 guests. The venue rental fee is $335. Wheelchair access to Italy Isola is through Isola West Plaza, so guests of other functions may come through your event.

The **Living Seas Salon** is a private event space with five large windows into the 5.7 million-gallon aquarium of The Seas with Nemo & Friends Pavilion. The food and beverage minimum is $2,450 for events before 4:00 pm and $3,500 for events after 4:00 pm. The venue rental fee is $500.

Living Seas Salon

The venue seats 25–104 guests at tables of six, and existing seating must be used. Although the tables cannot be removed or rearranged, you may bring in up to three 72-inch banquet rounds of 10 at an additional charge. Standard table linens are navy with a lime green overlay. The overlay may be exchanged for white at no cost, but there is an additional charge for changing out the navy linens for white floor-length linens or for replacing the overlay with other colors. The piano may not be moved, and food and beverage may not be displayed on it. If you're planning an evening reception, note that the lights in the aquarium are turned off beginning at 9:45 pm.

Epcot Reception Venues (continued)

The **United Kingdom Pavilion** offers two reception venues on World Showcase Lagoon. As with Epcot's other waterside venues, these offer buffet service only, which is limited to cold items and a small selection of hot items. The food and beverage minimums are $440 for dessert parties and $1,500 for a full meal at either site. There are restrictions on displaying and serving wedding cakes that should be discussed with your Wedding Event Planner. Restrooms are located outside these venues and are shared with theme park guests.

The secluded **United Kingdom Lochside** (formerly known as United Kingdom Lower Terrace) is set on the water at the end of a garden path. It is available for groups of 20-70 guests for dessert parties and just 20 guests for a full meal. The venue rental fee is $335. A maximum of five cocktail tables or four tallboy tables can be added to existing bench seating.

United Kingdom Lochside

The **United Kingdom Terrace** (formerly United Kingdom Upper Terrace) is separated from the walkway and United Kingdom Lochside by a wall and accommodates a minimum of 20 and a maximum of 50 guests for dessert parties and full meals. The venue rental fee is $250. One advantage of this site is its existing seating—seven wrought iron tables with umbrellas—which saves you a bit on the venue rental fee. No additional seating or tables may be added.

These are only the most popular reception venues in Epcot. There may be other venues available, like the Wonders of Life Pavilion, which is now used exclusively for special events. Or you may want to use more than one site for each part of your post-ceremony celebration. For example, you may wish to hold your cocktail hour and reception at two different venues, or you could move your group from reception to dessert party and back again. Your Wedding Event Coordinator will be able to suggest the venues and configurations that match your wedding-day vision.

The United Kingdom Pavilion's upper (left) and lower (right) terraces

Disney's Hollywood Studios Reception Venues

Only at Disney's Hollywood Studios can you dine inside a theme park ride! The **Great Movie Ride** offers you a choice of the Gangster scene, the Western scene, or the Wizard of Oz scene—or all three. The venue is available for up to 80 guests at a seated reception or up to 200 for a walk-around reception. Events start two hours after the park closes. The venue rental fee is $3,000, and the food and beverage minimum is $2,000. Use of the Great Movie Ride requires an $8,300 entertainment package, which includes a Director, two Gangsters, a Pianist, Ma and her Western Trio, and the Good Witch. You may wish to hire additional entertainment for dancing in the black-box room at the end of the ride or under the Sorcerer Mickey Hat in front of the ride. Prices start at $7,500 for a DJ. Restrooms are located outside the venue, near the ABC Theatre.

The **Tower of Terror Courtyard** reception takes place just outside the exit to the ride's gift shop, with the tower looming above. The venue rental fee is $2,000, and there is an $850 food and beverage minimum; menus can be either plated or buffet. Events must start at least 90 minutes after the park closes. A buyout of the ride itself costs $6,500.

There are also several reception opportunities inside the park's various show sets. A plated dinner for up to 50 at **Theater of the Stars**, home of *Beauty and the Beast - Live on Stage*, has a venue rental fee of $1,000 and a food and beverage minimum of $4,000. An entertainment package including six characters from the show, a pianist, and a Major Domo costs $10,395.

The "Event at a Parisian Cafe," held on the set of **Lights, Motors, Action!** has a venue rental fee of $1,000 and a food and beverage minimum of $5,500.

Possibly the most expensive event at the park, a dinner show on the set of the **Indiana Jones Epic Stunt Spectacular** has a venue rental fee of $3,000, a food and beverage minimum of $4,000, and an entertainment fee of $17,140 for a two-scene show, a DJ, a belly dancer, and stage decor.

A more economical option might be dinner inside the **Journey into Narnia: Prince Caspian** exhibit. The venue rental fee is $500, and the food and beverage minimum is $1,500. The venue holds up to 50 with no seating or 30 with 100% seating.

For a more traditional reception, check out the **Backstage Prop Shop**, which has the advantage of being available during park operating hours. The venue rental fee is $300, and food and beverage minimums are $520 for lunch and $1,500 for dinner. The venue seats up to 100 people, but capacity decreases with the use of entertainment and a dance floor. Another all-day location is **Hollywood Hideaway**, which is available for groups of up to 50. The venue rental fee is $300, and food and beverage minimums are $400 for breakfast, $520 for lunch, $800 for an evening reception, and $1,500 for dinner. Or buy out the **Hollywood Brown Derby** for breakfast or dinner for a $250 venue rental fee and a food and beverage minimum of $2,000 (an additional buyout fee applies at dinner.)

And for a traditional reception with a twist, consider a private tour and dinner for up to 90 in **The Magic of Disney Animation**. The venue rental fee is $1,000, and the food and beverage minimum is $1,000.

Disney's Animal Kingdom Reception Venues

These venues generally cannot be used until about two hours **after the park closes**. But, unlike the rest of the Disney parks, Animal Kingdom closes in the early evening, offering the possibility of holding dinner at a decent hour! If your event will be held during the park's Extra Magic Hours, no entertainment is permitted until after the park closes.

Belvedere Court in the palace ruins of the **Maharajah Jungle Trek** is available for groups of 10–80 guests, with a Roman table available for groups of 30 or fewer. The venue rental fee is $3,000, and the food and beverage minimum is $5,000. The package includes lighting but not a sound system; that will set you back an additional $900. The venue is not available from April–September due to the heat.

Tamu Tamu Courtyard

Festival of the Lion King is available for a plated dinner and private show for up to 104 guests. There is no venue rental fee, but the food and beverage minimum is $6,500, and there is a $5,000 charge if the show ends after 10:30 pm.

Flame Tree Gardens, the outdoor seating area adjacent to Flame Tree Barbecue, can seat up to 350 guests among its animal-themed pavilions. The venue rental fee is $500, and the food and beverage minimum is $3,500. Seating is a mixture of two-, four-, and six-top tables, and service is buffet-only. Individual pavilions have a venue rental fee of $250 and a daytime food and beverage minimum of $200.

Tamu Tamu Courtyard is located across from Tusker House in Africa. The venue seats up to 50 guests, with a venue rental fee of $250 and a food and beverage minimum of $2,500. Existing tables for four may be removed for a charge of $250. Restrooms are located outside the venue, a few feet away.

Disney also offers the **Safari and Karibu Dinner Package**, an economical way for smaller groups to host a unique event inside Animal Kingdom. For $67/person, groups of 20–60 get a ride on one of the last safaris of the day, followed by a buffet dinner at Tamu Tamu Courtyard. There are no additional fees for venue rental, event guides, or park admission. Entertainment, a bar, and floral and decor are available at an extra charge. The event is available to book within 45 days of your desired date.

Other Theme Park Reception Venues

If you still haven't found the perfect reception venue, check out Disney's Virtual Venue Tour at http://disneyweddings.disney.go.com/weddings/florida/vsi. Click on the "Reception" tab to see just about every event space inside **every park except Magic Kingdom**, which does not currently offer any reception venues. Venue availability must be determined by each park's management team, but the Virtual Venue Tour will give you an idea of the possibilities.

Special Venues

Ariel's at the Beach Club Resort

Disney's "Special Venues" category encompasses resort reception locations that aren't ballrooms or restaurants. Special Venues do not have venue rental fees, just food and beverage minimums.

Formerly an upscale table-service restaurant, **Ariel's** at the Beach Club is now available for breakfast, lunch, and dinner receptions. The split-level space features pastel colors and a tropical fish motif, from the light fixtures to the carpet. Ariel's can accommodate up to 80 guests with dancing, and the food and beverage minimum is $1,000. The price of the wedding cake does not count toward the food and beverage minimum, and menus are buffet-style only. Restrooms are located outside the venue and are shared with resort guests. Ariel's may not be available after December 2011; rumor has it the space will be returned to service as a restaurant.

© Nathan Root

Atlantic Dance Hall at the BoardWalk

The popular nightclub **Atlantic Dance Hall**, situated at one end of Disney's BoardWalk, is available for breakfast, lunch, and dinner receptions. This two-story Art Deco space accommodates up to 200 guests and offers buffet service only. The food and beverage minimums exclude the price of the wedding cake and vary depending on the day of the week and time of day.

	End Before 5 pm	End Between 5 pm & 8 pm	End After 8:30 pm
Sunday & Monday	$1,475	$5,000	$5,000
Tuesday–Thursday			not available
Friday & Saturday			not available

Guest access is through the BoardWalk Inn's main entrance. No outside vendors are permitted, with the exception of photographers and videographers.

Because it is a working club, Atlantic Dance Hall has a number of restrictions on seating arrangements. Existing seating is four-top marble cocktail tables, which will accommodate 96 guests on the first floor and 45 guests on the second floor. White linens can be added at no charge. There may be fees to bring in additional banquet tables.

Special Venues (continued)

Up to six 72-inch banquet rounds of 10 can be placed on Atlantic Dance Hall's dance floor, which will decrease its size. Additional 72-inch rounds can be brought in to replace the cocktail tables on the first floor, but there is a $2,500 removal fee. You and your guests must access Atlantic Dance Hall by entering the main lobby of BoardWalk Inn and walking along the BoardWalk to the venue.

Tucked away at the end of a long hall in the Disney Vacation Club wing of the BoardWalk Inn, **The Attic** sits atop Jellyrolls piano bar and overlooks Crescent Lake. This airy space features seaside cottage decor, a wall of windows, and a covered terrace with sweeping views of the BoardWalk, the Yacht & Beach Club,

© Nathan Root

The Attic at BoardWalk Inn

and even Epcot's Spaceship Earth. The venue accommodates 50 guests if both the indoor and outdoor spaces are used, with table seating for 36. Only the existing seating, consisting of wicker chairs, sofas, and love seats, may be used. However, there is room to bring in a sweetheart table and two chairs.

The food and beverage minimum for events ending before 5:00 pm is $1,000. Events ending after 5:00 pm have a minimum of $2,500. The price of the wedding cake does not count toward the venue minimum, and menus are buffet-style only. A dance floor is not available, although there is some space for ceremonial first dances on the terrace, and use of entertainment will decrease capacity. Because The Attic adjoins BoardWalk Villas guest rooms, only background-style music and non-amplified entertainment is allowed. Entertainment must conclude by 9:00 pm, and events must conclude by 10:00 pm.

The Attic's seating is a mix of overstuffed chairs, sofas, and rockers

The Grand Floridian's Summer House

Although technically considered part of the Grand Floridian Convention Center, the resort's Summer House, Marina Patio & Terrace, and Sago Cay Pointe are unique outdoor reception venues. Another distinction is that **wedding cake** does not count toward the food and beverage minimums at these locations.

The **Summer House** is an outdoor bar area adjacent to the beach, about halfway between the resort's theme pool and courtyard pool. This buffet-only venue is ideal for the cocktail hour or for an informal reception and has a food and beverage minimum of $1,000. There is no venue rental fee. The patio can accommodate up to 10 banquet rounds in addition to existing seating of six umbrella tables with four chairs apiece. Removal and replacement of existing furniture costs $250. The maximum capacity is 250 guests, but not everyone will get a seat if maximum capacity is reached. All entertainment must conclude by 10 pm.

The Grand Floridian's **Marina Patio & Terrace** and nearby **Sago Cay Pointe** are ideal spots to view the Magic Kingdom's Wishes fireworks over Cinderella Castle, making them great venues for an evening cocktail hour, dessert party, or buffet-style reception. They are also available for breakfast and lunch.

The Grand Floridian's Marina Patio

The food and beverage minimums are $1,000 for the Marina Patio & Terrace and $500 (dessert parties) or $1,000 (all other events) for Sago Cay Pointe. The Marina requires a minimum of 20 guests and has a maximum of 120, while Sago Cay Pointe accommodates up to 75 guests. Combined, the sites hold up to 300 people.

There are no venue rental fees for either site, but there is a $75 setup fee for tables and chairs in addition to the existing seating for 20 at the Marina. Sago Cay Pointe can accommodate a mixture of five cocktail tables, five tallboys, or two rounds of 10, but not everyone will get a seat if maximum capacity is reached.

Sago Cay Pointe

Both venues use only existing lighting, and there is a charge of $500–$1,050, depending on your group's size, to have the soundtrack to Wishes piped in. Figure on $500 for up to 50 guests and $650 for up to 150 guests. No characters are permitted, and only Disney floral, decor, and entertainment may be used; no non-Disney vendors or wedding guests may provide these services.

Food, Beverages, and Cake

For health reasons, all food served at Disney's Fairy Tale Weddings must be obtained from Disney, with the exception of edible wedding favors. While this precludes common money-saving practices like having a friend bake the wedding cake, it does open up a world of culinary possibilities through the extensive food-service network at Walt Disney World. In addition to providing numerous customizable brunch, lunch, and dinner menus, the Disney chefs can re-create family recipes and favorite dishes from restaurants at the parks and resorts. They also do an excellent job of accommodating **special dietary needs**, including those of Kosher, vegetarian, vegan, lactose-intolerant, and gluten-intolerant guests.

© Nathan Root

Caprese appetizer

Unless your reception will be held at California Grill, you may choose items from any of Disney's catering or restaurant menus. Menu prices range from about $40/person for a simple continental breakfast to $150/person for a multi-course dinner. Note that you may also customize any menu to suit your tastes and budget; you are not limited to what's on the menus your wedding consultant sends you.

To see sample menus, check out MagicalKingdoms.com's Wishes Collection section (http://www.magicalkingdoms.com/ftw/wdw/menus.html). Although the prices shown may not be current, these will give you an idea of the **myriad options** available.

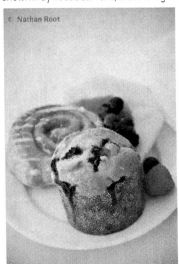
© Nathan Root

Brunch is a cost-effective choice

Remember that the per-person food and beverage minimum expenditure of $75–$125 required by Disney can be fulfilled by **any food and beverage** served on the day of your event, from the pre-reception cocktails to the wedding cake to the dessert-party treats.

However, if your reception venue has its own overall food and beverage minimum expenditure, only food and beverage **served there** will count toward it, and the cost of your wedding cake will not count unless the venue is part of Disney's Grand Floridian Resort & Spa.

All menu prices are subject a 21% service charge and 6.5% tax (which is also applied to the service charge).

Mickey waffles

If there will be **children** at your reception, you will be charged the adult per-person menu price for those ages 9 and older. However, you will not be required to meet the $75–$125 per person food and beverage minimum for guests under age 21 because they cannot drink alcohol. For younger children, you have the option of providing a lower-priced kids' meal or paying a reduced price for them to eat from the adult menu. Note that they will be charged at full price for pre-reception and dessert party food. Children under age 3 eat free at all meals.

If you would like to offer your photographer or videographer a meal during the reception, you may order a reduced-price **vendor meal**—usually a deli plate or a kids' meal—rather than pay full price for them to eat what your guests are served.

Plated vs. Buffet Meals

Unless your reception venue mandates buffet service due to its distance from a central kitchen, you will need to decide whether you want to have a plated or buffet meal. Some people have a strong preference for one over the other. Conventional wisdom holds that plated meals are more formal, elegant, and expensive, while buffets are more casual, convivial, and cost-effective. But with Disney's Fairy Tale Weddings, all bets are off. Your buffet may include **action stations** offering haute cuisine from around the world at a price equal to that of a plated meal. Or you may choose a sit-down meal of fun, inexpensive foods like you'd find at a barbeque or picnic.

Plated menus generally include an appetizer, a salad, a sorbet or "intermezzo" course, an entree, and dessert, but you don't have to serve all these courses. For instance, you may wish to skip dessert if you are serving wedding cake. You could choose the same entree for everyone or serve a duo plate featuring smaller portions of two entrees on the same plate. If you wish to offer your guests a choice of entree ahead of time, you must give their selections to your Wedding Event Planner before you make your final payment at 30 days out so that the balance may be accurately estimated. You can make changes as needed up to three business days before the wedding. Or you may choose to offer crown service, which lets guests select one of three entrees on the spot, just before the first course is served.

A duo-plate meal offers variety

Plated vs. Buffet Meals (continued)

Buffet menus generally feature appetizers, soup or salad, side dishes, main dishes, and desserts. These can be enhanced with—or entirely replaced by—action stations ranging from a build-your-own crepe bar to carving stations to a mashed potato martini bar serving up three kinds of potatoes in oversized martini glasses. You may choose items from different menus to suit your taste.

And if you can't decide between a plated meal and a buffet, Disney offers **family-style menus** that combine the two. Guests are

Mashed potato martinis

served individual plated appetizers and salads, and then main courses are placed on each table to be passed around and shared.

Pre-Reception

If you plan to take photos with your wedding party and family directly after the ceremony, you may wish to provide a pre-reception—also sometimes called a **cocktail hour**—for your guests while they wait. The pre-reception may be held in the same location as the reception or in a nearby space, and it usually lasts about an hour. Disney offers several pre-reception menus of hot and cold appetizers, or you may create your own. If your reception is being held in the same location as your pre-reception and you've chosen a buffet menu, you may be able to serve items from the reception buffet at the pre-reception instead, at no extra charge. If you are serving a sit-down meal, look for a plated menu that includes pre-reception food in the per-person charge.

Egg rolls	*Crab claw appetizer*	*Fruit display*

Beverages

Plated and buffet menus include coffee and tea at **no extra charge**. Brunch menus also usually include a choice of juices. A water station with pitchers of ice water is available for $25. If you want to offer your guests any other beverages, you will need to provide a bar. This doesn't mean you have to serve alcohol, however: One of the options is a soft drink, juice, and bottled water bar.

Disney also offers beer, house wine, call brands, premium wine and cocktails, and signature wine and cocktails. The following is a list of the offerings in each category.

Soft drinks: Coke, Diet Coke, and Sprite (no Pepsi products are sold on Disney property); orange, cranberry, and pineapple juice; Dasani water and Perrier mineral water

Beer: Bud Light, Michelob Ultra, Corona, Heineken, O'Doul's

House Wine: B.V. Century Cellars Chardonnay, Canyon Road Merlot, Beringer White Zinfandel

Call Liquor: Jim Beam, Cutty Sark, Canadian Club, Myers's Platinum, Captain Morgan, Beefeater, SKYY, SKYY Citrus, Sauza Gold

Premium Wine: Columbia Crest Two Vines Chardonnay, Canyon Road Cabernet Sauvignon, Mirrasou Pinot Noir, Casa Grande Pinot Grigio

A selection of house and premium wine

Premium Liquor: Jack Daniels, Dewars, Seagram's VO, Bacardi Superior, Captain Morgan, Tanqueray, Jose Cuervo Gold, SKYY Citrus, Stolichnaya

Signature Wine: Estancia Chardonnay*, Sonoma Junction Chardonnay, Sartori Pinot Grigio*, Sterling Vintners Collection Cabernet Sauvignon*, Simi Cabernet Sauvignon, Cupcake Vineyards Merlot, MacMurray Ranch Pinot Noir*, Lasorda Chianti

Signature Liquor: Knob Creek, Johnny Walker Black, Crown Royal, Tommy Bahama, Captain Morgan, Sauza Conmemorativo Anejo, Absolut, Absolut Citron, Hendrick's

Premium Cordials: Bailey's Irish Cream, Amaretto di Saronno, Kahlua, Frangelico Hazelnut Liqueur, Bushmills, Sambuca

Signature Cordials: Grand Marnier, B&B, Drambuie, Remy Martin VSOP, Starbucks Coffee Liqueur, Godiva Dark Liqueur, Godiva Light Liqueur

Sparkling Wine: Domaine Ste. Michelle Blanc de Blanc, Iron Horse Fairy Tale Cuvee

*Default choice for Signature Bar; others available with advance notice

Beverages (continued)

There are three different **ways to pay** for the bar. A package bar means you pay a set fee per guest, based on the length of your event, for unlimited drinks. With a hosted bar (also known as a bill-on-consumption bar), you pay based on how much your guests actually drink. Usually this is priced by the drink, but you may choose to pay by the bottle for wine,

There is a $100 service fee for each additional bartender

Champagne, and cordials. You may also offer a no-host or cash bar that requires guests to pay for their own drinks, although this is still a hot-button topic of wedding etiquette. If you choose this option you will be required to hire a cashier in addition to the bartender.

There is a **labor charge** of $100 for hosted and package bars that sell less than $500 in beverages. Additional bartenders can be requested for a $100 service fee each. If you request to have wine poured at the tables, it will be billed on consumption, not as part of a package. Any additional bar service will then be billed on consumption or cash.

Only guests age 21 and older may be served alcohol, and Disney is extremely vigilant about **checking IDs**.

All beverage prices are subject a 21% service charge and 6.5% tax (which is also applied to the service charge), except for Dasani water, which is billed only the service charge. If you request a brand of alcohol that is not on the Walt Disney World Catering list, you will be charged at cost for any opened product remaining at the end of the event, plus a 30% handling fee.

You may also **bring your own** beverages to your event. There is a taxable corkage fee of 50 cents per bottle or can for beer, soft drinks, and water and

Cocktail straws

$20 per bottle for liquor and wine. Liquor also incurs a $2.50 per drink charge to cover mixers, ice, and garnishes. While the corkage fee applies to all beverages brought to the event, Disney assesses a 21% service charge only on beverages opened at the event. The charge is calculated based on Disney's retail price for each beverage, not the price you bought it for.

Package Bar vs. Hosted Bar

It can be hard to decide which type of bar to offer at your reception because it is **difficult to estimate** how much your guests will drink. Certain factors can be clues, like the time of day or guests' religious restrictions. But ultimately you have to decide between the ease of a paying for a package and the potential cost savings—or spiraling!—of being billed on consumption.

Package bars are billed per guest, per hour of service. Usually they start with the pre-reception and last until the end of the reception, but some people choose to cut them off 30 minutes or more before the end of the event (coffee, tea, and ice water will still be available).

There are **seven categories** of package bar. The cheapest is Soft Drinks and Bottled Water, which starts at $8.50 per person for one hour of service and increases in $2 increments per person for each half hour thereafter. The most expensive is the Signature Wines & Liquor package, which starts at $27.50 per person for one hour and increases in $3.50 increments per person per half hour of service.

All alcoholic beverage packages also include soft drinks, juice, and bottled water.

The chart below shows the **starting price** per person and incremental increases for all seven categories.

Package Bar Category	First Hour (per person)	Additional Half Hours (per person)
Soft Drinks & Bottled Water	$8.50	$2.00
House Wines & Beer	$15.00	$2.50
Call Wines, Beer & Liquor	$18.00	$3.00
Premium Wines & Liquor	$20.50	$3.50
Signature Wines & Beer	$22.00	$3.50
Premium Cocktails & Signature Wines	$24.00	$3.50
Signature Wines & Liquor	$27.50	$3.50

Coffee, tea, and ice water are included in the price of buffet and plated menus

Beverages (continued)

If you choose a **hosted bar**, you will be billed per drink, based on Disney's standard 1 1/4-ounce pour. Cordials are served in 2-ounce pours, and soft drinks, bottled water, and juice are billed per container. If a guest requests a double pour or a mixed drink, you will be billed accordingly, and if a cocktail recipe requires more than one kind of alcohol, the price will be based on the total portion. The standard wine portion is 5 ounces.

© Nathan Root

Sparkling cider toast

Disney's estimate of two drinks per person for the first hour and one drink per person each hour thereafter is used to **calculate the cost** of your hosted bar when you make your final payment 30 days before the event. The per-drink price used in these calculations depends on the cocktail cost of the type of bar selected: $6.00 each for Call Brands, $7.00 each for Premium Brands, or $8.75 each for Signature Brands.

Pricing can be **adjusted** according to the needs of your group—for example, if you will have a considerable number of guests under drinking age. The actual drink charges will be calculated after the event, and your account will be credited or debited the difference.

Listed below is the **price per drink** for each of the various beverages Disney offers, along with the bottle prices on wine and cuvee.

Note that alcoholic beverages are priced 50 cents to $1.00 **higher for cash bars**.

By the Glass

• Soft Drinks, Perrier, & Dasani Water*	$4.00
• Juices	$5.00
• Beer	$6.00–$6.75
• House Wine	$6.75
• Call Cocktails	$6.00
• Premium Wine	$6.75–$7.50
• Premium Cocktails	$6.00–$7.00
• Signature Wine	$13.50
• Signature Cocktails	$6.00–$8.75
• Premium Cordials	$8.75
• Signature Cordials	$9.75

Dasani water is nontaxable

By the Bottle

• House Wine	$35
• Premium Wine	$39
• Sparkling Wine	$37
• Fairy Tale Cuvee	$62

Cake

From towering five-tier confections to individual mini cakes, wedding cake is the showpiece of the reception. And while Disney's Fairy Tale Weddings offers a catalog of popular cake styles, the team at the Grand Floridian Bakery can work from a picture or create just about **any style** of cake you dream up.

Disney offers eight wedding cake flavors and countless filling flavors, some of which are listed below:

Cake Flavors
- Yellow
- Chocolate
- Marble
- Carrot
- Red Velvet
- Lemon
- Orange
- Almond

Filling Flavors
- White Chocolate Mousse
- Dark Chocolate Mousse
- Milk Chocolate Mousse
- Raspberry Mousse
- Orange Mousse
- Amaretto Mousse
- Strawberry Mousse
- Passion Fruit Mousse
- German Chocolate
- Buttercream
- Cream Cheese
- Peanut Butter Mousse
- Peanut Butter Cup Mousse
- Bavarian Cream
- Bailey's Mousse
- Blackberry Mousse
- Mocha Mousse
- Fresh Strawberries
- Fresh Raspberries
- White Chocolate Mousse with Fresh Strawberries or Raspberries
- Bavarian Cream with Fresh Strawberries
- Passion Fruit Mousse with Fresh Raspberries
- Dark Chocolate Mousse with Fresh Raspberries
- Strawberry Mousse with Fresh Strawberries
- Raspberry Mousse with Fresh Raspberries

© Nathan Root

Chocolate cake with peanut butter cup filling and vanilla ice cream

Cake (continued)

While a traditional birthday cake is usually covered in buttercream frosting or whipped cream, most elaborate wedding cakes are covered in **fondant**, a malleable, edible substance that can be colored, shaped, and imprinted. These cakes have buttercream underneath the fondant to adhere it to the cake. Because many people do not like the taste of fondant, it is usually removed when the cake is served to guests.

You may request a cake covered only in **buttercream**, but be aware that there may be restrictions on where and how long it can be displayed to avoid spoilage. Also, many of the elaborate designs you see in magazines and in Disney's cake catalog cannot be replicated in buttercream. You could choose a simpler look or cover the cake with fresh flowers.

Mickey Wave Cake with white chocolate castle cake topper

The wedding cakes on Disney's list range from $7.50 to $17.50 per slice, and the **minimum guest count** required for each cake ranges from 50 to 200, depending on the cake style. The top layer of the cake, sometimes called the anniversary layer, is not included in the cake's guest count. It is assumed that the couple will take it with them after the reception.

Disney's **Mad Hatter** and Whimsy cakes are not priced per slice. They cost $450 for two tiers, $980 for three tiers, and $1,550 for four tiers. Miniature cakes range from $17 to $25 each and cannot be made with carrot cake or with German chocolate or fresh fruit fillings.

If you want a **custom** cake style, your Wedding Event Planner will

Cake detail

submit your design to the bakery for a price estimate. Asking for a loose interpretation may result in a lower quote than asking for an exact re-creation, and buttercream frosting will be less expensive than fondant.

Mad Hatter Cake with fresh flowers

A common money-saving tactic is to order a smaller wedding cake for display along with sheet cakes in the same flavors for serving guests. A quarter sheet cake serves 25 guests and costs $55, a half sheet cake serves 50 and costs $80, and a full sheet cake serves 100 and costs $120. These are covered in buttercream and are not meant for display.

Disney usually serves cake slices without the fondant

Two-tier Mad Hatter Cake

Many of the cakes on Disney's list include toppers or other inedible decorations. You may also provide your own topper, order fresh or sugar flowers, or purchase a white or milk **chocolate castle** cake topper. The castle costs between $100 and $200, depending on size, and the turrets can be painted the color of your choice for no extra charge. To custom paint the body of a small castle cake topper is an additional $50, while large castle cake toppers cost an extra $75 to paint. Disney also offers a chocolate sand castle cake topper; it's $165 for the small one and $285 for the large one. You may purchase Mickey's Wedding Gazebo topper for $85 (there is no charge for the topper if you order the Mickey's Wedding Gazebo cake).

There is a service charge on the price of the wedding cake, and a delivery and set-up fee will be charged at all but Grand Floridian reception venues. At the end of the reception, the staff will box up the **top layer** of the cake for you. If you have provided gift boxes, they will also pack up any leftover cake to give to your guests.

If your reception is held at the resort where you are staying, Bell Services can **deliver** to your room the cake top and other reception items, like the cake knife and server or your guest book. If you are staying anywhere else, you will need to make your own arrangements for transporting these items.

Custom cake with fresh flowers

Floral & Decor

One of the main ways to customize and **personalize** your wedding is through your floral and decor choices. When you get to this stage of the planning process, you'll find that Disney Floral & Gifts provides much more than just flowers. Every decorative element of the ceremony and reception, from the tulle canopy down to the aisle runner, can be arranged by working with your Floral Specialist.

This is one area of the planning process where **research** can really pay off. The more ideas you can provide your Floral Specialist—whether it's pictures from magazines, bits of fabric or ribbon, or even paint chips in your wedding colors—the easier it will be for him or her to help you create the look and feel you

Bridesmaid bouquet detail

envision for your wedding. If you aren't sure what you want, your Floral Specialist can show you pictures of individual flowers and popular arrangements, books of linen samples, and photos of past events to spark your imagination.

Wedding Pavilion pew decor

Unless your event is inside one of the parks, at Atlantic Dance Hall, or at an outdoor resort venue, you may also choose to work with **outside vendors** for floral and decor items. For in-park, Atlantic Dance Hall, and outdoor resort events, you are required to use Disney Floral & Gifts for everything except personal floral. You may also be able to bring in your own petals for tossing or scattering in the aisle, but you will have to designate a member of your wedding party or a guest to put them out; Disney will not set them up for you. Similarly, if you wish to move non-Disney floral items from the ceremony to the reception, you will need to make arrangements with your floral vendor or members of your group.

In this section we'll give you an overview of the **floral and decor options** provided by Disney Floral & Gifts, along with average prices for guideline purposes only. Floral prices, especially, can vary widely depending on the type of flower and its seasonal availability, as well as the size of each floral arrangement. Your Floral Specialist will be able to give you specific prices for your selections and work with you to find the combination of style and size that fits your budget.

Personal Floral

One of the first things many people think of when they think of a bride is her **bouquet**. The style and color of the wedding dress and the bride's height are among the factors that help your Floral Specialist determine the size and shape of the bouquet, so it is helpful to provide pictures of the dress. You may also choose to incorporate accessories like a cherished locket or even a few Hidden Mickeys. Bridal bouquets start at around $200.

Bridal bouquet with ribbon-wrapped handle

If you've scheduled an in-park bridal portrait session through Disney Event Group Photography within three days of your wedding, you may request a **floral refresh** to restore the bouquet to its wedding-day glory. Costs vary depending on the size and type of the flowers in the bouquet, but the service usually runs around $100. The bouquet will be collected directly after the ceremony and stored until the day of your photo shoot. Disney Floral & Gifts

The bride's bouquet arrives

will replace any wilted flowers and redeliver the bouquet to you that morning. If you wish to have the bouquet preserved, your Wedding Event Planner can recommend an independent floral preservation service. With prices north of $500, the process isn't cheap, but in the end you'll have the freeze-dried bridal bouquet framed with any other wedding memorabilia you wish to include.

If you have allergies or simply want a bouquet you can use again, you may want to investigate **artificial flowers**. Disney Floral & Gifts can make a silk bouquet to your specifications, or you can buy or make your own. A quick Google search will turn up numerous online resources for bouquets and floral supplies. Some interesting alternatives include flowers made from paper or clay and non-floral bouquets of crystals, beads, or feathers.

Because they are smaller than the bride's bouquet, **bridesmaids' bouquets** are usually less expensive, starting at around $100. Some low-cost alternatives are a rose wand, which requires only a few flowers, or a single presentation rose. A basket of petals for the flower girl starts at $55.

Complementary bride's and bridesmaids' bouquets

Personal Floral (continued)

Like the bridesmaids' bouquets, the groom's **boutonniere** could be based on the flowers used in the bride's bouquet. You may want it to be slightly different than the boutonnieres of the rest of the wedding party in size, color, or type of flowers. Boutonnieres start at $10.50, and crystal hidden Mickeys are available for $3 each.

Corsages for mothers of the bride and groom or other members of the family start at $21. Disney Floral & Gifts also offers presentation roses that the bride and groom may give to a special guest during the ceremony. These cost $20 for a single stem or $30 for a double stem.

Groom's boutonniere with hidden Mickey

Ceremony Decor

Whether you want to deck the aisle at the Wedding Pavilion with candelabra and piles of flowers or need nothing but a unity candle to complete your ceremony, you can work with Disney Floral & Gifts to achieve the look you've envisioned for your ceremony. The following are some of the most popular offerings.

Altar arrangement and unity candle at the Wedding Pavilion

One or more **altar arrangements** can dress up the altar at the Wedding Pavilion or delineate an altar area in less formal settings like the World Showcase venues at Epcot. Prices range widely depending on your selection, but you can figure on $175 or more for a floral arrangement or potted tree and less for alternatives like branches, leaves, or feathers. Vases, baskets, columns, and stands will need to be rented at an additional cost. Depending on the distance and time between the ceremony and reception, it may be cost effective to have your altar arrangement transferred to the reception site as decoration for an additional fee.

Disney Floral & Gifts offers a basic chuppah for $250, with optional floral rings averaging $100 and ribbons around $80. Unity candle sets start at $65, but adding a floral arrangement will run another $100-$200, depending on the flowers. A popular alternative to the unity candle is a sand ceremony, in which two different colors of sand are poured together into a single vase. Disney Floral & Gifts has sand ceremony sets starting at $25. Unity candles and sand ceremonies are easy to buy or make yourself, and you can provide them to your Wedding Event Coordinator along with other ceremony items, like programs, a day or two before the wedding.

Aisle decor includes standing or hanging floral arrangements, swagging, or ribbons along the pews or chairs, and petals strewn in or around the aisle. Mixed floral arrangements that can later be reused as centerpieces average $175, plus $25 each for columns with or without skirting. Tall vase arrangements average $170, including the vase rental, while swagging averages $150.

Aisle runners range from $75 for a basic white paper runner to $1,500 for a customized fabric runner. At the Wedding Pavilion, which has a longer aisle than most outdoor ceremony sites, simple fabric runners start at $275. If you will be bringing your own, the dimensions for the Wedding Pavilion aisle are 90 inches wide by 54 feet from the door to the bottom step of the altar or 69 feet up the steps to the top of the altar.

Aisle decor at Sea Breeze Point

Aisle petals in Morocco

The cost of **aisle petals** varies depending on the amount of coverage and length of the aisle. It could be as low as $50 for a scattering of rose petals down a short aisle or as high as $2,000 for mounds of petals on both sides of the aisle at the Wedding Pavilion. If you know the approximate square footage of the aisle or have a quote from Disney on the size of an aisle runner, you can calculate the number of cups of petals required for different amounts of coverage at http://flyboynaturals.com/suqu.html.

Disney Floral & Gifts offers several options for the couple's staged (or real) exit from the ceremony. **Toss petals** are probably the most popular choice. These start at $3.50 per person for bunches of petals in individual organza bags or paper cones. You may also choose to provide a big basket of petals for guests to scoop from for around $2 per person. Bottles of bubbles for guests to blow during your exit cost $3 per guest, or you can provide your own. Disney does not allow non-biodegradable materials for outdoor staged exits, including artificial rose petals and confetti.

If you're on a budget or want more choice, try a Google search of online vendors for aisle runners and freeze-dried flower petals. Note that you may be required to designate a member of your party to set up any decor not provided by Disney.

Bags of toss petals

Ceremony Decor (continued)

If your ceremony is not being held in the Wedding Pavilion, you may want to consider **alternatives** to the plastic lawn chairs Disney provides at outdoor venues or the standard banquet chairs provided at indoor venues. Basic chair covers include a sash in the color of your choice and cost $8.50. The price goes up from there depending on the style and fabric you select. Upgraded chairs range from white wooden folding chairs for $5 apiece to elegant Chiavari chairs starting at $12.50 apiece. Sashes and other chair decor cost extra, and there is a delivery fee of $100-$250, depending on venue, for bringing in different chairs. If your ceremony is not being held inside a park, at Atlantic Dance Hall, or at an outdoor venue, you may be able to use an outside vendor for chairs and chair covers.

Chair covers and sashes

Reception Decor

If you thought there were a lot of options for ceremony decor, just wait until you start planning the reception! Disney Floral & Gifts provides more than just centerpieces and flowers for the cake—there's also a range of themed backdrops, lighting options, and decorative accents, not to mention the myriad table settings and linen styles. You can also purchase place cards, menus, table numbers, and favors through Disney, although many people provide their own. If your reception is not being held inside a park, at Atlantic Dance Hall, or at an outdoor resort location, you may use an outside vendor for chairs, chair covers, tables, table linens, and floral arrangements.

Choosing wedding colors makes it easy to coordinate reception decor

Disney's **Magical Backdrops** include the $1,875 Storybook Entrance, which allows you and your guests to literally step into the pages of a storybook when they enter your reception, and the $3,700 Rustic Entrance, featuring an arched gate, a fountain, greenery, and fresh roses. The "life-size scale replica" Cinderella Castle Façade reaches almost to the ceiling and includes topiaries, fresh flowers, and two fountains for $13,000. Or the happy couple can watch the reception from gilded red or purple Royal Thrones for $830.

© Nathan Root

There are several **lighting options** in addition to the atmospheric lighting provided as part of the DJ package (see "Music & Entertainment," beginning on page 104). The canopy of white tulle and twinkle lights extends from the ceiling above the center of the room to the edge of the dance floor and costs $2,385. Pin spotting places a small spotlight directly over the head table, cake table, or guest tables for dramatic effect. The cost is $125 per pin spot. You can add ficus trees with lights at a cost of $490 for 4 trees, $845 for 6 trees, $1,140 for 8 trees, or $1,975 for 10 trees. And for $350 you can select from an array of projected light patterns, known as gobos, including a castle, the moon and stars, or even your monogram.

Tulle and twinkle-light canopy

Among the other **themed accents** available are fog machines, priced at $950 for a maximum of 20 minutes' operation, and confetti, which rains down on guests after the last dance at a price of $500. A standard dance floor is available for ballrooms and banquet rooms at no extra charge if you arrange for your DJ or band through Disney. If you use an outside vendor at one of these venues, Disney will charge a setup fee of $950 (DJ) or $1,550 (band) to cover lighting, staging, and a dance floor. For reception venues that are not part of a convention center, there is a fee for bringing in a dance floor. A standard 9-foot-by-12-foot dance floor is usually around $450, while a white or black-and-white dance floor costs $675.

Confetti cannons, used here during the recessional, also have a big impact during the last dance at the reception

And for the ultimate cap to your ceremony or reception, Disney offers a private **fireworks display** starting at $3,000. This 30-second photo opportunity is only available at the Wedding Pavilion, where fireworks are launched as the couple crosses the footbridge leading back to Franck's and their guests.

Reception Decor (continued)

The number of **tables** used and their size depends on the number of guests and may be restricted to existing options at certain reception venue. The standard sizes are rounds of 8 or 10, but rounds of 6 or even 4 may be available in some venues.

There are also several different **head table** styles for the bridal couple. The traditional setup is to seat the wedding party at a head table on a riser at one end of the room, creating a focal point. A roman table allows the entire wedding party, and potentially their partners, to be seated with the bridal couple at one long table in the center of the room. A reserved head table places the wedding party at a round table like all the others, but in the center of the room. And a sweetheart table accommodates just the bridal couple for the first meal of their union.

Sweetheart table on a riser, with castle gobo

Assigned seating arrangements can be one of the trickiest aspects of planning a wedding reception, but the options for dressing those chairs and setting those tables can be just as overwhelming. The standard setup at most reception venues includes banquet chairs, white poly-cotton overlays and underlays on the tables, glassware, dishes, and flatware. (Some exceptions include the navy and green or white standard table linens at the Living Seas Salon and the wicker and upholstered chairs at The Attic.)

Any changes or upgrades to the **linens, chairs, or place settings** will incur additional charges. Basic chair covers include a sash in the color of your choice and cost $8.50. The price goes up from there depending on the style and fabric you select. Elegant Chiavari chairs start at $12.50 apiece

Chiavari chairs and upgraded linens at the Yacht Club

and cost as much as $25 apiece depending on the color, sashes, and other decorative accents selected. Delivery fees for bringing in different chairs range from $100–$250, depending on location. Various combinations of base plates, chargers, and napkins range from $3 to $20 per place setting, and an overall table style featuring coordinated chairs, linens, place settings, and a centerpiece can cost anywhere from $300 to $1,600 to seat 10 people. To see the colors and fabrics offered by Disney Floral & Gifts, check out http://www.linenshowroom.com.

Individual floral **centerpieces** start at $75, not including the rental fee for vases and other containers. You may be able to lower the cost by using scattered petals or non-floral items like candles instead. Another idea is to place the bridesmaids' bouquets in vases on the tables.

You may also **bring your own** containers for the floral arrangements provided by Disney Floral & Gifts or provide your own floral arrangements. If you choose to bring your own, you will be responsible for designating a member of your party to set them up.

Glow cubes in a centerpiece

The bride's bouquet doubles as decor

Mickey and Minnie topiaries can be rented for $1,050 each. **Floral arrangements** for the gift and cake tables and flowers for the cake start at $75, and the official Disney's Fairy Tale Weddings cake knife and server set costs $50. You may use the venue's standard cake knife and server for free or provide your own. Toasting glasses are also provided by the venue, but you may bring your own or purchase a commemorative set from Disney Floral & Gifts for $50. And because most brides would rather not part with their bouquets (and those bouquets can be extremely heavy), Disney offers toss bouquets starting at $35.

Disney Floral & Gifts can provide place cards, table cards, and menus, as well as a number of favors, from personalized mouse ears to chocolate place cards. Many of these are on display at Franck's. You are **not required** to use Disney for these, even if your event is in a park or at an outdoor venue. If you bring your own favors, place cards, menus, or table cards, Disney will set out up to two items per place setting free of charge. Any more than that will incur a set-up fee of $35 per hour, with a minimum of one hour.

Chocolate favor

Personalized menu

Table number

Music & Entertainment

Music is an integral part of the ceremony, and it sets the tone for the reception. Entertainers and costumed characters add fun, humor, and a unique touch found only at Disney's Fairy Tale Weddings. As you'd expect from one of the world's largest entertainment companies, Disney offers numerous music and entertainment choices for your big day. These fall into **four categories**: musicians and DJs, audiovisual and technical services, themed Disney entertainers, and Walt Disney World characters.

Musicians & DJs

Disney can provide a wide range of **solo musicians and ensembles** for the ceremony and reception. The starting price includes three hours of the

musicians' time, with additional performance time available at an hourly rate. Union rules require musicians to take a 20-minute break for every hour of service, so you will get 40-minute sets interspersed with 20-minute breaks.

Some performers bring recordings of their music to play during these breaks, or you may provide your own. Depending on the venue,

Classical String Trio

there may be ambient music playing in the background already. You may also need to provide sheet music if you select songs that are not in the standard repertoire. Because there is a **three-hour minimum** for musicians, it can be cost-effective to have ceremony musicians play during the pre-reception or first part of the reception. Note that the services of an organist are included in the venue fee for the Wedding Pavilion.

The list on the next page is just a **sampling** of the kinds of musicians available. Your Wedding Event Planner will work with you to find the type of musicians or band you're looking for. The bands offered include swing, country, pop, and even an 11-piece mariachi band. The prices listed are for the first three hours of performance, except for most styles of live band, which have a four-hour minimum.

Classical/Jazz Guitarist

Disney Musicians

- Flute $575
- Classical/Jazz Guitarist $575
- Key West-Style Guitarist $745
- Harpist $800
- Pianist (includes piano rental) $820
- Violinist $575
- Vocalist (ceremony) $650
- Bagpiper $575
- Violin/Flute Duo $1,030
- Harp/Flute Duo $1,200
- Jazz Trio $1,515
- Classical String Trio $1,515
- String Quartet $1,980
- Calypso Trio with Steel Drum $1,710
- Live Band $7,000

A DJ leads guests in "YMCA"

If you prefer to have a **disc jockey** for your reception, prices start at $1,500 for four hours and include a lighting package. The price doubles for the month of December. Disney contracts with local DJs, and you will be assigned one about 30

Live bands start at $7,000

days before your event. If you want a specific DJ on Disney's list, you may be able to contact him or her directly and ask to be penciled in before 30 days out to ensure availability, but your Wedding Event Planner will handle all the details of confirming and hiring the DJ.

If your cocktail hour and reception are held in the **same location**, you will need to pay for the DJ from the beginning of the cocktail hour—even if your ceremony musicians will be playing during that time—because the DJ must set up in time for the start of the event.

Non-Disney musicians and DJs are not allowed at functions held inside the parks, at Atlantic Dance Hall, or at outdoor resort venues. This also prohibits you from having any of your guests perform at these venues. If your event is held elsewhere and you choose to bring in your own DJ or band, Disney **charges a fee of** $950 (DJ) or $1,550 (band) to cover lighting, staging, and a dance floor.

Calypso Trio with Steel Drum

Audiovisual & Technical Services

Whether you need microphones for your outdoor ceremony or you want to create your own reception playlist on your iPod, Disney's Audio Visual Services department can provide the necessary **equipment and technicians**. The cost of equipment and setup varies depending on the requirements of each venue, but some of the options available are CD players, iPod setups (but not iPods themselves), speakers, mixers, microphones, and lighting, along with qualified technicians to run the equipment.

An **iPod setup** includes two speakers, an audio mixer, and the appropriate cables and starts at $250 for resort venues. At park venues, the cost is $300 for those with an existing sound system and up to $650 for those without. You will need to have one of your guests run the system, or you can hire a Disney sound tech. If you need wireless lavaliere microphones for your ceremony,

You may also bring your own iPod sound system and have a guest run it

Disney provides an $800 package with a two-speaker sound system and a tech to run it. If you want to play recorded music at the ceremony, you can add a CD player to the package for a nominal fee. And if you want to feature a slideshow of childhood pictures of the bridal couple at the reception, or if you just want something to entertain younger guests, a TV and DVD player are available for $165.

Themed Entertainers

Disney offers a variety of themed entertainers to add a special bit of magic to your ceremony or reception. For $675, a Major Domo in full regalia will carry your wedding rings down the aisle in a glass slipper. Or you could have an English Butler in tails present the wedding rings on a silver platter. Both characters may also be able to make **announcements**, assist with a petal toss, direct guests between events,

or even collaborate in a practical joke on the Best Man involving "misplaced" rings—talk to your Wedding Event Planner if you have something in mind. Disney also offers a costumed Herald Trumpeter to play a fanfare during the processional and announce the arrival of the bride and groom at the reception. Prices start at $700 for one and $1,100 for two.

The Major Domo announces the bridal couple

The reception can be your chance to really cut loose, and Disney's themed entertainers will help everyone get into the spirit. For $1,800 a pair of **Uninvited Guests** will "crash" your event and mingle with guests for three hours; each additional hour costs $350. Wearing loud polyester outfits and armed with an inside knowledge of your guests (which you provide), this "husband and wife" pair

Caricatures make great party favors

will provide improvisational comedy during dinner and through to the end of the reception. Similarly, $1,500 gets you a pair of Tacky Tourists, either two women or a man and a woman, who stumble on your reception and share their Disney obsession through tidbits and trivia. And for $900 for three hours and $175 for each additional hour, a Clumsy Waiter will guide guests to their tables, make outrageous comments, and provide physical comedy throughout the meal.

Themed entertainers can also be a **great alternative** to a DJ or band and dancing. A caricature artist is available for $585 for three hours, with a three-hour minimum, and $195 for each additional hour. The artist can draw 8-10 black-and-white caricatures per hour or 4 in color; an additional artist would be required for parties of more than 40 guests (based on four hours of service). Caricatures are 11x14 inches and do not include envelopes or tubes for transport. Other choices include a magician ($760), a face painter ($420), a balloon artist ($700), a fortune teller ($700), and a juggler ($640). All prices are for three hours, and there is a three-hour minimum. If your reception will be held in one of the theme parks, you may be able to request an appearance by some of that park's entertainers, like an animal encounter in Animal Kingdom ($450) or Chinese acrobats in Epcot's China Pavilion. For the acrobats, prices are $1,830 for four acrobats or $2,525 for seven acrobats, and they are only available after 8:00 pm.

Walt Disney World Characters

For that extra-special Disney touch, you can have costumed characters like Mickey, Minnie, and Donald or face characters like Cinderella and Prince Charming make an appearance at your reception. Prices start at $900 for one character, $1,350 for two, and $1,800 for three for **30 minutes** of interaction. Some characters may have multiple costumes to choose from, although these may increase the price. Certain characters may not appear together, but you can schedule them to arrive at different times. Non-overlapping character appearances—like Pluto during the pre-reception and Lumiere during dinner—are billed as separate, individual appearances. Due to licensing and theming restrictions, not all characters may be available at every venue, and some characters, like Winnie the Pooh & Friends, are not available at all. Characters may not appear at outdoor in-park receptions until the park has closed to day guests. Also, alcoholic beverage service must stop during character appearances.

Transportation

Walt Disney World spans 47 square miles, which makes transportation arrangements for the bridal party and wedding guests an important part of the planning process. Although Disney offers a range of free transportation options to resort guests, these may not be practical to the schedule and venues used on the day of your event. Disney's bus service does not make direct connections between the Disney resorts, so guests would have to change buses at one of the theme parks or Downtown Disney to reach a ceremony or reception at one of the resorts—a process that can take more than an hour and is only possible during park operating hours. And if your event is being held inside a park, Disney requires you to charter transportation for guests.

Limos arrive from backstage at Epcot

That said, it can be fun to incorporate public **Disney transportation** options in your day if your group is small. For example, the bride and groom may choose to depart the reception for their hotel on the Monorail or a Friendship boat, which makes for great photo opportunities and surprises and delights vacationers.

In addition to basic options like limos and motor coaches, Disney's Fairy Tale Weddings offers **specialty transportation** for staged entrances and exits, including a replica of Cinderella's Glass Coach. These methods are more for show than actual transportation, so you will also have to arrange regular transportation for the rest of the day.

With the exception of specialty transportation, Disney makes all arrangements through local company Mears Transportation. If you have your heart set on a **nontraditional choice** like a stretch Hummer or just want to make your own transportation arrangements, you may work with another vendor for any event not located inside one of the Disney parks.

The rates listed here are for transportation provided by Disney's Fairy Tale Weddings within Walt Disney World. It is possible to arrange transportation to and from locations **outside** Walt Disney World, but it will substantially increase the amount of travel time for your guests and, therefore, the cost of the transportation. If you have off-site guests, Disney recommends that they meet at one of the Walt Disney World resort locations on your transportation route to catch a ride.

Transportation for the Bridal Party

Ceremony transportation for the bridal couple and their attendants could be as simple as a walk from their rooms at BoardWalk Inn to Sea Breeze Point, or it could involve a fleet of limos dispatched to all corners of the World. Among the **factors** in play are where the couple is staying the night before the wedding, whether they will be taking pictures together before the ceremony, and whether their attendants and families will be taking pre-ceremony pictures with them.

If the bridal couple and any other members of the wedding party plan to take formal pictures between the ceremony and reception, they will require **separate transportation** from the guests. Otherwise, the entire group may travel to the reception site together. After the reception, the bride and groom usually have their own transportation to their resort, while guests and the wedding party depart together or make their own way to their next destinations.

Transportation for Guests

Depending on where your ceremony and reception are held and whether your guests have **cars**, you may want to provide transportation to the ceremony, from the ceremony to the reception, and from the reception back to their resorts. Smaller parties can make use of limos, town cars, vans, or minibuses.

For larger groups, you will need to rent one or more **motor coaches**, which accommodate up to 50 passengers each. These are luxury coaches like the ones used by Disney's Magical Express and the Disney Cruise Line, not the city-bus style of Disney's free transportation to the parks. You may even be able to have the driver play a slideshow of your childhood pictures for guests using the coach's DVD player!

The bridal couple might take a limo while guests board a private motor coach

Transportation Costs

The chart below lists the various **types of transportation**, the number of guests each one accommodates, and the prices of each kind of trip. There are three types of trips: one-way, round trip, and charter. One-way trips are only available on Disney property and travel just from Point A to Point B. Round trips travel from Point A to Point B and back to Point A. Charter transportation can make an unlimited number of stops but must be hired for a minimum of three or five hours, depending on vehicle type.

You may be able to **save money** and avoid having to charter transportation by adding one stop to a one-way or round trip for $20–$50, depending on the vehicle type. For example, if all your guests are staying at just two Disney resorts, you can hire a one-way motor coach and add an extra stop. However, trips with more than two stops or a transfer that lasts longer than 15 minutes automatically become charters. So if your guests are scattered among four different resorts, you will be required to charter a motor coach for a minimum number of hours that may be longer than you need. Therefore, it's important to consider transportation when you're setting up your room block.

Type	Capacity	One Way	Round Trip	Charter
Town Car	4	$25	n/a	$40/hour (3-hour min.)
Limo	8	$166	$332	$94.16/hour (3-hour min.)
Van	11	$163	$221	$68.25/hour (3-hour min.)
Minibus	25	$273	$321	$87.15/hour (5-hour min.)
Motor Coach	50	$325	$410	$97.65/hour (5-hour min.)

Note: There is no tax or service charge on transportation.

Specialty Transportation

Disney offers a number of specialty transportation options that make for great **photo opportunities** and a dramatic entrance or exit from the ceremony or reception. For three hours, you can have one of dozens of vintage cars, with the Model A Ford ($600) and vintage Rolls Royce ($800) being the most popular. A Horse-Drawn Landau Coach costs $1,700 for two hours. Cinderella's Glass Coach comes with white ponies and costumed footmen at a rate of $2,700 for two hours. The Model A and the Rolls are a tight squeeze for more than two people, while the coaches seat up to four people. The coaches are only available at the Wedding Pavilion, Grand Floridian, BoardWalk Inn, and Yacht Club, as well as at morning Epcot ceremonies in every venue except the United Kingdom.

Cinderella's Glass Coach at Sea Breeze Point

Another fun transportation option might be one of Disney's **boats**. The reproduction Hacker-Craft runabout Breathless II can ferry up to six people between venues at Epcot, Disney's Hollywood Studios, the Yacht & Beach Club, and the BoardWalk. The price is $105 for 30 minutes. For $250 one way, up to 50 people may ride a Friendship boat between any of the same locations. Over on Seven Seas Lagoon, the Grand 1 yacht travels between the Wedding Pavilion and the Grand Floridian, the Contemporary Resort, the Polynesian Resort, and Wilderness Lodge. This 52-foot Sea Ray is staffed by a captain and a deckhand and seats 17; the price is $520 per hour, with a minimum of one hour.

One thing to keep in mind when considering specialty transportation is the limited amount of time you spend in it. In particular, the two coaches don't actually take you from your hotel to the ceremony and back. For example, if you are being married at the Wedding Pavilion and are not staying at the Grand Floridian, you must arrange transportation to the Grand Floridian to meet the coach. The bride gets a **short ride** to the Wedding Pavilion, and after the ceremony the bride and groom make a staged exit in the coach for the photographs, then circle back to the Wedding Pavilion for pictures with family and friends.

The Model A Ford arrives at the Grand Floridian

Photography

Photos and video provide **lasting memories** of the wedding day, from the first time the bride and groom see each other to the last dance at the reception. For many people, the choice of photographer is highly personal and depends a lot on the style they want and their rapport with the vendor. While Disney provides skilled photographers, there is no guarantee you'll get the one you request or be able to meet with him or her prior to the day of your event. This is one reason that couples frequently seek outside vendors for photography. In addition to covering the packages and products Disney offers, we'll discuss the advantages of hiring your own photographer.

Not to be confused with Disney's PhotoPass service in the parks, Disney Event Group Photography is a team of professional photographers, photo retouchers, and album designers who capture the priceless moments at your event. In addition to a range of photography packages, products, and services, Disney offers the bridal couple a number of **unique photo opportunities**, including portrait sessions inside the theme parks before they open.

Disney Event Group Photography assigns photographers to each event based on **availability**. If you have a preference or a recommendation, Disney will attempt to match you with the photographer you request but cannot guarantee it. You can see a sample of each photographer's work at http://www.disneyeventphotography.com.

Among the **advantages** of using Disney Event Group Photography are the ability to apply the cost toward your overall minimum expenditure and to get images from every event Disney shoots on one disc: wedding, dessert party, Magic Kingdom Portrait Session, etc.

However, it is important to note that the "proof disc" that comes with some of Disney's packages contains images that are 450x300 pixels and 72 dpi. Disney describes these as suitable for archival purposes and e-mailing. Professional photo printers and online consumer services like Snapfish and Shutterfly require a minimum resolution of 300 dpi and 540x360 pixels to print a 4x6 image; larger photos require larger numbers of pixels.

Disney offers Wishes Collection couples a disc of **high-resolution images** from all events photographed by Disney for $1,000. The price drops to $500 three years from the date of the wedding. Couples who only use Disney for an in-park bridal portrait shoot may purchase the disc right away for $750 or wait for it to drop to $500 after three years. Disney retains digital copies of your photos for five years.

All photo packages include a proof book with thumbnail versions of the images, and photos are posted on a password-protected **web site** two weeks after the event. You can order reprints up to 8x10 inches on the web site, or you can call Disney Event Group Photography about larger prints or canvas prints. Prices are listed on the following pages.

Photography Packages

The $5,225 **Enchanted Rose** package includes up to 10 hours of event coverage, 4x6-inch prints, 10 6x6-inch softcover books featuring 24 photos each, and a proof disc of low-resolution images. (You can get a disc of high-resolution images by giving up the prints and albums.) You have a choice of one of the four albums described below, plus up to two hours of the Album Designer's time. You will also receive two Family Albums—either the Traditional Album, with 30 5x7-inch prints, or the Artist Commissioned Album, with 20 prints. The package includes a Magic Kingdom Portrait Session, with one 20x24-inch portrait and 12 5x7-inch prints in a Disney-themed album, plus a 4x6-inch print of every shot.

The $3,650 **Dreams** package includes up to eight hours of coverage, 4x6-inch prints, a proof disc of low-resolution images, and one Traditional Family Album of 30 5x7-inch prints. Also included is your choice of either the 50-print Artist Commissioned album or the Signature Album and two hours with an Album Designer. You can get a disc of high-resolution images by giving up the prints and albums and paying an additional $200.

The $2,800 **Romance** package includes six hours of coverage, 4x6-inch prints, and a Signature Album, plus two hours with an Album Designer. You can get a disc of high-resolution images by giving up the prints and albums and paying an additional $400.

If you will be using an outside photographer for all but the in-park portion of your event, Disney offers two **stripped-down packages**. Both include one photographer for a maximum of three hours and a 4x6-inch print of every image. The $1,700 Celebration A package comes with 24 8x10-inch photos of your choice in a white Premier album, while the $1,900 Celebration B package will get you 40 8x10-inch photos of your choice in a white Premier album.

A $200 fee applies whenever you break up the photography time included in each package—for example, if you wanted to have the photographer leave the reception early and return later for a dessert party.

Albums

Disney's **Signature Album** is a 12x12-inch leather, library-bound album. Depending on the photography package you choose, you will have a certain amount of credit toward the cost of prints to put in the album. The package includes a two-hour session with an Album Designer, who works with you to select and lay out the images. The session can be scheduled as soon as your wedding contract is signed, and additional hours cost $75.

The 11x14-inch **Digital Montage Album** includes 65 prints with a modern photo finish and a two-hour session with an Album Designer. You select the images, and the Album Designer determines their layout. The 12x12-inch **Artist Commissioned** album includes 50 prints with custom mats and frames. The design and layout are determined by the Album Artist. The **Brilliance Album** is a 12x12-inch photo book with metallic-finish cover and pearlescent pages. The design and layout are determined by the Album Artist.

Prints and Portraits

Print Prices

• 4x5	$10
• 4x6	$10
• 5x7	$15
• 8x10	$30
• 8x12	$30
• 11x14	$55
• 16x20	$85
• 20x24	$115
• 30x40	$250
• 8 wallets*	$15
• 16 wallets*	$24
• 24 wallets*	$31

*same image

Print Packages
(Includes U.S. shipping)

Print Package A - $300
1 – 11x14 portrait
4 – 8x10
3 – 5x7
8 – 4x6

Print Package B - $288
1 – 16x20 portrait
1 – 11x14 portrait
2 – 8x10

Print Package C - $207
1 – 16x20 portrait
2 – 8x10

Print Package D - $109
2 – 8x10
2 – 5x7
8 – wallets (same image)

Portrait Prices

Portraits are mounted on GatorBoard, a rigid polystyrene foam. They include basic retouching to diminish lines, spots, glare, and minor facial blemishes. Retouching is available for regular prints at $50 per hour, with a minimum of one hour. For canvas portrait prices add 50%.

• 11x14	$120
• 16x20	$165
• 20x24	$225
• 24x30	$275
• 30x40	$380

 Pros & Cons of Hiring Outside Vendors

Unless your event is being held inside one of the Disney theme parks, you may hire outside vendors for nearly every aspect of your wedding but food and beverage. This includes floral, decor, transportation, photography, and videography. The exceptions are floral, decor, and entertainment at outdoor venues anywhere in Walt Disney World—these must be provided by Disney. The following is a list of pros and cons that may help you decide whether to seek your own vendors.

Pros
• Cost savings or more bang for your buck
• Ability to choose and meet with a specific vendor
• Ability to select from a range of vendors with a variety of styles
• More options to choose from

Cons
• Costs don't count toward Disney's overall minimum expenditure
• Requires time and effort to research
• Requires individual contract negotiation
• Outside vendors prohibited at certain venues

Additional Photography Packages

One of the most popular Disney photography packages is the **Magic Kingdom Portrait Session** because it is most couples' only opportunity to wear wedding attire in the park. The session is open only to the couple, who are picked up from the lobby of their Disney resort at either 5:00 am or 6:00 am to be photographed before the Magic Kingdom opens. The one-hour session takes place at Cinderella Castle and Prince Charming Regal

A popular Magic Kingdom photo spot

Carrousel. Other locations may be available on request. The cost is $1,100 for an album of 12 5x7-inch prints and loose 4x6-inch prints of every image from the photo shoot.

A similar package is available for **Epcot, Disney's Hollywood Studios, or Disney's Animal Kingdom** at a cost of $650 for 12 5x7-inch prints in an album and a 4x6-inch print of every image. The same package, under the name Trash the Dress, is available at either of Disney's **water parks**.

For $1,400 couples may schedule portrait sessions at the Magic Kingdom and an additional park on the same day. Along with a 4x6-inch print of every image, this package includes a 30-print album of 5x7-inch images that can be customized with your names and wedding date.

Also offered is a **Walt Disney World Resort Portrait Session** at the hotel of your choice for $450. Like the in-park sessions, it is for the bridal couple only; however, the pickup time is flexible. You will receive a 6x6-inch soft cover photo book containing 24 images and a 4x6-inch print of every image. For $125 you can upgrade to an album of 12 5x7-inch prints, and $180 gets you the same album with 20 prints.

If Disney Event Group photography is shooting your wedding, these portrait sessions **do not have to be held on the same day as your event** in order to count toward your overall minimum expenditure.

Another option is the $310 **Honeymoon Photographic Session**, which is available only at Epcot and takes place during normal operating hours. Wedding attire is not permitted, and park admission is not included. Couples receive a 6x6-inch, soft-cover photo book with 24 images, one 4x6-inch print of every image, and online posting of the images. For $65 you can upgrade to an 8x8-inch, hard-cover photo book. For $400 you can upgrade to the 7x9-inch black leather Digital Montage 24 album, which includes 10 pages and 24 images laid out by a graphic artist. Each additional 2-sided page costs $30. For $300 you can purchase all the high-resolution images on disc (note that if you use Disney for your wedding photography and purchase that on disc, the portrait session photos can be added at no charge.)

If you are planning an IllumiNations or Fantasmic! dessert party, Disney offers a $350 **dessert party photo package** that includes two hours of photography, 30–50 photos, and 4x6-inch prints of every image.

Hiring Your Own Photographer

Finding your own photographer allows you to work with a **specific vendor** based on his or her entire body of work and generally gets you more bang for your buck, including high-resolution digital copies of all your photos and savings on packages and reprints. Disney no longer charges a fee for bringing in an outside photographer, but they are prohibited at in-park events.

- **Choose your photographer—**Just about any wedding magazine or web site will advise you to interview multiple photographers to view samples of their work—including all the photos from a single event—and see if you will feel comfortable entrusting your wedding-day memories to them. Some photographers offer couples engagement portrait sessions as an introduction. These will give you an idea whether you feel comfortable working with the photographer and let you see a better sampling of his or her work, not just a few highlights.

- **Digital copies of photos—**In these days of digital photography and online or home photo printing, many of us have come to expect access to more than just physical copies of our pictures. Although wedding photographers used to control the negatives to their clients' pictures and require couples to buy prints directly from them, most now give their clients the rights to digital versions of their pictures to use as they please. The disc of photos may be included in the package or available for a fee. It allows couples to print their own photos, share them electronically with others, and create photo albums or coffee table–style books of their pictures.

- **Significant cost savings—**Many independent Orlando-area photographers offer packages at significantly lower rates than Disney's or offer more hours, products, and service for a similar price. They are also usually willing to work with you to customize a package to suit your budget by reducing the number of hours of coverage or the number of prints and albums. And because their packages usually include digital copies of all your images, you will be able to save money by making your own prints and albums too.

Videography

Although Disney's video services are contracted through outside vendor Bruno White Entertainment (http://www.brunowhite.com/), your Wedding Event Planner and Disney Event Group Photography will be your contacts. As with photography, the **advantages** of choosing a Disney package are convenience and the ability to apply the cost to your overall minimum expenditure. There is also a 10% discount if you use Disney for both photography and videography.

Among the **disadvantages** of choosing Disney video packages is that videographers are assigned to each event based on availability, so you may not know who will be shooting your wedding or be able to see samples of his or her work. However, if you have a preference or a recommendation, Disney will attempt to match you with the videographer you request. Disney no longer charges a fee for bringing in an outside videographer; however, they are prohibited at in-park events.

Wedding Videography Packages

Disney's $5,200 **Enchanted Memories** package includes an 8–12-minute opening montage of the couple telling their love story over footage from the entire day, along with 8 hours of multi-camera video coverage, 4 hours of cinematic glide-cam coverage, digital enhancements, DVD menus, wedding-party credits, four copies of the DVD, and 10 Internet downloads of the ceremony footage for friends and family (note that these are after the fact; the ceremony will not be webcast live). Couples may submit photos for the opening montage and any music they wish to include in addition to the original audio and music from the ceremony and reception. For ceremonies at the Wedding Pavilion, the package includes three mounted cameras and two manned cameras. For ceremonies at all other venues, the package includes four camera angles (not all are manned). The package provides two manned cameras for the reception.

The $3,300 **Memories** package is available in two styles: Romantic, which features more slow-motion, fairy tale–style shots, and Modern, which is fast-paced like a music video. The package includes 6 hours of coverage, a 5-7-minute montage of wedding-day highlights, digital enhancements, DVD menus, wedding-party credits, 2 copies of the DVD, and 5 Internet downloads of the ceremony footage for friends and family. Couples may submit any music they wish to include in addition to the original audio and music from the ceremony and reception. For ceremonies at the Wedding Pavilion, the package includes four camera angles. Ceremonies at all other venues receive three camera angles. The package provides two-camera coverage for the reception.

The $1,200 **Celebration Package** captures the ceremony only, from the couple's arrival at the site to their staged exit. It includes one-camera coverage of the arrival and departure, which is edited to music. The ceremony is covered by three cameras and includes original audio.

Additional DVD copies are $100 each. With the $1,000 **High-Definition Upgrade**, all your footage is shot on high-def video, and you get two copies of the final product on Blu-ray disc.

Among the other enhancements is the $500 **Through the Years Montage**, which sets 40 of your family photos to music and can be shown at any pre-wedding or wedding-day event. It is also added as a special feature on your wedding DVD.

The $500 **Dessert Party** package is a 2-minute montage of your dessert party, including guest testimonials, that can be added as a special feature to your wedding DVD. It includes one-camera coverage and is edited to the song of your choice. The $800 **Love Story Interview** allows the bride and groom to share the story of their journey to the altar and can be added to the wedding DVD.

The **Bridal Spotlight** is the video equivalent of a Theme Park Portrait Session—a music video of you in the theme park before it opens, set to the song of your choice. The price is $1,000 for the Magic Kingdom, $800 for any of the other Disney parks, $1,400 for the Magic Kingdom plus another park, or $1,000 for two of the other parks. A 15% discount is available if you use Disney videography for your wedding.

Childcare

There are several options for entertaining and **supervising** children on the day of your event. These range from catered children's parties in a separate venue to simply setting up a television or activities in one corner of your reception venue. If you are having an adults-only event, you may wish to provide your guests with information about in-room childcare and resort kids' clubs.

All private and special-event childcare is provided by bonded and insured service Kid's Nite Out (http://www.kidsniteout.com). Resort children's clubs are staffed by trained Disney cast members.

Children's Parties

If you will have **11 or more** children at your event, you may wish to provide a separate children's party in a private room. Generally this option is only available at convention center reception venues, but certain special venues and restaurants may have a private room nearby that would work. There is a four-hour minimum, including one hour of preparation time, and children must be at least 6 weeks old. The price is $9.50/hour per child ages 3 to teen and for younger children who are toilet-trained. Children ages 6 weeks to 3 years cost $11.50/hour each, and there is a $2.50/hour per child surcharge if you have fewer than 11 children; there is a seven-child minimum. Rates include tax but not the automatic 10% gratuity.

Prices include wristbands and security cards, games, toys, sing-alongs, group activities, and arts and crafts. You may also choose to provide a **buffet** of kids' foods catered by the resort at an additional charge. You will need to supply the name and age of each child when you reserve the party so that Kid's Nite Out can provide the appropriate number of caretakers.

If you will have 25 or more children, you may request a **themed party** that includes everything in the children's party package plus decorations, prizes, themed projects, games, and entertainment. Rates are $2 more per hour per child than the standard rate for each age category, including tax but not the automatic 10% gratuity.

Other Entertainment

If you will have fewer than seven children at your event but still wish to provide entertainment, you might consider setting up a **kids' table** stocked with inexpensive toys, books, and art supplies in one corner of your reception room. If the area is secluded enough, you could even rent a TV and DVD player from Disney's Audio Visual Services department for $165.

A kids' table keeps younger guests entertained

In-Room Service

Kid's Nite Out also offers in-room childcare at Disney resorts, off-property hotels, and vacation homes in the greater Orlando area. In-room service is available for children between the ages of 6 weeks and 12 years, and there is a **four-hour minimum**. There is no charge for combining families, so you might consider offering the service in lieu of a children's party if there will be fewer than seven kids at your event.

Rates

1 child	$16.00/hour
2 children	$18.50/hour
3 children	$21.00/hour
4 children	$23.50/hour
5 children	$26.00/hour

Groups of more than **five children** require multiple caregivers, assigned at a maximum of three children each and charged at the rates above. For example, a group of six children would require two caregivers at a rate of $21/hour each, for a total of $42/hour.

Services are provided 24 hours a day, seven days a week by sitters who are at least 18 years old and are certified in child/infant CPR and basic first aid. Sitters bring their own supplies, including books, games, and activities.

To book, call 407-828-0920 between 8:00 am and 9:00 pm seven days a week. Cancellations must be made at least four hours in advance to avoid the minimum charge.

Resort Children's Clubs

Walt Disney World has five kids' clubs open to children **ages 3–12** from 4:00 pm or 4:30 pm until midnight every day. The clubs offer supervised entertainment, including games, movies, and activities, at a rate of $11.50/hour per child, with a 2-hour minimum. Dinner is included in the price and is usually served between 6:00 pm and 8:00 pm. Parents are given a pager when they drop off their children.

Reservations and a credit card number are required, and there is a 24-hour cancellation policy. Children must be **toilet-trained**. To book, call 407-WDW-DINE. If you have a last-minute need for childcare, you can call each club directly after 4:00 pm to check for availability. Club locations and phone numbers are listed below.

The Polynesian Resort	The Never Land Club	407-824-2000, ext. 2184
Yacht & Beach Club Resorts	Sandcastle Club	407-934-3750
Wilderness Lodge Resort	Cub's Den	407-824-1083
Animal Kingdom Lodge	Simba's Clubhouse	407-938-4785
Grand Floridian Resort & Spa	Mouseketeer Club	407-824-2985

Although the clubs are at Deluxe resorts, they are open to all Disney resort guests.

Money-Saving Tips

We've compiled some of the many ways to save money on your Disney's Fairy Tale Wedding. Some of these tips help you shave a few dollars off the cost here and there, while others can have a **major impact** on the bottom line. Many of the best ways to save big—like cutting the guest list and having a morning event—only work if you know them before you get too far into the planning process. But no matter where you are along the way, the more tips you use, the more you'll save!

Big Ways to Save

- Hold your event on a weekday and avoid major holidays
- Invite fewer guests
- Hold your ceremony in the morning
- Shorten your reception by an hour or more, or skip the pre-reception
- Pick a reception venue that doesn't need as much (or any) decoration
- Cut down (or cut out) floral like altarpieces, pew decorations, and centerpieces
- Use outside vendors for linens and chairs or chair covers
- Serve brunch or lunch instead of dinner
- Don't serve alcohol
- Skip the rehearsal dinner or limit the guest list
- Make iPod playlists or CDs for the reception instead of hiring a band or DJ
- Use outside vendors for photography and videography
- Make your own invitations, programs, table names, and place cards
- Rent Disney Vacation Club points for your resort stay

Other Ways to Save

- Buy bridal accessories, cake toppers, favors, and more on eBay
- Rehearsal dinner alternatives: miniature golf, hayride at Fort Wilderness, meet 'n' greet in your resort room or lobby
- Limit the number of attendants
- Choose a bridesmaid's bouquet for the bride
- Choose rose wands or single stems for bridesmaids

- Buy or make your own artificial bouquet for the Magic Kingdom Portrait Session instead of refreshing your bridal bouquet

- Provide enough toss petals for fewer guests than you have

- Bring your own toss petals

- Move ceremony floral to reception (unless you can get separate decor for the reception that costs less than the move fee)

- Use non-floral centerpieces

- Decorate the cake table with bridesmaids' bouquets

- Use rehearsal dinner menus instead of reception dinner menus

- Serve one or two items from the reception buffet as your pre-reception food instead of ordering a separate menu

- Cut out any desserts included with the reception menu

- Select a two-tier cake for display and have sheet cakes in the back to make up the difference

- Serve half glasses of Champagne for the toast or just toast with drinks in hand

- Bring your own Champagne

- Offer beer and wine only

- Serve one signature cocktail or serve alcoholic punch by the gallon instead of a call brands bar

- Use chair covers instead of Chiavari chairs

- Eliminate chargers under the plates, gobos on the walls, and other details no one will remember

- Cut out welcome bags and/or favors

- Make your own favors

- Block rooms at only one or two resorts and charter one-way transportation for guests

- Have guests meet a guide at the entrance for in-park dessert parties instead of chartering transportation, if possible for your venue

- Ride your charter bus to the ceremony site before it picks up your guests instead of using a limo or specialty transportation

- Ride the charter bus with your guests after the reception

- Pay bills with your Disney Rewards Visa or other rewards card to earn Disney Dollars or cash back for your trip

How to Find Your Own Vendors

One of the advantages of having a Disney's Fairy Tale Wedding is the one-stop-shopping aspect of planning your event: Disney offers just about every wedding-day service you'll need. But if you're looking for more options, a lower price, or a different kind of offering, the prospect of finding vendors on your own—especially if you don't live in the area—can be daunting. Fortunately, there is a wealth of information available through several avenues **online**.

Wedding Web Sites
National web sites and magazines like Wedding Channel (http://www.weddingchannel.com), Brides (http://www.brides.com), The Knot (http://theknot.com), Wedding Bee (http://www.weddingbee.com), and OneWed.com (http://www.onewed.com) have regional vendor listings. Although these are usually paid for by the vendors, they can be a good place to start looking.

Message Boards
The best way to get vendor **feedback and recommendations** from real couples is through online communities and message boards specifically for Disney's Fairy Tale Weddings. The largest public site is the Disney Weddings and Honeymoons forum on the DIS Boards (http://www.disboards.com/forumdisplay.php?f=55), an active community of past, present, and future Disney brides and grooms.

There are also several private message boards, including the DisneyBrides (http://www.disneybrides.com)forum and the Disneymooner forum (http://www.disneymooner.com/).

Although not specifically for Disney weddings, the Central Florida forum on the Knot Boards (http://forums.theknot.com/Sites/theknot/Pages/Main.aspx/local-wedding-boards_florida-central-florida) is populated by locals who can give you the scoop on Orlando-area wedding vendors.

These communities offer a wealth of information, pictures, and opinions—just keep in mind that the vendors preferred by their users are not the only game in town.

Search Engines
Sifting through umpteen pages of Google search results for the phrase "Orlando wedding photographer" may not be your cup of tea, but you should be able to turn up enough relevant results in the first few pages for significant research and comparison. This can also be a good way to investigate vendors recommended on the various message boards.

Another resource to try is Craigslist for Orlando (http://orlando.craigslist.org).

Wishes Collection Time Line

The following is an overview of the typical time line for a Wishes Collection Event. Don't worry if you have less than a year to plan yours—Disney's Fairy Tale Wedding planners are there to guide you through the process and take on the heavy lifting, so to speak. Most of the details aren't finalized until the end of the process anyway, and legend has it that Disney once pulled off a Wishes wedding in less than a month!

16 to 24 Months

❏ Contact a Wedding Consultant to **discuss options** and narrow down your top three choices for ceremony and reception space.

❏ Begin to envision the **style** and formality level of your event.

❏ Begin compiling a **guest list** and decide on your event's approximate size. Gather complete names and addresses.

❏ Schedule a **site visit**.

❏ Select a tentative **date**.

16 Months

❏ For events at **theme park or non-convention-center venues** you may create a room block, sign a Letter of Agreement, and return it with the $2,000 deposit. E-mail the guest list to your Wedding Consultant. You will be assigned a Wedding Event Planner and sent a planning kit.

❏ **Tentatively hold** space at all other ceremony and reception venues.

12 Months

❏ If you haven't already, review, sign, and return the Letter of Agreement, along with the $2,000 deposit to **confirm your event locations**.

❏ E-mail the **guest list** to your Wedding Consultant.

❏ Disney will e-mail your guests a **save-the-date announcement** after you return your signed Letter of Agreement.

❏ You will be assigned a **Wedding Event Planner** and sent a planning kit.

8–12 Months

❑ If you haven't done so already, select Disney resorts for your guests and work with your Wedding Consultant to create a **room block**.

❑ Complete the information you want on your Disney **Facebook page**.

❑ Discuss who pays for what and start a **budget**.

❑ Send your engagement **photo and announcement** to the local paper.

❑ Schedule an in-park **portrait session**, if desired.

❑ Use *PassPorter's Disney Weddings & Honeymoons* to track your plans and house all your event-related scraps and ideas in one place.

❑ Choose your **attendants** and ask them to be in the wedding party.

❑ Begin gathering **ideas**, pictures, and samples to share with your Wedding Event Coordinator and Floral Specialist.

❑ If you will be using them, interview and get prices from such **outside vendors** as photographers, videographers, florists, DJs, and bands.

❑ If you plan to use frequent flyer miles to travel to Walt Disney World and/or your honeymoon destination, book your **flight** now.

❑ Start shopping for a **bridal gown**.

❑ Decide on and contact your **officiant** to discuss ceremony structure and religious requirements like counseling.

❑ If you will be honeymooning somewhere other than Walt Disney World, make your **honeymoon reservations**.

Additional Tasks
❑
❑
❑
❑
❑

7 Months

❏ Begin looking over the **planning kit** and filling in as much information as you can.

❏ Schedule a formal **planning session** with your Wedding Event Planner and Floral Specialist for 4-6 months before your wedding.

❏ Make or modify your reservations for your stay at Walt Disney World to take advantage of your **event discount.**

❏ Order the bridal gown. Be sure it is scheduled to arrive at least **one month** before you leave so there is time for alterations.

6 Months

❏ Disney's Fairy Tale Weddings confirms **pricing** for all elements of the event.

4 to 6 Months

❏ Make necessary Walt Disney World **dining reservations.**

❏ Shop for and order **bridesmaids'** dresses.

❏ Finalize **contracts** with outside vendors.

❏ **Register** for wedding gifts. The rule of thumb is three stores with a variety of locations and price ranges.

❏ If it is not being handled by your Wedding Event Planner, **book** the rehearsal dinner.

❏ Narrow down selections and details for **floral, decor, food, and cake.**

❏ Line up **cosmetology** services for the wedding day or in-park portrait session. Schedule a cosmetology trial if you will be visiting Walt Disney World for a planning session.

❏ Attend your planning session or **discuss planning details** via telephone, e-mail, fax, and/or mail.

❏ Purchase **rings** and send for engraving.

❏ If you will be making **welcome bags** for guests, start collecting items.

❏ Make or buy **favors**, if necessary.

❏ Book your **flights.**

❏ Order or make your invitations, announcements, and other **stationery.**

❏ Work with mothers to select their **dresses.**

❏ Sign up for **dance lessons**, if desired.

2 to 4 Months

❏ Buy or make a guest book and such **accessories** as a cake topper, cake knife and server, ring pillow, toasting flutes, garter, candles, etc.

❏ **Finalize** details with outside vendors.

❏ Send your **invitations**, with an RSVP date of at least one month before the event.

❏ Prepare **maps** and directions or transportation schedules for the ceremony and reception.

❏ Get anything you need for an **international** honeymoon (passport, birth certificate, visas, vaccinations, etc.).

❏ Pick out or design a **ketubah** or other marriage contract required by your religion.

❏ Have the groomsmen's measurements taken and order their attire.

❏ Confirm delivery date for bridal gown and **schedule fittings**.

❏ Talk to people you'd want to do special **performances or readings** as part of the ceremony.

❏ Select your **music** for the ceremony, pre-reception, and reception and review with musicians/singers.

Additional Tasks
❏
❏
❏
❏
❏
❏
❏

90 Days

❏ Full **overall minimum expenditure** is due.

❏ Adjust the number of nights in your **room block**, if necessary.

1 to 2 Months

❏ Confirm that formalwear has been ordered for groom and groomsmen. Schedule **formalwear fittings**.

❏ Confirm that guests are making their Walt Disney World resort reservations before the **30-day deadline**. Call the Wedding Group Reservations number to see who has made reservations.

❏ As you receive presents, be sure to **update** or add items to your registries and track the gifts you get.

❏ Have your first bridal **gown fitting**.

❏ Arrange for a **babysitter** for the reception, if necessary.

❏ If you will be obtaining your marriage **license by mail**, contact the Brevard County Courthouse to order the paperwork. The license must be used within 60 days.

❏ Your Wedding Event Planner will provide a detailed **final budget**.

❏ Submit your wedding **announcement** to newspapers, if desired.

❏ Plan the **seating** for the reception and start writing place cards.

❏ Make sure all bridesmaids' attire has been **fitted**.

30 Days

❏ **Full balance** of Estimated Budget is due. Any reductions made within 30 days are subject to cancellation charges as outlined in your Letter of Agreement.

❏ $1,000 of your initial deposit will be applied to your **Estimated Budget**.

❏ Signed copies of the **BEO** are due.

❏ All vacant rooms in the resort Room Block will be **released**.

❏ Last day for any **entertainment** reductions or cancellations.

❏ Last day to change the style of your **cake**.

❏ Double-check your **floral choices** and notify your Wedding Event Planner of any changes.

3 to 4 Weeks

❑ Finalize your **vows**.

❑ Attend **final** bridal-gown fitting.

❑ Schedule wedding-related **grooming appointments**.

❑ Finish and print ceremony **programs**, if desired.

❑ Finalize your "must play" and "don't play" **music lists** and review with ceremony and reception musicians or DJ.

❑ Pick up rings and check the **inscriptions** before you leave the store.

❑ Have a follow-up meeting or phone call with the officiant to go over **ceremony** timing and details.

❑ Confirm wedding and honeymoon **reservations**, and give loved ones your itinerary in case of emergency.

❑ Contact bridal party with **critical information** related to rehearsal and ceremony (dates, times, directions, duties).

❑ Create a **ceremony box** to gather your ceremony accessories (candles, ring pillow, petal basket, etc.).

❑ Create a **reception box** to gather your reception accessories (favors, cake topper, guest book, place cards, cake knife and server, etc.).

15 Days

❑ Last day to make changes to **floral and decor**.

❑ Final guest count for **cake** due.

Additional Tasks
❑
❑
❑
❑
❑

1 to 2 Weeks

❏ Pick up your bridal gown and make sure all of your **accessories** are together. Ship the gown to a formalwear dealer for storage, steaming, and delivery to your resort, if desired.

❏ **Ship** boxes of ceremony and reception accessories to your hotel if you will not be bringing them yourself. Disney's Fairy Tale Weddings cannot store these items.

❏ Finalize your wedding-day **schedule** and share with attendants, parents, and outside vendors. Distribute directions, schedule, and contact list, unless these will be placed in welcome bags.

❏ Confirm all **final payment** amounts and wedding-day schedule with your outside vendors. Make sure they all have directions and access to the site.

❏ **10 days out:** Finalize your seating arrangements, prepare place cards, and give seating chart to your Wedding Event Planner.

❏ Call guests who haven't sent in their reply cards for the reception or rehearsal dinner to get a final **head count.**

❏ If you're having a **receiving line**, determine the order you want everyone to stand in.

❏ Check in with your **officiant** and give him/her rehearsal details and wedding-day schedule.

❏ Prepare your **toasts** or thanks to friends and family.

❏ **Assemble** welcome bags.

❏ Put cash **tips** in marked envelopes and give them to a designated family member or friend to distribute on the wedding day.

One Week

❏ Schedule time to go pick up your **marriage license** at the courthouse, if necessary. The three-day waiting period applies only to Florida residents, not out-of-state and international residents.

❏ Pick up **formalwear** and try it on or have it delivered for a fitting.

❏ Review any seating details with the ushers.

❏ Finalize your rehearsal dinner arrangements or other plans. If these were arranged through your Wedding Event Planner, the final guest count is due four days before the dinner by 12:00 pm.

❏ Distribute welcome bags to guests' resorts.

Three Days

❑ Submit **final guest count** and meal selections to your Wedding Event Planner by 12:00 pm.

❑ Finalize all **food and beverage** with your Wedding Event Planner.

❑ Arrange to **deliver** ceremony and reception boxes to Franck's.

One Day

❑ Attend the wedding **rehearsal**.

❑ Hand out **assignment** lists and checklists to ensure everyone knows their tasks, including the person responsible for transporting gifts.

❑ Assign someone to mail your **wedding announcements**.

Wedding Day

❑ Don't forget the **rings and marriage license**.

❑ Make sure two witnesses **sign** the marriage license.

❑ Be sure to **eat** properly.

❑ Don't let the day pass by in a blur—take time to stop and **enjoy** it!

Additional Tasks
❑
❑
❑
❑
❑
❑
❑

Chapter 4
Couture Collection

Disney's Fairy Tale Weddings collaborated with celebrity wedding planner David Tutera to create the Couture Wedding Collection, four luxurious reception themes with a complementary ceremony theme that will transform your big day into a **magazine-worthy event**. Tutera has parlayed his unique wedding-planning style into a media empire that includes books, professional speaking engagements, and a TV show. While your primary contact will be a Disney Wedding Event Planner trained by Tutera, he has been known to work with Couture Collection couples on certain aspects of their events, and he even made an appearance at the first Couture Collection wedding.

Although Disney classes the Couture Collection as a separate category of event, what you're getting is basically an elaborate **decor package** overlaid on a Wishes Collection event. This is an easy way to get a glamorous modern look without having to decide on all the elements yourself. However, the overall minimum expenditure, the decor package, the amount of the deposit, and the per-person food and beverage minimum

Couture Collection ceremonies are usually held at Disney's Wedding Pavilion

expenditure are significantly higher for Couture Collection events.

Accordingly, this chapter is designed to be used in conjunction with Chapter 3 Wishes Collection, which will answer your questions about the **basics of planning** a customized wedding, vow renewal, or commitment ceremony at Walt Disney World.

On these pages we'll cover the starting costs of the Couture Collection and tell you what is and **isn't included** for the price. We'll also go over the basics of booking and the deposit and give you an overview of the four different reception themes.

Couture Wedding Basics

When you choose a Couture Collection event, you get a reception decor package that includes invitations, floral, props, linens, lighting, and a DJ—and **nothing else**. Food, beverages, cake, additional entertainment, the ceremony site fee, personal floral, photography, videography, and transportation are an additional charge. You may choose to add a Couture ceremony decor package, which includes altarpieces, aisle decorations, and other coordinating elements but doesn't include personal floral like bouquets and boutonnieres.

Ceremonies are held at Disney's Wedding Pavilion, in a ballroom at Disney's Contemporary Resort, or at any of the other Walt Disney World ceremony venues. However, Couture wedding receptions must be held in one of the ballrooms at the **Contemporary Resort** because the decor packages were designed exclusively for this location.

Minimum Expenditures

There are **three sets** of minimum expenditures for Couture Collection Events.

The **Overall Minimum Expenditure** for a Couture Collection event is $65,000 for up to 50 guests. This works like the $10,000-$15,000 overall minimum expenditure for Wishes events, except that it may increase if you have more than 50 guests.

There is also a **Decor Minimum Expenditure** of $55,000 for up to 50 guests, which is applied to the Overall Minimum Expenditure. Adding guests may increase the cost of the decor package.

The third requirement is a **Food and Beverage Minimum Expenditure** of $175/person (plus 6.5% sales tax and 21% service charge) for the reception only. This includes the cost of the cake but not food and beverages from any other events that day, like a dessert party. There are no venue-specific food and beverage minimum expenditures for Couture Collection events.

Optional **Couture Wedding Ceremony Decor packages** start at $8,500 and do not include personal floral. The Couture ceremony decor package must be purchased in conjunction with a Couture reception decor package, although you can purchase the reception package by itself.

Guest Accommodation Requirements

Couture Collection events require the same **guest accommodation requirements** as Wishes Collection events, which are outlined in Chapter 3: Wishes Collection. Your guests can take advantage of the same discounts on room rates, and you will receive a complimentary night at the Walt Disney World resort of your choice if you fulfill your minimum room-night requirement.

Booking & Deposit

A Letter of Agreement is sent as soon as Disney's Fairy Tale Weddings can confirm availability of your venues. You will need to sign and return it with a nonrefundable **$10,000 deposit** to reserve your locations. The deposit may only be made by credit card, check, money order, or wire transfer. Your final payment of the entire balance is due 30 days before the event date.

Reception Decor Package Elements

David Tutera designed four unique **reception looks** – Classic Elegance, Enchanted Garden, Simply Chic, and Cocktail Soiree—but every reception decor package includes the following elements:

- Use of a ballroom at the Contemporary Resort
- Draping to enhance the space
- Custom-designed table linens for cocktail hour and reception, including the escort and gift tables
- Chiavari chairs
- Custom-designed beverage bars
- Themed decor props appropriate to each look, such as urns, gilded mirrors, and floor lamps
- Custom-designed floral centerpieces
- Custom-designed ceiling decor like chandeliers, lanterns, butterflies, and lamps
- Designer lighting package tailored to each look
- DJ and standard dance floor
- Coordinating invitations and save-the-date announcements for 50 guests (excluding postage, maximum of 100 invites)
- Some looks include place cards and table numbers
- Personal wedding web site
- Disney Wedding Planner trained by David Tutera

Because these packages were carefully crafted by David Tutera, Disney states that the individual design elements **cannot be modified**. However, couples who have had Couture Collection events report that they were allowed to make some changes, and on a few occasions David Tutera has worked with couples to customize elements of their events.

Couture Reception Looks

The four reception looks created by David Tutera range from elegantly romantic to modern and chic. All of them feature complementary lighting schemes that can change color as the event progresses. To see **pictures** of each theme, check out http://disneyweddings.disney.go.com/weddings/florida/couture/ceremony-reception/detail.

The **Classic Elegance** theme is a modern take on fairy tale opulence featuring gold wall draping, gilded mirrors and candelabra, crystal chandeliers, and pink- and gold-fringed linens. Complementary floral arrangements include masses of pink, white, and lavender roses accented with hydrangea and cherry blossoms, and the lighting design washes the room in pink and lavender.

© Patrick Johnson

Classic Elegance table decor

The **Enchanted Garden** theme is similarly romantic, but the emphasis is on flowers and butterflies. Butter yellow draping and trailing ivy create the backdrop for an indoor garden of topiaries, iron plant stands, and high and low arrangements of hydrangea, roses, heather, and tulips in pink, yellow, coral, and green. Butterflies floating overhead lend a whimsical touch, and the theme is carried through the centerpieces and on the cake.

White draping, linens, and flowers create the clean lines and fresh look of the **Simply Chic** theme, which is accented with pops of chartreuse green. Water, candles, and flowers fill Lucite runners on rectangular tables and glass cylinders on round tables, and candles positioned on and around large mirrors appear to be floating. Overhead, large Asian lanterns are suspended like bubbles in the pure white space.

Cocktail Soiree is the most modern look, designed to emulate the feel of a hip new hotel or lounge in shades of ice blue, chocolate brown, and white. Rather than traditional round tables, guests choose from stools at the oversized illuminated bar, lobby-like arrangements of sofas and benches, long communal tables with stools, or square dining tables set with Lucite lamps, candles, and flowers. The backdrop is ice blue draping, with giant lamp shades in blue and brown suspended from the ceiling.

© Patrick Johnson

A variation on the Enchanted Garden look

Food & Beverage

Although the price of food and beverage is not included in the Couture reception decor package, Disney offers private consultations with the Contemporary Resort's culinary team to customize a **gourmet menu**. You will meet with a chef to plan a reception menu that reflects your personal taste and the reception theme, and an executive pastry chef will help you design a custom wedding cake. A Disney sommelier can provide advice on wine pairings for your reception meal, and David Tutera has recommended signature drinks to coordinate with each theme.

Below are sample cocktail hour and reception menus designed to coordinate with the Simply Chic theme.

Simply Chic Sample Menu

Cocktail Hour
- Mini Shrimp Martinis
- Lobster Cocktail
- Mini Mint Poulet Rouge Mojitos
- Long-stem Strawberry Stuffed with Goat Cheese
- USDA Prime Beef Tenderloin Fork
- Lychee Nut Stuffed with Prosciutto and Asiago
- Truffle Cracker with Asiago Foam

First Course
- Wasabi Seared Scallop Encrusted in Lemon Grass and Black Sesame Seeds served over a Nishiki Rice Cake with Orange Tobiko Roe
- Tatsoi Greens with Japanese Chrysanthemum and a Plum Wine and Soy Vinaigrette
- Asian Cucumber Essence with Rice Wine Vinegar and Dark Sesame Oil in a Wonton Cup

Second Course
- Cantaloupe Ginger Sorbet with Sake Toast

Third Course
- Tsao-Style Prime Beef Filet with Sweet Thai Chili Butter
- Braised Grouper with Daikon Radish Pureed Potatoes and Petite Asian-Style Vegetables
- Fresh Baked Lavosh, Prawn Chips, Rice Paper, and Wonton Chips Served With Whipped Flavored Butters to include Garlic and Herb, Wasabi and Soy, and Candied Ginger and Sake

Fourth Course
- Friandise Selection
- Banana Caramel Custard Accented with Ginger
- Coffee and Decaffeinated Coffee and a Selection of Teas

Notes

Chapter 5
Additional Events

The wedding day may be the focus of your stay at Walt Disney World, but it probably won't be the only time your group gathers during the trip. These days, more and more couples are making their celebrations **multi-day events** featuring welcome parties, bridesmaids' teas, park-hopping, and even excursions to watch or play sports. Walt Disney World offers numerous options for entertaining your guests, including the unique opportunity to host a dessert party during one of several fireworks shows, making for a memorable pre- or post-wedding get-together.

In this chapter we'll look at wedding-day additions like dessert parties and specialty cruises, wedding-related gatherings like rehearsal dinners and farewell brunches, and other group activities you might want to offer your guests. Your Disney Wedding Services Coordinator or Wedding Event Planner may be able to arrange some of these events for you, but we'll also provide information on **how to book** these yourself. (Note that only catered events held on the day of your wedding, vow renewal, or commitment ceremony will count toward the overall minimum expenditure for the Wishes Collection. Also, there is a $50 small-party fee for private catered events for fewer than 20 people.)

We'll also take a look at Disney's **Grand Gatherings**, events and services designed for groups of eight or more people staying at Walt Disney World resorts. Because all of the planning is done for you, these make a natural addition to your festivities.

For more **detailed information** on the restaurants mentioned here, check out *PassPorter's Walt Disney World*. Another great resource is *PassPorter's Festivals and Celebrations at Walt Disney World*, which can help you take advantage of any special events being held during your trip.

© Patrick Johnson

A specialty cruise offers guests a unique view of fireworks shows like HalloWishes

Dessert Parties

One of the more popular additions to Disney's Fairy Tale Weddings are dessert parties held during Walt Disney World's fireworks shows. These events include a **private** viewing area and dessert buffet during IllumiNations: Reflections of Earth at Epcot, Fantasmic! at Disney's Hollywood Studios, or Wishes Nighttime Spectacular at the Magic Kingdom.

Fantasmic! and IllumiNations parties are in-park events, while Wishes parties are held at the Grand Floridian. At this time Disney does not offer private dessert parties inside the Magic Kingdom.

Dessert parties can be a fun addition to the wedding day, whether they occur after the reception or function as a

Dessert party treats at Epcot

cocktail hour between the ceremony and the reception. They also make great **welcome parties** or rehearsal dinners—although they are referred to as "dessert parties," a limited selection of hot and cold food is available. (Note that food and beverage minimums will be higher if you choose to serve a full breakfast, lunch, or dinner.)

Outdoor Event Requirements
Except for personal floral like bouquets, boutonnieres, and corsages, **all floral** and decor at any outdoor event on Disney property must be provided by Disney Floral & Gifts. Additionally, any talent or entertainment must be secured through your Wedding Event Planner.

In-Park Event Requirements
For in-park events, a $12.95 viewing fee will be charged for each guest who does not have park admission. Couples who wish to wear **wedding attire** in the park must hire transportation to take them backstage or, in some cases, meet an event guide at the park entrance. You may also be required to hire transportation for your guests, although it is sometimes possible for the group to meet an

Guests enjoy chocolate fondue

event guide at the park entrance for admission. Check with your Wedding Consultant or Coordinator to see if your event qualifies.

Only **Disney photographers** and videographers are allowed at any in-park event, including dessert parties. Characters and amplified entertainment are not allowed at outdoor in-park events (existing background music will be played).

IllumiNations at Epcot

The United Kingdom, France, Morocco, Japan, and Italy pavilions all boast prime IllumiNations viewing areas for dessert parties. Usually only smaller venues like Canada, Morocco, Japan, and Africa are available to Escape weddings, but occasionally larger Escape groups have been able to use the United Kingdom Terrace or the Rue de Paris (formerly known as French Island Arm). Another choice for Escape events is one of the **standing-room-only venues** Epcot has carved out in Norway, Morocco, and France.

Each site has its own food and beverage minimum and venue rental fee. The venue rental fee will be waived if you are holding your reception in the park immediately before or after the dessert party. There is a choice of black or white standard table linens included in the fee, and you are welcome to work with Disney Floral & Gifts to add centerpieces or decor elements.

Epcot offers a variety of dessert menus ranging from $23 to $33 per person, but you can customize them to suit your tastes and budget. The dessert choices run the gamut: cupcakes, cookies, cheesecake, pastries, ice cream floats, cheese trays, and even a build-your-own-sundae buffet. There is also a selection of cordials and liqueurs, along with the option to add a bar. All menus include fruit punch, coffee, and tea, along with flavored syrups and sticks, sugars, cream, and honey.

Restrooms are located outside these venues and are shared with theme park guests. IlluminNations is rarely cancelled due to weather conditions. In case of rain, your party will be moved indoors and guests will be offered umbrellas to use if they wish to view the fireworks.

Dessert parties usually start 30 minutes before IllumiNations and last **one hour**. You may extend the time of the party by 30 minutes or more at no charge. Extending food service beyond one hour will cost you a prorated amount per person based on the price of the menu you select and the amount of time you wish to add. However, most people find one hour of food service to be enough even for longer parties.

Isola West Plaza offers spectacular views of IllumiNations: Reflections of Earth

IllumiNations at Epcot (continued)

Canada Overlook is directly across from the Refreshment Port, between the entrance to World Showcase and the Canada Pavilion. This venue accommodates parties of 20–50 and has a food and beverage minimum of $22/person. The venue rental fee is $335. A maximum of six cocktail tables or six tallboy tables can be accommodated.

View from Canada Overlook

United Kingdom Lochside

The **United Kingdom Terrace** (formerly United Kingdom Upper Terrace) is separated from the walkway and United Kingdom Lochside by a wall and holds a minimum of 20 and a maximum of 50 guests. The venue rental fee is $250, and the food and beverage minimum is $440. One advantage of this site is its existing seating—seven wrought-iron tables with umbrellas and chairs—which will save you a setup fee. No additional seating or tables may be added.

The secluded **United Kingdom Lochside** (formerly known as United Kingdom Lower Terrace) is set on the water at the end of a winding garden path. It is available for parties of 20–70, and the venue rental fee is $335. The food and beverage minimum is $440. A maximum of five cocktail tables or four tallboy tables can be brought in.

United Kingdom Terrace

The **Terrace des Fleurs** (formerly known as French Island Upper) is available for dessert parties of 50 or more guests, with a venue rental fee of $335 and food and beverage minimums of $22/person. The staircase adjacent to the site may be used by guests of other functions held at the lower terrace. **Eau de France** (formerly French Island Lower) is also available to parties of 50 or more guests. The venue rental fee is $335. Unlike the other areas of the French Island, Eau de France is not wheelchair accessible.

Terrace des Fleurs

Eau de France   *Rue de Paris*

Rue de Paris (formerly French Island Arm) has a 50-person minimum and a $335 venue rental fee. Wheelchair access to Terrace des Fleurs cuts through this site.

The **Morocco Oasis** is the area between the Morocco boat dock and the shop on the edge of the lagoon. It is available to parties of 10–60 guests and has a $285 venue rental fee. The food and beverage minimum is $440.

The Morocco Oasis sits between the boat dock and the shop

The five-story pagoda at the **Japan Pavilion** is open to dessert parties of 10 or fewer guests, who view the fireworks from the Taiko drummers' area of the balcony. The venue rental fee is $285.

Isola West Plaza is a small terrace adjacent to Italy Isola's larger bridge. A wall of hedges is usually brought in (at an additional cost) to separate the

View from Japan dessert party area

area from the main walkway during private events. A minimum of 50 guests is required for this venue, with a maximum of 125. The food and beverage minimum is $440, and the venue rental fee is $335. (See page 139 for a photo.)

IllumiNations at Epcot (continued)

Linked to **Italy Plaza** by two stone bridges, Italy Isola sits on the waters of World Showcase Lagoon and offers prime fireworks viewing. A minimum of 100 guests is required, with a 150-guest maximum, and the venue rental fee is $585. The food and beverage minimum is $1,650.

Italy Isola

Located across the main path from the African gift shop, **Outpost Overlook** is a small pocket that accommodates 10-20 guests. The food and beverage minimum is $22/person, and the venue rental fee is $250. Seating is at existing patio tables and chairs, which cannot be removed or rearranged.

Outpost Overlook in Africa

More **pictures** of the viewing areas at the United Kingdom, France, and Italy pavilions can be found in Chapter 3: Wishes Collection.

Standing-Room-Only Venues

Epcot also offers three **small dessert party venues**—in France, Morocco, and Norway—that offer standing room only. The food and beverage minimum is $22/person at all three locations.

Parisian Point holds a minimum of 10 guests and a maximum of 20, and the venue rental fee is $250. No tables or chairs are available.

Parisian Point in France

Kazbah Point holds a minimum of 10 guests and a maximum of 25, and the venue rental fee is $335. A maximum of two tallboy tables may be brought in, but no chairs are available. **Vikings Landing** holds a minimum of 10 guests and a maximum of 25, and the venue rental fee is $250. A maximum of two tallboy tables may be brought in, but no chairs are available. Benches may be present but are not guaranteed.

Kazbah Point in Morocco

Vikings Landing in Norway

Fantasmic! at Disney's Hollywood Studios

The Hollywood Hills Amphitheater has **two private patios** for Fantasmic! Dessert parties. Both have a $250 venue rental fee and a $750 food and beverage minimum. The Small Patio accommodates up to 40 guests, while the Large Patio is available to groups of 40 to 100 guests. If you opt to use both patios, the venue rental fee is $500 and the food and beverage minimum is $1,500.

Both venues have a $75 **setup fee** for tables and chairs, which is usually rolled into the venue rental fee on your bill. The standard table linens are black and cannot be exchanged. Dessert parties begin 30 minutes before the show and conclude at the end of the show. Show times may change without notice, and Fantasmic! may be postponed or cancelled due to weather. No amplified entertainment or characters are allowed at these locations.

Disney's Hollywood Studios offers customizable **dessert menus** ranging from $23 to $33 per person, along with such decadent culinary action stations as flambé and hand-dipped ice cream. There is also a selection of cordials served in chocolate liqueur cups and the option to add espresso and cappuccino service or sparkling wine. All menus include fruit punch, coffee, and tea.

Wishes at the Grand Floridian

The Grand Floridian's Marina Patio & Terrace and nearby Sago Cay Pointe are both great spots for viewing Wishes. The food and beverage minimums are $1,000 for the Grand Floridian Marina and $500 (dessert) or $1,000 (all other meals) for Sago Cay Pointe, but there are **no
venue rental fees**. Both venues have a $75 setup fee for bringing in tables and chairs, although the Marina has existing seating for 20. The Marina holds 20-300 guests, while Sago Cay Pointe holds up to 75 guests.

The **menus** provided by the Grand Floridian's catering department are more expensive than those at Epcot and Disney's Hollywood Studios, ranging

Private party at the Grand Floridian Marina

from $35–$55 per person for one hour of service, but they can be cut down to suit your budget. The choices include cookies, pastries, fondue, flambé, fruit and cheese platters, Bananas Foster, and a chocolate fountain. All menus include coffees with whipped cream, shaved chocolate, cinnamon sticks, orange peel, and flavored coffee syrups. There is a charge to have the music from Wishes piped in—figure on $500 for up to 50 guests and $650 for up to 150 guests. The fee includes a sound technician and a backup CD in case the live audio feed cuts out.

Sago Cay Pointe has castle views

Specialty Cruises

Another option is to book a specialty cruise to view Epcot's IllumiNations: Reflections of Earth from the International Gateway or the Magic Kingdom's Wishes fireworks from Seven Seas Lagoon. Cruises depart from the Grand Floridian, Contemporary, Fort Wilderness, Wilderness Lodge, Polynesian, or Yacht & Beach Club marinas about

View of IllumiNations from a specialty cruise

30 minutes prior to the fireworks shows and include a tour of the lake and light snacks. These are better suited to **small groups**, and a post-dinner cruise on the Grand 1 yacht is especially popular for Escape Collection events.

25-foot pontoon boat

Standard fireworks cruises on pontoon boats last about an hour, while the Breathless II and Grand 1 Yacht can be booked for longer periods. Cruises include soda, water, and bagged snacks, but you may arrange an **onboard meal** for all but the Breathless II by calling Private Dining at the resort from which your cruise departs.

An **audio feed** of the Wishes soundtrack is available for a fee—ask for a Premium Cruise when you book. IllumiNations cruises do not require audio because they stop under the International Gateway, directly in front of the show. For $25 more, you can book a Celebration cruise, which adds decorations to the standard package.

For the pontoon boats, the maximum number of guests is 10, or 12 if the party includes children. Reservations can be made 180 days in advance by calling 407-WDW-PLAY (407-939-7529); a credit card is required to book, and there is a 24-hour cancellation policy. IllumiNations cruises are especially popular, so be sure to call **exactly** 180 days from the date you want, and start dialing a few minutes before the call center opens at 7:00 am ET.

21-foot (l) and 25-foot (r) pontoon boats

The chart on the next page shows the prices of the various packages including tax.

Cruise	Boat Size	Price incl. tax	Max # Guests	Extras
Wishes Cruise – Basic	21-foot pontoon boat	$292.88	8	none
Wishes Cruise – Premium	25-foot pontoon boat	$346.13	10	Audio feed
Wishes Celebration Cruise – Basic	21-foot pontoon boat	$317.88	8	Decorations
Wishes Celebration Cruise – Premium	25-foot pontoon boat	$371.13	10	Audio feed & decorations
IllumiNations Cruise	25-foot pontoon boat	$346.13	10	none
IllumiNations Celebration Cruise	25-foot pontoon boat	$371.13	10	Decorations

Breathless II: This reproduction Hacker-Craft runabout **seats six** and departs from the Yacht & Beach Club marina. During the day it can be booked at a rate of $105 + tax for 30 minutes. IllumiNations cruises cost $325 + tax and include snacks. Call 407-WDW-PLAY or 407-939-8687 to reserve the Breathless II. IllumiNations cruises are especially popular, so be sure to call exactly 180 days from the date you want, and start dialing a few minutes

Breathless II

before the call center opens at 7:00 am ET. [Note: At press time, the Breathless II had been removed from service indefinitely due to a maintenance issue.]

Grand 1 Yacht: This 52-foot Sea Ray **seats 17** and is staffed by a captain and a deckhand. Cruises depart from the Grand Floridian Resort. The rate is $520 + tax per hour, with a 1-hour minimum most of the year and a 2-hour minimum on holidays. Snacks are not included, but you may arrange for Private Dining service from the Grand Floridian, complete with butler! Call 407-WDW-PLAY or 407-824-2682 up to 180 days in advance to reserve the Grand 1. Call 407-824-1951 to arrange for Private Dining.

Another option is the **Pirate and Pals Fireworks Voyage**, and evening cruise around Bay Lake that departs from Disney's Contemporary Resort. Your group will enjoy snacks and beverages before setting sail with Captain Hook and Mr. Smee from Disney's Peter Pan. They'll entertain you with songs and trivia before the start of the Electrical Water Pageant and the Magic Kingdom's fireworks show. When you get back to shore, Peter Pan will be waiting to sign autographs and pose for pictures. Prices are $53.99 for ages 10 and up and $30.99 for ages 3-9.

Group Meals

Rehearsal dinners, welcome parties, farewell brunches, and bridesmaids' teas give your group a chance to meet before and after the big day, **extending** the celebration and giving everyone the opportunity to get to know each other.

In most cases, your Disney Wedding Event Planner or Coordinator can make Disney dining reservations for you or help you plan a private event. If you will be making your own arrangements, you can **book a reservation** at any Walt Disney World restaurant by calling 407-WDW-DINE (407-939-3463) for groups of up to 12 guests or 407-

Whispering Canyon's lively atmosphere is fun for groups

939-7700 for groups of 13 or more. Larger groups are usually given the first seating (around 5:30 pm) or the last seating (around 9:00 pm). Some restaurants cannot accommodate groups of more than 50, and many can't guarantee your party's tables will be next to each other. The Group Dining Information chart in Chapter 2: Escape Collection includes phone numbers, prices, and requirements for making group reservations at some of the most popular restaurants.

If you have a large group or just want something more private, you can arrange for a **private room** at a restaurant like California Grill or use a reception location like Ariel's. The same venue rental fees and food and beverage minimums apply. Another idea is to try one of the restaurants at Downtown Disney, such as Fulton's, Portobello, or Raglan Road. Many of these have private rooms or semi-private seating areas and special group menus. Check out the Private Rooms/Restaurant Buyouts chart in Chapter 2: Escape Collection for full details on many of the private dining options.

The light-filled Grand Floridian Cafe would be a great spot for a farewell brunch

Welcome Parties & Rehearsal Dinners

Traditionally, a rehearsal dinner is just for the bridal party and immediate family, while a welcome party is for all guests. However, it is also customary to invite out-of-town guests to the rehearsal dinner, so, unless your guests live in Orlando, that means everyone! No matter what you call it, you may wish to host

© Photography By Taz

an event before the big day so that people have an opportunity to **meet and mingle** with you and other guests. Often this means dinner in a restaurant, but you may prefer a private party or just a casual gathering by the pool.

By far the most popular location for rehearsal dinners is **Ohana** at the Polynesian Resort. The festive

Ohana is a favorite for welcome parties atmosphere and fixed-price menu are conducive to group gatherings, and if you time your meal just right, you may be able to see fireworks over the Magic Kingdom! Other popular choices include Chef Mickey's, at the Contemporary Resort, and 1900 Park Fare, at the Grand Floridian.

Your Wedding Event Planner or Coordinator can arrange a **private party** complete with decor and themed entertainment at any of the convention center ballrooms or even outdoors. Hurricane Hanna's Grill and Shipwreck Beach at the Yacht & Beach Club are popular locations for beach-themed parties.

For something a little more **casual**, consider booking a suite, a cabin or campsite at Fort Wilderness, or a Disney Vacation Club Villa for an open-house-style party. Or meet in a public area of your resort or by the pool. You can have food delivered or pick it up from a nearby grocery store. Just be sure to be respectful of other resort guests.

Farewell Brunch

Hosting brunch on the **morning after** your event gives you an opportunity to send off your guests in style. Your Wedding Event Planner or Coordinator can help you arrange a private event at venues like The Attic and the Whitehall Room & Patio, or you can make your own group reservation at a popular breakfast spot like the Grand Floridian Cafe or Chef Mickey's. Private locations require the venue-specific food and beverage minimums outlined in the "Reception Venues" section of Chapter 3: Wishes Collection.

Another fun idea is House of Blues' **Sunday Gospel Brunch** at Downtown Disney, which features a full buffet of traditional and Southern breakfast specialties and a live gospel performance. Seating times are 10:30 am and 1:00 pm. Tickets are available up to two weeks in advance by calling House of Blues directly at 1-407-934-BLUE (for groups of up to 19) or 407-934-2622 (for groups of 20 or more). Prices are $33.50 for ages 10 and up and $17.25 ages 3–9, plus service charge.

Bridesmaids' Tea

A bridesmaids' **luncheon or tea** can be a great way to thank the women who helped you plan your event. Your Wedding Event Planner or Coordinator can help you arrange a private Mad Hatter-themed tea at any of the convention center locations or on the lawn at BoardWalk Inn. In addition to colorful linens and floral enhancements, Disney offers a number of oversized Mad Hatter tea party props, including

Whitehall Patio can be reserved for a tea

mushrooms, teapots, a clock, sections of white picket fence, and even the giant caterpillar. These can be quite pricey, however, and there is a $500 fee to set up less than $2,000 worth of props. A three-tier Mad Hatter cake will set you back another $980 and feeds 85, while a two-tier, 50-person version runs $450. You may also arrange for a surprise appearance by the Mad Hatter, the White Rabbit, or Alice at standard character-appearance rates of $900 for one, $1,350 for two, or $1,800 for three for 30 minutes.

The Grand Floridian's **Gardenview Tea Room** is a great place for a bridesmaids' tea. Located at the far end of the hotel lobby, the restaurant looks out over the Grand Floridian's grounds. Tea menus range from $13.50–$25.50/person, and there are a la carte sandwiches and pastries.

Gardenview Tea Room does not allow speeches, games, or gift opening. Parties of up to 12 may book by calling 407-WDW-DINE, while parties of 13–25 should call 407-824-2351. Groups of 13 or more are seated at 2:00 pm or 4:40 pm and must order off the large-party menu. A credit card is required to hold the reservation, and there is a 48-hour cancellation policy. The card will be charged the full cost of the menu for no-shows.

Gardenview Tea Room at the Grand Floridian

You may also **buy out** the restaurant for a private event from 11:00 am to 1:00 pm on Tuesday or Saturday; there is a $500 food and beverage minimum. To buy out the restaurant from 7:00 pm to 9:00 pm any day of the week, the food and beverage minimum is $1,000. The restaurant seats 50 people.

Other Group Activities

One of the great things about Walt Disney World is the **myriad activities** available without setting foot in a theme park. Whether you want to plan group excursions for your guests or just want to give them ideas to explore on their own, this section will show you some of the possibilities.

Fun at Fort Wilderness

Fort Wilderness Resort & Campground offers several **fun and inexpensive** group activities that are a great alternative to a traditional welcome party or rehearsal dinner. Note that Fort Wilderness has an internal bus system to transport guests from the main parking area, so be sure to allow enough time to get to your destination.

Fort Wilderness Trading Post

Campfire Sing-Along & Movie
This free event is held nightly near Meadow Trading Post, usually around 7:00 pm in the winter and 8:00 pm in the summer. The campfire begins with a 40-minute sing-along and **marshmallow roast**. You may bring your own or buy sticks and marshmallows for $2; a s'mores kit is available for $5. Chip 'n' Dale stop by to visit and sign autographs during the sing-along. Afterward, guests move to benches and bleachers or lay out their blankets to watch an animated Disney feature on a large outdoor screen. On Friday and Saturday nights, you may be able to catch a double feature. The sing-along will still be held on rainy nights, although it is relocated to the porch.

Private Wagon Rides
Another fun group activity at Fort Wilderness is the horse-drawn wagon ride, which departs from Pioneer Hall at 7:00 pm and 9:30 pm nightly. This **45-minute** scenic

Wagon ride at Fort Wilderness

tour of Fort Wilderness may offer views of the Magic Kingdom's fireworks show, depending on the park's schedule. The price is $8 for those ages 10 and up and $5 for those ages 3–9, and reservations are not accepted. However, for $300 you may schedule a private wagon ride for your group of 30 adults or 35 adults and children. Private rides depart at 5:30 pm and 8:15 pm, and you can call 407-WDW-PLAY (939-7529) up to 180 days ahead to book.

Golf & Spectator Sports

Walt Disney World offers four 18-hole golf courses, one 9-hole course, and two miniature golf courses. If you'd rather **watch** sports than play, check out Disney's Wide World of Sports Complex, which offers an ever-changing calendar of spectator sports. Any of these would be a great place for a group outing in the days leading up to your event.

Golf

Disney's Palm and Magnolia golf courses are located across from Disney's Polynesian Resort, the Osprey Ridge course is located at the Bonnet Creek Golf Club, and the Lake Buena Vista Course is situated near Downtown Disney and Disney's Saratoga Springs Resort & Spa. The par-36 Oak Trail walking course is located near Disney's Magnolia golf course.

Rates at the four championship courses are $109 for resort guests and $124 for the general public. A **discounted Twilight Rate** of $59 is available after 2:00 pm or 3:00 pm, depending on the season. Rates at the Oak Trail course are $38 for ages 18 and over and $20 for ages 17 and under. The replay rate is 50% of full price, good that day only.

To reserve a tee time, call 407-WDW-GOLF between 7:00 am and 10:00 pm EST or log on to http://www.disneyworldgolf.com. Times are guaranteed with a credit card, and they must be canceled at least 48 hours beforehand to avoid a penalty. If you have a Disney resort reservation, you may book up to 90 days in advance, while non-resort guests may book up to 60 days in advance. Resorts guests receive **complimentary transportation** from their hotels to the golf course. To arrange a group outing, call 407-938-3870 or e-mail WDW.Golf.Reservations@disney.com.

Miniature Golf

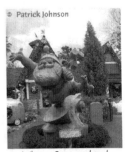
© Patrick Johnson

Walt Disney World has two miniature golf courses, the Fantasia-themed Fantasia Gardens and the Christmas-themed Disney's Winter Summerland. One round of miniature golf costs $12.78 for ages 10 and up and $10.65 for ages 3–9. There is a 50% discount for Annual Passholders.

The price includes a **souvenir** Walt Disney World logo golf ball for each round. Tee times cannot be reserved over the phone, but if you pay in person you may reserve a time for later in the day.

Winter Summerland

ESPN Wide World of Sports Complex

This 220-acre facility offers more than 170 amateur and professional sporting events every year, including Atlanta Braves Spring Training and Tampa Bay Buccaneers Training Camp. A **schedule** of events is available at http://espnwwos.disney.go.com. General admission is $13.50 for ages 10 and up and $10.00 for ages 3–9, but certain events may cost more.

Dinner Shows

Although tickets can be expensive, Walt Disney World's dinner shows are an easy way to incorporate a **meal and entertainment** into group gatherings. Reservations can be made up to 180 days in advance by calling 407-WDW-DINE, and tables are assigned in the order in which they are reserved. Full payment is required at the time of reservation but may be refunded up to 48 hours in advance.

Hoop-Dee-Doo Musical Revue

This vaudeville-style show at **Fort Wilderness'** Pioneer Hall offers an all-you-can-eat barbeque dinner and country western singing, dancing, and slapstick comedy.

It is one of Walt Disney World's longest running shows, and it can sell out during certain times of the year. Tickets are available in three sections: Category 1 is on the floor and closest to the stage, Category 2 is on the floor behind Category 1 or in the center of the balcony, and Category 3 is in the balcony on the right-hand or left-hand side. Category 1 costs $61.99–$65.99/ ages 10 and up and $31.99–$33.99/

Hoop-Dee-Doo Musical Revue

children ages 3–9. Category 2 seats are $56.99–$60.99/adults and $27.99–$29.99/ children, while Category 3 seats are $52.99–$56.99/adults and $26.99–$28.99/ children. There is no charge for children under age 3, and all prices include tax and tip.

Spirit of Aloha

Held at Luau Cove at Disney's **Polynesian Resort**, this show features Polynesian music and dancing, plus a family-style dinner. The show is very popular and can

Spirit of Aloha dinner show

sell out at certain times of year. Tickets are available in three sections: Category 1 is on the lower level, front and center. Category 2 is on the left or right side of the stage on the lower level or on the upper level directly behind Category 1. Category 3 is on the far left or right side of the stage on the lower level or on the upper level surrounding Category 2. Category 1 costs $65.99–$69.99/adults and $33.99–$35.99/ children. Category 2 costs $60.99–$64.99/adults and $29.99–$31.99/children. Category 3 costs $56.99–$60.99/adults and $28.99–$30.99/ children. There is no charge for children under age 3, and all prices include tax and tip.

Mickey's Backyard Barbecue

Mickey's Backyard Barbecue is more of a character buffet than a dinner show, but the dancing and musical entertainment set it apart. The show is held from 6:30 pm–8:00 pm on Thursdays and Saturdays at **Fort Wilderness'** Outdoor Pavilion. Tickets are $44.99 for ages 10 and up and $26.99 ages 3–9. There is no charge for children under age 3, and all prices include tax and tip. Seating is first-come, first-served, so a line forms as much as an hour before showtime.

Grand Gatherings

Groups of **eight or more** people staying at Walt Disney World resort hotels qualify for Disney's Grand Gatherings travel-planning services and events. The concierge-like services include arranging restaurant and dinner show reservations, tours and recreation, photo packages, floral service and gift baskets, and merchandise delivery.

In addition to these perks, Grand Gatherings' exclusive **events** offer an easy way to add another activity to your wedding, vow renewal, or commitment ceremony celebration without a lot of planning on your part. While not completely private, the events are open only to other Grand Gatherings groups, making them something your guests might not otherwise get to enjoy. You can register your group as a Grand

The Odyssey at Epcot

Gathering and get event dates and times by calling 407-WDW-MAGIC. Events can be booked 3-180 days in advance; full payment is required 45 days beforehand. Prices include tax and tip, and children under age 3 are free. Groups of 20 or more may book a custom event by calling 407-828-3200.

International Dinner and IllumiNations Dessert Reception
This event begins with a **family-style dinner** of international cuisine at the Odyssey in Epcot, including singing, dancing, storytelling, and character appearances. Afterward, your group will be escorted to a dessert buffet in a private viewing area for the IllumiNations fireworks show. Prices are $69.99 (regular season)/$73.99 (peak season) for ages 10 and up and $33.99/$35.99 for ages 3-9. Theme park admission is required.

Safari Celebration Dinner
Your group will enjoy a **private ride** on Animal Kingdom's Kilimanjaro Safaris, followed by an all-you-can-eat African-inspired dinner at Tusker House Restaurant. The evening is capped by a visit from some exotic wildlife and their handlers in the restaurant's courtyard and a chance to meet Disney characters. Prices are $69.99 (regular season)/$73.99 (peak season) for ages 10 and up and $33.99/$35.99 for ages 3-9. Theme park admission is required.

Good Morning Gathering
Meet Tony from *Lady and the Tramp* at Tony's Town Square Restaurant for an all-you-can-eat breakfast with some Disney characters. Afterward your group will be escorted to **reserved seating** at Mickey's PhilharMagic. Prices are $34.99 (regular season)/$38.99 (peak season) for ages 10 and up and $20.99/$22.99 for ages 3-9. Theme park admission is required.

Information on the **Pirate and Pals Fireworks Voyage** can be found in the Specialty Cruises section of this chapter.

Chapter 6
Everything Else

Although Disney offers services for just about every aspect of your wedding, vow renewal, or commitment ceremony, there are still a few you'll have to plan **on your own**. This includes obtaining a marriage license, if necessary, and finding someone to officiate at the ceremony, as well as renting formalwear and arranging for cosmetology services. And once you've lined up all these vendors, you'll probably need to know whom and how much to tip!

In this chapter, we'll cover the **basics** of obtaining these services and what to consider when selecting a vendor. Disney's Fairy Tale Weddings will provide you with lists of vendors who have worked on Disney events before, but you are not restricted to the names on those lists. One of the best ways to find a vendor and read reviews of his or her work is to browse the various online message boards devoted to Orlando-area and Disney weddings, vow renewals, and commitment ceremonies. Check out "How to Find Your Own Vendors" on page 122 of Chapter 3: Wishes Collection for tips on locating vendors.

Goin' to the chapel...

The **marriage license** is the most important piece of paper related to your wedding. We'll tell you how to get one by mail or pick it up in person, including what documentation you'll need to bring with you. Once you have a license, you'll need someone to sign it and preside over the ceremony. We'll tell you who is authorized to perform marriages in the state of Florida, how to bring your own officiant, and what the options are for Catholic ceremonies.

Unless the groom and his attendants own appropriate **formalwear**, chances are they will need to rent tuxedos or suits. We'll cover the options for picking up and/or returning formalwear in Orlando and detail the process. Some vendors also provide gown steaming services for the bride and her attendants, along with a gown shipping and delivery service to eliminate the hassle of carrying the wedding dress on a plane.

Many brides and their attendants choose to hire **cosmetologists** to do their hair and makeup on the wedding day. We'll cover the options for in-room and on-site services and offer tips for finding a vendor with the style you're looking for.

And finally, we'll tell you which vendors you may want to consider **tipping** and how much they usually get. Although tipping isn't mandatory, most couples plan to do it. You may be surprised to find out how few are really necessary!

Marriage License

Unless you are having a vow renewal or a commitment ceremony, Disney requires you to obtain a valid **Florida** marriage license. (For a vow renewal, you may be required to show your original marriage license or a certified copy.) You can either pick one up at a courthouse near Walt Disney World or, if you are not a Florida resident, apply by mail. A Florida marriage license is valid in any county in the state, so it doesn't matter which county you get yours from.

Requirements

Applicants must be at least 18 years of age, and no blood test is required. There is **no waiting period** for out-of-state and international residents or for Florida residents who have completed at least four hours of premarital counseling. All other Florida residents must wait three days from the license-issue date to marry.

You will be required to show **identification** such as a driver's license or a passport—a certified copy of a birth certificate is only required for applicants who do not have one of these or who are between the ages of 16 and 18. (Applicants younger than 18 will need the permission of both parents to apply.) If you are a

resident of the United States you will also be required to provide your Social Security number, naturalization number, or immigration number, while international residents must provide a passport number.

If you have previously been married, you may be required to provide a copy of your marriage license. If you have been **divorced** within the last

The couple and the officiant must sign the license

90 days in Florida, or within the last 12 months elsewhere in the United States, you may be required to provide a copy of your divorce decree. However, many Florida counties only require you to state when and how your previous marriage ended (e.g., divorce, annulment, or death), so check with the courthouse where you plan to apply.

Most Florida counties' marriage licenses are valid for **60 days** from the date of issue, but some may only be valid for 30 days—check with the Clerk of the Court where you plan to obtain yours. The cost is $98, and you may pay by cash, credit card, traveler's check, money order, or cashier's check; personal checks are not accepted.

There is a **discount** for couples who can provide proof of at least four hours of premarital counseling by a qualified provider no more than one year prior to the date of application.

Qualified providers include official representatives of a religious institution, such as a minister or pastor, and, for Florida residents, a licensed psychologist, clinical social worker, marriage and family therapist, or mental-health counselor. If you have completed premarital counseling, you'll need a certificate of completion or a letter from the provider stating your names, the date

The officiant presiding over a sand ceremony

of completion, and whether the course was conducted in person, by videotape or other electronic medium, or by a combination of these methods. Note that Osceola County will only give the premarital counseling discount to Florida residents.

Although there is space for two witnesses to sign the marriage license, Florida does not require witness signatures for the license to be valid. The completed license must be returned to the county clerk's office within **10 days** of the wedding—usually the officiant mails it in. You should receive a certified copy of your marriage license within a month of the wedding.

Apply in Person

There are **two courthouses** within half an hour's drive of Walt Disney World. The Orange County Courthouse is about 25 miles away in downtown Orlando, while the Osceola County Courthouse is about 17 miles away in Kissimmee. Both are open Monday through Friday from 8:30 am to 4:30 pm. They are closed on certain U.S. holidays, so it is a good idea to call before you go.

Note that both applicants must be present to obtain the license. Licenses obtained from Osceola and Orange counties are valid for 60 days from date of issue.

Osceola County Courthouse
2 Courthouse Square, 2nd Floor
Kissimmee, FL 34741
407-742-3530
http://www.osceolaclerk.com

Orange County Courthouse
425 N. Orange Avenue, Room #355
Orlando, FL 32801
407-836-2067
http://www.myorangeclerk.com/service/marriage.shtml

If you are a Florida resident, you may find it more convenient to obtain your license from your local Clerk of the Court rather than at a courthouse. A list of clerks by county can be found at http://dlis.dos.state.fl.us/fgils/coclerks.html.

Apply by Mail

Unless you are a Florida resident, you may apply for your marriage license by mail through the Brevard County Circuit Court. This can save time in the days leading up to the wedding and potentially the cost of a long taxi ride. Although there are services that will help you apply by mail for a fee, you can easily **do it yourself** for just the cost of the license.

To apply, call the Marriage License Information Clerk at 321-637-5413, e-mail marriagelicenseinformation@brevardclerk.us, or visit http://199.241.8.125/index. cfm?FuseAction=MarriageLicenses.Forms to download the Mail Away Marriage License form.

After you fill out and return the form, the clerk will prepare and send to you an Application to Marry (not a valid license) and an affidavit. These must be signed by the bride and groom in the presence of a **notary public**. You will return them to the clerk's office along with the application fee and a copy of each applicant's photo ID, as well as proof of premarital counseling, if desired. You can download a Marriage Course Provider Affidavit from the Brevard County Circuit Court web site to complete and return with the Application to Marry.

Once your notarized application has been received, the clerk will mail you a marriage license valid for **60 days** from the date of issue.

Officiant

Disney provides a list of officiants who have previously performed weddings at Walt Disney World, but you are welcome to find another local officiant or bring your own. If you choose an officiant who is not on Disney's list, he or she will be counted

Any ordained clergy member may officiate

as a **guest** at the ceremony and any other event he or she attends (Memories Collection ceremonies excluded).

According to Florida state law, any "regularly ordained minister of the gospel or elders in communion with some church, or other ordained clergy" may perform the marriage, along with all Florida judicial officers, including retired judicial officers, clerks of the circuit courts, and notaries public. The state also recognizes Quaker officiants and marriages. Anyone who falls under these guidelines may perform the ceremony without filling out any special paperwork, except to sign the **marriage license** at the time of the ceremony.

If you would like to be married by a **friend or a family member**, he or she will need to be ordained as a clergy member through an organization such as the Universal Life Church (http://www.themonastery.org) or the Church of Spiritual Humanism (http://www.spiritualhumanism.org/), which offer free ordination online within a few days. Although certain states require additional documentation for clergy members of these churches to perform marriages, Florida has not historically been one of them. If you have concerns, check with the clerk of the Florida county that will be issuing your marriage license.

The Orlando Catholic Diocese does not officially recognize wedding ceremonies performed outside the **Catholic Church**, so a Walt Disney World ceremony is not considered valid. Speak with your church's clergy about your situation and the alternatives. Some couples choose to have a marriage blessing, convalidation ceremony, or Mass at their hometown Catholic church before or after the Walt Disney World wedding. Others hold the ceremony at an Orlando-area Catholic church and the reception at Walt Disney World. And some couples may be comfortable forgoing the official Catholic wedding but work with the officiant to incorporate their religious beliefs in the Disney ceremony. You can even hire a retired priest to officiate at your wedding—check out http://www.rentapriest.com for a list of Orlando-area officiants. Although the ceremonies they perform are not recognized by the Catholic Church, they may be close enough to the traditional Catholic ceremony for your needs.

Unless your officiant is a friend or someone you brought with you from home, you should not feel obligated to mail an invitation or invite him or her to the reception. The officiants on Disney's list usually excuse themselves after the ceremony.

Tips for Writing Your Own Vows

Choosing to write your own vows is a great way to personalize your ceremony and share the depth of your commitment with your partner. However, it can be daunting to craft a heartfelt declaration to be made in front of all your friends and family and potentially captured on video for posterity! The key is to be **sincere, specific, and concise**. Don't feel you need to come up with stunningly original vows—it would be difficult to say something about love that no one's ever said before. Just say what you truly feel. Describe what you love about your partner and what you promise to do, and say it succinctly. And feel free to depart from traditional language ("I take you," for example) to use words and phrases that feel more natural to you. You may wish to work on shared vows with your partner or each write your own and surprise the other at the ceremony. It can be helpful to follow an outline like the sample below:

Opening: I, _____, take/choose you, _____, to be/as my_____.

Middle: Describe what you love about your partner and what you two will accomplish together.

Pledge: What you promise to do for your partner.

Formalwear Services

If you are flying to Walt Disney World, you can save the hassle of traveling with a **tuxedo or suit** by renting one in Orlando. This also eliminates the possibility of being charged late fees or extended-rental fees by your local formalwear dealer for keeping the clothes more than a few days. The information packet sent by Disney's Fairy Tale Weddings includes a list of Orlando-area formalwear dealers.

In addition to renting tuxedos and suits, many of the dealers on Disney's list will deliver and pick up formalwear, offer wedding **gown steaming** and preservation, and can even ship the wedding gown back to your home.

Tuxedo Rental

If you don't plan to bring your own, there are several ways to handle tuxedo rental. Usually the members of the wedding party are fitted at formalwear dealers in their hometowns, send their **measurements** to the dealer in Orlando,

and then pick up formalwear or have it delivered to a hotel. If the dealer you choose is part of a national network of formalwear dealers, you may wish to have the members of your party measured at a local branch of that network.

You can schedule a **fitting** at the Orlando dealer's shop or in your hotel room a few days before the event to be sure the formalwear fits properly. If you have your fitting on-site, the dealer may be able to exchange or alter the pieces right away and send you off with a complete outfit in the correct size. You will then need to drive the tuxedo back to the store the day after the event. If you have the fitting at your hotel, the formalwear dealer will take the tuxedo back the shop, exchange or alter any pieces that are the wrong size, and then redeliver the outfit in time for the event. After the event you simply leave the

Several vendors offer both tuxedo rental and gown steaming

tuxedo with Bell Services at your hotel, and someone from the dealer will pick it up. If you will be doing an in-park bridal portrait session, you may be able to keep the tuxedo a few extra days at no charge, depending on the policies of the vendor used by your formalwear dealer.

Some dealers keep only a **limited range** of tuxedo sizes and styles on hand and may need to exchange your pieces at an off-site warehouse. During the week this can be done fairly quickly, usually within a day or two. But because these warehouses are closed on weekends and holidays, the dealer may not be able to exchange pieces for you if your event takes place on a Monday or the Tuesday after a holiday. In this case, only the sleeve lengths and pants hems can be altered.

If this sounds like a risky proposition, you may wish to bring your formalwear with you. Although this can be a hassle if you are traveling a long way, there is the option of **"one-way"** formalwear rental. The national chain MW Tux (http://www.mwtux.com), formerly After Hours Formalwear, lets you rent your tuxedo or suit at any branch in the United States and drop it off at an Orlando-area store. If you are staying at a Walt Disney World resort, you can even have them pick up the tuxedo at your resort. If you are interested in this service, your first call should be to the Winter Garden branch of MW Tux (407-656-7700) so they can work with your local store to set up the rental.

Gown Steaming & Shipping

No matter how carefully you pack your wedding gown, chances are it will be wrinkled by the time you get to Orlando. Disney provides the names of two local formalwear dealers and a wardrobe stylist who can come to your hotel room to steam or **press your dress** before your event. The cost depends on the style and fabric content of your gown, but it usually ranges from $65 to $100.

Carolyn Allen's Bridal & Tuxedo (http://www.carolynallens.com) also offers a wedding gown **shipping and storage** service. Instead of lugging your wedding gown and accessories on the plane, you can ship them directly to Carolyn Allen's within two weeks of the wedding and have them delivered to your hotel for steaming on the morning of the wedding. After the wedding, the company will pick up your dress and accessories from Bell Services at your resort and ship them back to your home. The only charge is $15 for storage and delivery, plus the actual cost of shipping the dress to and from Carolyn Allen's. Accessories may include a veil, wrap, or shawl but not shoes.

Pack your dress any way you want and steam it later

The store also offers a gown **cleaning and preservation** service, which starts at around $175 and includes the price of return shipping. The service takes anywhere from 3 to 10 weeks, and you can have accessories or even paper goods like programs and invitations preserved with the dress.

Cosmetology Services

Your Disney's Fairy Tale Weddings information packet includes a list of some of the many local cosmetologists, several of whom used to work for Disney's now-disbanded cosmetology department. The list also features salons that provide services off-site or that will send cosmetologists to your room. Most

independent cosmetologists provide **in-room services**, although some charge a travel fee. If you plan to schedule cosmetology for the morning of your Theme Park Portrait Session, note that some cosmetologists are not available that early in the morning or charge an additional fee for early service.

In-room cosmetology services offer convenience

If your wedding is later in the day, you may also wish to investigate the cosmetology services of the four **salons** on Disney property. Ivy Trellis Salon, at Disney's Grand Floridian Resort & Spa; Casa De Belleza Salon, at Disney's Coronado Springs Resort; American Beauty Salon, at Disney's Contemporary Resort; and Perriwig Salon, at Disney's Yacht & Beach Club Resorts are all operated by Niki Bryan Spa, and more information about their services and hours can be found at http://www.relaxedyet.com. Cosmetology services are also offered at the Mandara Spa at the Walt Disney World Swan and Dolphin Resort (http://www.swandolphin.com/activities/spa.html).

Selecting a cosmetologist can be a very personal decision, and the various online message boards devoted to Orlando-area and Disney weddings offer a good way to see their work and get recommendations. If you have the opportunity to visit Walt Disney World before the wedding, it can be especially helpful to arrange a **trial run** with the cosmetologist you're considering. And if you can schedule the trial before an engagement portrait session with your

Ivy Trellis Salon at the Grand Floridian

photographer, you'll have the advantage of knowing exactly how your hair and makeup will look in photos! You may wish to bring any hair accessories you plan to wear with your wedding gown, along with inspiration pictures and possibly even a photo of your gown to give the cosmetologist an idea of the look you're going for. And if you have no idea what you'd like, your cosmetologist can make recommendations based on your coloring and face shape.

Tipping

Many different people will provide services on the day of your event, and trying to figure out whom to tip can be confusing—especially when you consider Disney's built-in 21% service charge on food and beverage. Of course, tipping is **never compulsory**, but it is nice gesture of appreciation for those who make the day go smoothly.

The rule of thumb is that you don't need to tip wedding professionals or people who own their own businesses. Traditionally this includes wedding planners, photographers, videographers, florists, and cake bakers. However, it is customary to tip **service people** such as drivers, bartenders, food servers, and business owners' assistants.

With Disney's Fairy Tale Weddings, many of these employees and service people are already accounted for in the 21% food and beverage **service charge**, including bartenders, servers, and the catering manager. You are not expected to tip Disney employees who make deliveries or set up, since you are already paying fees for these services. And, unlike traditional hotel weddings, Disney's Fairy Tale Weddings do not usually require valets, coat-check staff, or restroom attendants.

Figuring out whom to tip and how much to tip can be tricky

Until recently, Disney **cast members** have been prohibited from accepting tips. However, those in certain positions—including just about anyone you would work with through Disney's Fairy Tale Weddings except consultants—are now allowed to accept cash tips. Alternatively, you may choose to express your appreciation for a wedding professional with a thank-you note, a small gift, or a gift card in lieu of a tip.

Cosmetologists who own their businesses are frequently tipped by Disney brides, although you can make a case either way. One school of thought is that cosmetologists who travel to your hotel are already charging higher prices or a travel fee and don't have to pay rent to a salon to work, so there is no need for a tip. However many people feel that cosmetologists should be tipped regardless of the location or their status as an owner or employee.

If your **officiant** charges a fee, you are not expected to tip him or her, and civil officiants may not be allowed to accept a tip. Some consider it offensive to tip members of the clergy. If you bring your religious officiant with you and are not charged a fee, you may want to consider making a donation to his or her church.

Tipping (continued)

It's a good idea to calculate tips and put them in envelopes for each vendor **ahead of time** to expedite tipping on the day of the event. Traditionally the best man or the father of the bride or groom distributes these, but any reliable friend or family member can do this. Tips are usually given in cash and distributed toward the end of the event according to the level of service provided.

The charts below show you who is usually tipped and who is only tipped for going beyond the call of duty, along with average tip amounts for each. Those not listed below are generally **not tipped**.

Usually Tipped	Amount
Limo/Bus Driver	15%–20%, capped at $150
Cosmetology Assistant	15%–20%
Photo/Video Assistant	$25–$50

Tipped for Exceptional Service	Amount
Cosmetologist	15%–20%
DJ	$50–$100
Floral Specialist	Thank-you card, gift, or gift card
Formalwear Steamer	$10–$20
Musicians	$15–$25 each
Officiant (if no fee charged)	$50–$150
Wedding Coordinator, Event Planner, or Consultant	Thank-you card, gift, or gift card

© Nathan Root

Disney catering staff and bartenders are covered by the 21% service charge

Chapter 7

Disney Cruise Collection

A Disney Cruise Collection event is a unique and potentially economical way to combine your celebration and a honeymoon or vacation. Like the Escape Collection, it combines all the **basic elements** needed for a wedding, vow renewal, or commitment ceremony in a convenient package for a flat fee. Other similarities are the fixed nature of the package elements and limited options for customization, which keep the price down.

© Sarah R. Gennaro

"Secret" Deck 7 is one of several ceremony locations

But unlike the collections offered at Walt Disney World, the Cruise Collection functions as an **add-on** to the cruise you select, rather than a special event with separate contract and minimum requirements. This means that, depending on the itinerary and stateroom category you select, you could have an entire wedding and honeymoon, including meals, for less than the cost of an Escape Collection event at Walt Disney World.

The Cruise Collection is also ideal for those looking for a more casual affair—especially if you want one on the beach! At the same time, it adds a level of luxury to the standard cruise experience, including **concierge service** and the ability to book excursions and onboard amenities like spa and salon appointments 105 days in advance, instead of the usual 75, if your cruise has been paid in full.

This chapter will cover the **basic elements** included with the Cruise Collection package and describe which can be customized or provided by you. We'll also explain the special circumstances surrounding your marriage license, look at formalwear rental, and discuss tipping. And we've included a sample itinerary for the day of your event and a 12-month time line leading up to it.

The Basics

The Disney Cruise Line offers **add-on packages** of $2,500 or $3,500 per couple on top of the cost of the cruise. These include a ceremony onboard or on Disney's private island, Castaway Cay; an officiant; a pianist; a two-tier cake; a bottle of Iron Horse Fairy Tale Cuvee and a bottle of Martinelli's Sparkling Cider; a bouquet and boutonniere; dinner for two at Palo on the night of the ceremony; steaming for one gown and one tuxedo; an onboard wedding coordinator; concierge service; a complimentary 8x10-inch photo; a Disney's Fairy Tale Weddings cake serving set; a $100 onboard credit; and a keepsake Disney Cruise line certificate. You may also request Disney Cruise Line postcards to use as save-the-dates or announcements.

Package prices are $2,500 for an onboard ceremony and $3,500 for a Castaway Cay ceremony, and they are added to your cruise booking.

If you have more than four people (including the bridal couple) you will be charged for an additional bottle of Fairy Tale Cuvee or the beverage of your choice. If you have more than 10 people total, an **additional guest fee** of $20/person will be charged prior to the voyage. The fee does not cover additional drinks. No fee is charged for children under age 3, and they do not count toward the guest limit.

Special permission from the ship is required for groups of more than 50 people. Taxes, government fees, and shore excursions are not included in the Cruise Collection package price. The $100 stateroom credit may be used for merchandise, spa treatments, shore excursions, and other onboard activities, and any unused portion is not refundable or transferable. Certain package enhancements, including floral upgrades, may require **advance payment** by credit card if they do not originate from the ship's facilities.

Although there are no wedding discounts offered on the price of the cruise, you are eligible for any of the standard discounts, bonuses, or promotions offered by the Disney Cruise Line, Disney Rewards Visa, AAA, or your travel agent. If you will be traveling with guests and require eight or more staterooms, a travel agent can set up your trip as **group travel**, which entitles you to a discounted rate and group seating at meals.

All guests will be required to have valid **passports** to enter or reenter the United States. U.S. residents who are not U.S. citizens are required to travel with their Alien Registration cards (Green Cards). For security reasons, all adult guests must show a picture ID to embark and disembark the ship at each port, including Castaway Cay. A parent, guardian, or other responsible adult must be present at the gangway to authorize anyone under the age of 18 to go ashore unaccompanied.

Disney Cruise Collection events can be booked up to **12 months** in advance.

The specific **location, date, and time** of your event cannot be confirmed until 30 days before sailing, and they may be changed at any time due to circumstances like inclement weather. Only one Castaway Cay wedding is available per cruise, while there may be up to two onboard weddings. Onboard ceremonies on the Disney Wonder are held on the

Ceremony setup on the beach at Castaway Cay

Nassau day, while onboard ceremonies on the Disney Magic are held on a sea day. If it rains, outdoor ceremonies will be moved indoors, and no refunds will be issued.

Castaway Cay ceremonies take place at 10:00 am, while onboard ceremonies are usually held at 4:00 pm, 4:30 pm, or 5:30 pm. The **ceremony location** at Castaway Cay is on the beach. On the Wonder, ceremonies take place on Deck 7 Aft, at Cadillac Lounge, or at Outlook Cafe. On the Magic, ceremonies take place on Deck 7 Aft or at Sessions. There is a 20-person limit on Deck 7 Aft, a 30-person limit in Cadillac Lounge/Sessions, and a 25-person limit at Outlook Cafe.

The 15–20-minute ceremony is followed by a short reception with **cake cutting**, toasts, ceremonial first dances, and time for more photos. If your ceremony is onboard, the cake cutting will be held at the ceremony site. If your ceremony is held on Castaway Cay, you will first take photos on the beach and then be transported back to the ship to have the cake cutting at a private venue—usually Palo. No additional food may be ordered for the reception, but light refreshments may be available at a Castaway Cay ceremony. If you will be dining immediately after the reception, you can have the cake boxed up to bring with you to dinner.

That evening, the couple may choose to **dine alone at Palo** or reserve tables for a group, subject to availability. Only the bridal couple's meal at Palo is covered in the package price. Guests under age 18 may attend a cake cutting at Palo, but they will not be allowed to dine there that night.

There is **no deposit** required by Disney's Fairy Tale Weddings, but you must have a deposit on a cruise in order to book your ceremony package. Full payment for the entire cruise, including the ceremony package, must be made to the Disney Cruise Line 90 days before departure for Stateroom Categories 1–3 or 75 days before departure for Stateroom Categories 4–12. Any fees for additional guests or floral will be charged 30 days prior to departure, while enhancements provided onboard, like photography, will be billed to your stateroom on the day of service.

Although you will not receive a separate contract for your Cruise Collection event, Disney's Fairy Tale Weddings will send you a **confirmation letter** with your wedding-day itinerary and choices two or three weeks prior to sailing.

Marriage License

Disney Cruise Collection packages no longer include a Florida marriage license, so you will need to obtain one yourself. Disney will provide you with the name of a service that can help you get a license for a hefty fee, but you can easily **do it yourself** for just the cost of the license by using Brevard County Circuit Court's mail-away license service. (Note that Florida residents must apply at a courthouse in person to

© Laura Stickles

The legal ceremony may be held in front of the Walt Disney Theatre

obtain a license.) Castaway Cay ceremonies also require a Bahamanian marriage license, but your wedding coordinator will provide you with all the paperwork. More general information about Florida's marriage license requirements can be found in the Marriage License section starting on page 154 of Chapter 6: Everything Else.

To apply by mail, call the Marriage License Information Clerk at 321-637-5413, e-mail marriagelicenseinformation@brevardclerk.us, or visit http://199.241.8.125/index.cfm?FuseAction=MarriageLicenses.Forms to download the Mail Away Marriage License form.

After you fill out and return the form, the Clerk will prepare and send to you an Application to Marry (not a valid license) and an affidavit. These must be signed by the bride and groom in the presence of a **notary public**. You will return them to the Clerk's office along with the application fee and a copy of each applicant's photo ID, as well as proof of premarital counseling, if desired. You can download a Marriage Course Provider Affidavit from the Brevard County Circuit Court web site to complete and return with the Application to Marry.

Once your notarized application has been received, the Clerk will mail you a marriage license valid for **60 days** from the date of issue.

Because Disney's ship captains cannot perform legal ceremonies, you will meet privately with a notary public to sign your marriage license **before** the cruise departs. A certified copy of the signed license will be mailed to you by the Clerk of the Court about 21 business days later.

Your Florida marriage license will list the ship's **sailing date** as your legal wedding day, but many couples choose to celebrate the day of their ceremony as their anniversary. However, Disney recommends that you wait until after the wedding to print or engrave items with that date, since the ship's itinerary is subject to change and your ceremony may be rescheduled for another time during the trip.

Customizing Your Event

Due to the limited facilities onboard the ship, the basic elements of the Cruise Collection package are set, with just a few options to choose from. However, you may customize your ceremony with several additions.

Floral

Cruise Collection packages include a **bouquet** for the bride and a matching boutonniere for the groom, and only the choices listed in the planning kit are available.

The Solid French Bouquet is made of solid-colored roses in a classic round shape with sheer ribbon. It is available in red, white, ivory, light pink, hot pink, lavender, yellow, and orange or any combination of these colors. The Tropical Bouquet is a mix of brightly colored tropical flowers in a free-form arrangement tied with ribbon. For an **additional $75** you may upgrade to the Calla Lily Bouquet, a contemporary arrangement with satin ribbon-wrapped stems and pearl pins available in Crystal White, Garnet Glow, Majestic Red, Orange Mango & Florex Gold. For the same fee, Disney also offers a Holiday Bouquet, available in November and December; an Autumn Bouquet, available in September, October, and November; or the Romance bouquet. Your Wedding Consultant can provide information on the styles available at the time of your event.

© Elizabeth Donahue

Tropical Bouquet

Additional floral is available at an extra cost and will be charged to your credit card prior to sailing. Although prices vary depending on the type of flower, season, and size of each arrangement, the following list will give you an idea of the average prices, excluding 7% tax.

• Bridesmaid Bouquet	$125.00
• Single Rose Pin-On Corsage	$20.00
• Single Rose Wrist Corsage	$30.00
• Boutonniere (Pin-On)	$14.00
• Dendrobium Orchid Leis	$56.00
• Flower Girl Basket with Rose Petals	$55.00
• Presentation Rose	$30.00
• Rose Wand	$30.00
• Crystal Hidden Mickey	$6.00
• Rose Petals — Small (approx. 10 roses)	$17.50
• Rose Petals — Medium (approx. 50 roses)	$87.50
• Rose Petals — Large (approx. 100 roses)	$137.00
• Palm Branches & Shell Aisle Decor (Castaway Cay)	$150.00

Floral (continued)

To purchase floral arrangements for your **stateroom** from Disney, check out http://disneycruise.disney.go.com/planning-center/gifts-and-amenities/. You may also use approved outside vendor The Perfect Gift (http://www.theperfectgift.cc or 800-950-4559) for floral arrangements and gift baskets. There is a $14/item delivery fee, and you may be told that the ship cannot refrigerate floral arrangements for you.

Although you are not allowed to bring live, potted plants ashore when you disembark, Customs will allow you to bring **cut flowers** through.

You may also choose to bring your own **silk arrangements**, ceremony decor, and accessories, such as an aisle runner, swagging, cake serving set, or guest book. Your onboard wedding coordinator will arrange to have these items set out for you.

Cake & Champagne

The Disney Cruise Line offers a two-tier cake with fondant over buttercream icing and a Mickey & Minnie topper in one of three styles: Classic Round, Elegant Square, and Contemporary Round. The color and style of the decorations on the standard cakes may not be modified. However, you may bring your own cake topper or upgrade to a floral topper. If you provide your own, it must weigh 1 lb. or less and be 6 inches in diameter or smaller, and it must be approved by the ship. Standard cake **flavor choices** are Chocolate, White, Yellow, and Marble; standard filling flavors are Chocolate Mousse, White Chocolate Mousse, Strawberry Mousse, Bavarian Cream, and Buttercream.

Fairy Tale Cuvee set up at ceremony

You will receive **one bottle** of Iron Horse Fairy Tale Cuvee and one bottle of Martinelli's Sparkling Cider for a celebratory toast at your cake cutting. Additional bottles are available at $64 plus 7% tax and 15% service charge for the Fairy Tale Cuvee and $22 plus tax and service charge for sparkling cider. You may upgrade the bottle included with your package for an additional charge to Moet and Chandon White Star, Krug Grand Brut, Perrier Jouet, or Moet Chandon Dom Perignon, Epernay.

You may also add soft drinks or other **nonalcoholic beverages** for the cake-cutting reception; ice water is available at no charge. Another option is to bring your own alcohol on board. There is a 15% service charge for serving it at your cake-cutting reception. Note that no additional food may be ordered for onboard receptions, but you may be able to add light refreshments to a Castaway Cay ceremony.

Music & Entertainment

The Cruise Collection package includes a **keyboard player** at the ceremony and cake-cutting reception. You may choose selections from a list of traditional and Disney songs or provide sheet music or a CD for the pianist. If you prefer recorded music, you may provide a CD of your selections in the desired order to the Onboard wedding coordinator. If you have no preference, the standard music selections played during the ceremony are as follows.

Prelude/Seating: "Trumpet Voluntary" ("Prince of Denmark's March") by Clarke

Processional: "Bridal Chorus" ("Here Comes the Bride") by Wagner and "Trumpet Voluntary" ("Prince of Denmark's March") by Clarke

Recessional: "Wedding March" ("There Goes the Bride") by Mendelssohn

It may also be possible to arrange for an appearance by one or more Disney **characters** during your reception. However, the selection and availability of characters is limited, and Disney may not be able to confirm their appearance until a few days before your event. Prices are $900 for one character, $1,350 for two, and $1,800 for three for 20 minutes of interaction. Talk to your Wedding Consultant about whether this option is available during your cruise.

Dining at Palo

The package includes dinner for two at Palo, and the bridal couple will be automatically booked there for the night of the ceremony. If you prefer to dine on another day, at brunch instead of dinner, or with a group, you must make your own reservation at http://www.disneycruise.com.

One of the perks of the Cruise Collection package is the ability to book 105 days (rather than 75 days) before the voyage if your cruise has been paid in full. You are guaranteed a table for two as part of the package, and you may book tables of **four or six** online or at Palo once onboard. Although the bridal couple's meals are complimentary, there is a $15 charge for each additional person.

Palo has a dress code, and guests must be age 18 or older. Those who wish to have a **family dining** experience on the night of the ceremony are asked to attend their regular dining rotation and arrange for their dinner for two at Palo on another day.

Parties of 12-14 adults may request to reserve Palo's **private room** for their celebratory meal. The room is available at either 6:00 pm or 9:00 pm. Booking cannot be confirmed until 60 days before departure, but your Wedding Consultant can help you make arrangements.

Photography

Although photography is **not included** in the price of the Cruise Collection package, you may add on one of the packages provided by the ship's photographers. The price will be charged to your onboard account, and you will receive your prints before you leave the ship. This means you will need to look through all your photos to select the ones for your album and enlargements, so be sure to leave time to do this—especially if your ceremony will be held toward the end of the cruise.

The ship photographer sets up a shot

The **Celebration Package** costs $349.95 and includes 20 5x7-inch prints, five 8x10-inch prints, and one 8x10-inch folio. Castaway Cay ceremonies incur an $85 surcharge with this package to cover the additional photography time required. The **Wishes Package** is $549.95 and includes 30 5x7-inch prints, 15 8x10-inch prints, and one 5x7-inch photo album. The **Magic Package** costs $999.95 and includes 30 5x7-inch prints, 30 8x10-inch prints, 25 wedding announcements, one 5x7 photo album, one 8x10 photo album, and a CD of all images. All packages include **one hour** of photography, but additional photography may be purchased at $85 per hour.

Additional 5x7-inch prints cost $6.95 each, while 8x10-inch prints cost $19.95 each. A pack of 25 wedding announcements costs $24.95. You may also purchase a **disc of all your images** for $399.95 in addition to the cost of a photography package; the disc is not available by itself.

Couples who have a Disney Cruise Collection event are entitled to purchase a Magic Kingdom Portrait Session (or other in-park bridal portrait session) from Disney Event Group Photography. See page 115 for more details.

Formalwear Service

While many couples choose more casual attire for Cruise Collection events, the Disney Cruise Line does have an **onboard** tuxedo vendor for its seven-night cruises. If you will be sailing on a three- or four-night cruise, you will need to arrange your own formalwear services—check out the Tuxedo Rental section of Chapter 6: Everything Else for some ideas.

Onboard tuxedo rental is provided at an additional charge by Cruiseline Formalwear (http://www.cruiselineformal.com). Although there may be some inventory available at the time of sailing, it is recommended that you preorder tuxedos **two weeks** or more before sailing. Tuxedo packages range from $85–$160 and include one or two jackets, pants, two shirts, cummerbund, bow tie, cuff links and shirt studs. Shoes, vests, and other accessories may be rented separately.

The package will be delivered to your stateroom on the day of sailing, and you will return it to your cabin attendant after the event. Minor alterations and some exchanges can be made onboard, but it is recommended that you have your measurements taken at a local formalwear dealer before you place your order. Children's tuxedos are available by preorder only.

Basic dress and tuxedo **steaming** for the bride and groom is included in the Cruise Collection package, but if the gown is very elaborate, you may wish to arrange for steaming or pressing before you board the ship. Other guests' attire may be steamed for a fee.

Salon & Spa Services

The cost of salon and spa services is not included in the Cruise Collection package, but, unlike other guests, you have the ability to **book salon** appointments before departure. Just let your Wedding Consultant know if you would like to arrange this service for the day of your event. Prices range from $24 to $75 for a wash, cut, and style, with a $30 surcharge for an updo. A wash and blow dry runs $32–$48. At press time, no makeup services were available.

Such **spa services** as massages, manicures, pedicures, facials, and body wraps are available to prebook online at http://disneycruise.disney.go.com/ships-activities/onboard-activities/fitness-spa. Passes to the Tropical Rainforest—which features steam rooms, heated loungers, and scented showers—may not be booked online but can be arranged through your Wedding Consultant.

Note that the Vista Spa & Salon is open only guests 18 years of age and older.

Tipping

First, remember that tipping is **never** mandatory, but it can be a nice gesture to those who go above and beyond to make your wedding day run smoothly.

While there is a fairly detailed set of tipping guidelines for the regular staff on your Disney Cruise, the wedding services provided by the captain, onboard wedding coordinator, and pianist are included in the price of your Cruise Collection package, so these people are not traditionally tipped. However, a note of thanks is always appreciated. If you wish to reward exceptional service, **cash** may be more useful than gifts or gift cards to Disney Cruise Line cast members, who live in cramped quarters and may have few opportunities to leave the ship during their months-long contracts.

If your ceremony will be performed on Castaway Cay by a **local officiant**, check out the tipping guidelines at the end of Chapter 6: Everything Else.

Getting the Ball Rolling

The first time you call Disney's Fairy Tale Weddings (321-939-4610) a Sales Lead Associate will take down your name, contact information, and preferred ceremony location. Then you will be assigned a **Wedding Consultant** to coordinate the details of the wedding. You will need to contact the Disney Cruise Line directly (1-800-511-1333) to price out sailing dates, get stateroom category information, and book your cruise. The Disney Cruise Line requires a deposit determined by the price of your cruise at the time of booking.

After you have booked your cruise, you will need to give your Wedding Consultant your cruise **confirmation number** and sailing dates. She will then send you a Disney Cruise Line Intimate Wedding Planning Guide, and the cost of the Cruise Collection package will be added to your cruise booking. The planning guide confirms the details of your event and outlines the options and add-ons. This and the charge to your cruise booking are your only confirmation—you will not receive a Letter of Agreement from Disney's Fairy Tale Weddings.

Although cruises can be booked a year or more in advance, the work on your Cruise Collection wedding doesn't start until about **60 days** before your sailing date. At that time, you will return your completed planning guide and submit your marriage license application, if necessary. About 30 days before your sailing date, your Wedding Consultant will turn your file over to the Disney Cruise Line and begin working on a confirmation letter. When you receive the letter, you will have a chance to look over the details and make any necessary changes to the final order.

On departure day, you will meet with the **Guest Services Groups Manager** on the ship. He or she will act as your onboard wedding coordinator for the duration of the trip.

As with Disney's Escape Collection, it can be a good idea to **take a relaxed approach** to your Cruise Collection event planning. Cruise couples do not get a lot of hand-holding from the Wedding Consultant because their events are very simple to arrange. Additionally, at press time there was just one Cruise Collection Wedding Consultant. When you consider that there are up to three weddings on each sailing, you can imagine how busy she is!

If you have a year until your wedding, don't be surprised if you go months without hearing from your Wedding Consultant. This is not because she doesn't care, it's just that there really isn't that much that needs to be done in advance. If all your requests are reflected in your **confirmation letter**, you can be assured that they will be met. So if you are the super-organized type who likes to take advantage of every spare moment, channel that energy into planning the details that you control, like making favors or invitations.

Sample Wedding Day Itineraries

Onboard Ceremony

Approximately 1 hour

- ❏ Flowers are delivered to the stateroom a few hours before the event
- ❏ Bride has hair appointment at Vista Spa
- ❏ 30 minutes before the ceremony, groom arrives at wedding location
- ❏ 20 minutes before the ceremony, groom and wedding party are introduced to ship's captain
- ❏ 15 minutes before the ceremony, bride is escorted to wedding location
- ❏ Onboard wedding coordinator greets bride and coordinates ceremony
- ❏ Ceremony begins
- ❏ Cake-cutting reception held immediately following the ceremony
- ❏ Photographer takes bridal couple around the ship for photographs
- ❏ Bridal couple dines at Palo

Castaway Cay Ceremony

Approximately 90 minutes

- ❏ Flowers are delivered to the stateroom a few hours before the event
- ❏ Bride has hair appointment at Vista Spa
- ❏ 45 minutes before the ceremony, groom meets guests in the Atrium Lobby for transportation to Castaway Cay
- ❏ 30 minutes before the ceremony, bride will meet onboard wedding coordinator for transportation to Castaway Cay
- ❏ Ceremony begins
- ❏ Immediately following, bride, groom, and guests pose for pictures on the island
- ❏ Bridal party and guests are transported back to the ship for cake-cutting reception at Palo
- ❏ Photographer takes bridal couple around the ship for photographs
- ❏ Bridal couple dines at Palo that evening

Cruise Collection Time Line

This 12-month **checklist** will show you one way to structure your time, but don't worry if you have less than a year or don't plan to do everything on the list. Disney's Fairy Tale Weddings doesn't really begin working on your Cruise Collection event until about 60 days out.

12 Months or More

❏ You may contact the Disney Cruise Line to **book** your cruise.

❏ Check out *PassPorter's Disney Cruise Line and Its Ports of Call* to begin preparing for your trip.

10 to 12 Months

❏ Contact Disney's Fairy Tale Weddings with your cruise **reservation number** and dates.

❏ Discuss who pays for what and start a wedding **budget**.

❏ Send your engagement **photo and announcement** to the local paper.

❏ Schedule an in-park **portrait session**, if desired.

❏ Begin compiling a **guest list** with complete names and addresses.

❏ Use *PassPorter's Disney Weddings & Honeymoons* to track your plans and keep all your inspiration pictures and ideas in one place.

❏ Choose your **attendants** and ask them to be in the wedding party.

❏ Begin gathering **ideas**, pictures, and samples to share with your Disney's Fairy Tale Wedding Consultant.

7 to 9 Months

❏ **Finalize** the guest list.

❏ If you plan to use frequent flyer miles to travel to Florida, book your **flight** now.

❏ Start shopping for a **bridal gown**.

❏ Order or make your invitations, announcements, and other wedding **stationery**.

4 to 6 Months

❏ Look over the Disney Cruise Line Intimate Wedding **Planning Guide** and begin filling in as much information as you can.

❏ Order the bridal gown. Be sure it is scheduled to arrive at least **one month** before you leave so there is time to have it altered.

❏ Shop for and order **bridesmaids' dresses**.

❏ **Register** for wedding gifts. The rule of thumb is at least three stores with a variety of locations and price ranges.

❏ Narrow down selections and details for extra **floral, decor,** and **food**.

❏ Purchase **rings** and send for engraving.

❏ If you will be making **welcome bags** for guests, start collecting items.

❏ Make or buy **favors**.

❏ Work with mothers to select their **dresses**.

❏ Sign up for **dance lessons**, if desired.

❏ Send your **invitations**.

105 Days

❏ If your cruise has been paid in full, you may **book** excursions, spa treatments, and your dinner at Palo.

❏ Book your **flights**.

Additional Tasks
❏
❏
❏
❏
❏
❏

90 Days

❏ **Full payment** is due for Stateroom Categories 1-3.

3 Months

❏ Buy or make a guest book and such **accessories** as a cake topper, cake knife and server, ring pillow, toasting flutes, garter, candles etc.

❏ Get any **documentation** you need for your cruise, including passport, Alien Registration Card, visas, etc.

❏ Pick out or design a **ketubah** or other marriage contract required by your religion.

❏ Have the groomsmen's measurements taken and **order their attire**.

❏ Confirm delivery date for bridal gown and **schedule fittings**.

❏ Talk to people you'd want to do special **performances or readings** as part of the ceremony.

75 Days

❏ **Full payment** is due for Stateroom Categories 4-12.

❏ You may **book** excursions, spa treatments, and your dinner at Palo.

Additional Tasks
❏
❏
❏
❏
❏
❏
❏

60 Days

❏ **Return** your planning guide and, if necessary, your marriage license information sheet.

1 to 2 Months

❏ Have your marriage **license application** notarized and mail it in.

❏ Work with your Wedding Consultant to schedule any wedding-day hair **appointments** at Vista Spa & Salon.

❏ Confirm formalwear has been ordered for groom and groomsmen. Schedule tux **fittings**, if available.

❏ As you receive presents, be sure to **update** and/or add items to your registries and track the gifts you get.

❏ Have your first bridal **gown fitting**.

❏ Submit your wedding **announcement** to newspapers, if desired.

❏ Make sure all bridesmaids' attire has been **fitted**.

❏ Select **songs** for the ceremony and work with your Wedding Consultant to see if the pianist needs the sheet music.

30 Days

❏ Your Wedding Consultant will turn your file over to the Disney Cruise Line and begin work on your **confirmation letter**.

❏ The cost of additional floral and any fees for additional guests will be **charged** to your account.

3 to 4 Weeks

❏ Finalize your **vows**.

❏ Attend **final** gown fitting.

❏ Prepare a must-have **shot list** for your photographer.

❏ Schedule pre-departure **grooming appointments**.

❏ Finish and print ceremony **programs**, if desired.

❏ Pick up rings and check the **inscriptions** before you leave the store.

❏ Confirm **reservations**, and give loved ones your itinerary in case of emergency.

❏ Contact wedding party with **critical information** related to the ceremony (times, duties).

1 to 2 Weeks

❏ Pick up your bridal gown and make sure all of your **accessories** are together.

❏ Prepare your **toasts** or thanks to friends and family.

❏ **Assemble** welcome bags.

❏ Put cash **tips** in marked envelopes and give them to a designated family member or friend to distribute on the wedding day.

❏ Pick up **formalwear** and try it on (if you will not be renting onboard).

❏ If you are a Florida resident, schedule time to go pick up your **marriage license** at the courthouse, if necessary. A three-day waiting period applies.

Sailing Day

❏ If necessary, meet with the **notary** at the Disney Cruise Line terminal to sign the marriage license.

❏ Meet with your **onboard wedding coordinator** to finalize logistics and set the wedding-day itinerary.

Ceremony Day

❏ Don't forget the **rings**.

❏ Be sure to **eat** properly.

❏ If possible, begin looking through ceremony photos to **select favorites** for albums and enlargements.

❏ Don't let the day pass by in a blur—take time to stop and **enjoy** it!

Additional Tasks
❏
❏
❏
❏
❏

Chapter 8

Honeymoons & Anniversaries at Walt Disney World

Although it is best known as a family vacation spot, Walt Disney World consistently ranks among the top **honeymoon** destinations in the world. In addition to its numerous restaurants and resorts and staggering array of activities, Walt Disney World offers the kind of hospitality that will make your trip unforgettable.

Another advantage to honeymooning in the World is the **variety** of experiences. In one trip you can relax on a beach, go sightseeing in downtown Hollywood, stroll through 11 countries, explore Asian jungles and African savannas, and step into the past, the future, and the land of fantasy!

In this chapter we'll look at some of the things you can do to add **extra romance** to your Walt Disney World vacation.

Arguably the most romantic spot in Walt Disney World

Although the terminology is geared toward honeymoons, any of the ideas presented here would be a great addition to an **anniversary or engagement** trip.

First we'll cover ways to **let people know** you're celebrating a special occasion and how to take advantage of Disney's Honeymoon Registry for activities, meals, and merchandise on your trip.

Then, because Disney doesn't currently offer special honeymoon packages at Walt Disney World, we'll look at the **VIP experiences** that might approximate one.

And finally, we'll cover romantic options and ideas for dining and transportation, as well as **memory-making** activities like tours, photography sessions, and spa services.

Let People Know You're Celebrating!

Cast members often go out of their way to provide **extra magic** to honeymooners, and your fellow guests may pitch in too! Many couples report receiving well wishes, free desserts, special seating, and other perks just for celebrating their honeymoon at Walt Disney World. But first you have to let people know that you're celebrating.

Reservations
The first thing you can do is to have a reservations agent **note your honeymoon** on your resort reservation and on each dining reservation. This is the quickest and easiest way to get the word out.

Buttons
You can pick up **free** "Happily Ever After" or "Happy Anniversary" buttons at Guest Relations inside the parks or at your Disney resort's front desk—although chances are the resort cast member will see the note on your reservation and offer them to you first!

Wedding mouse ear hats

Mouse Ears
If you don't mind a little **extra attention**, you can announce your honeymoon by wearing the bride and groom mouse ears sold inside the Disney parks and at the Disney Store at Downtown Disney. For the groom, Disney offers a black top hat with attached mouse ears or a set of classic black mouse ears with a mini top hat, a tuxedo front, and tails in the back. Both styles cost $14.95 each. Brides can buy a headband with white sequined mouse ears and attached veil for $16.95 or a bejeweled white mouse ear hat with a mini rhinestone tiara and veil for $15.95. If you'd like to buy them before you get to Walt Disney World, call Merchandise Guest Services at Walt Disney World (407-363-6200) or Disneyland (800-362-4533) to have them shipped to you. You can also find bride and groom ear hats at http://www.disneystore. com/accessories/ear-hats/disney-parks-authentic/mn/1000292+1000809/.

Crafty Ways to Send the Message
Many people make their own Disney-themed **bridal gear**, including personalized T-shirts, custom bride- and groom-ear baseball hats, and even door signs for their hotel rooms. If you have a creative bent, this can be a fun and unique way to let people know you're celebrating your honeymoon.

So what can you expect to receive once you're decked out in all this honeymoon gear? Nothing. That is to say, in order to avoid disappointment, the best policy is just to enjoy spending time together in Walt Disney World without expecting special treatment. Not everyone will get every perk, but if you make your own magic, you'll be that much more surprised if you do receive some honeymoon-related pixie dust.

Disney's Honeymoon Registry

If you are honeymooning at a Disney-owned resort or aboard the Disney Cruise Line, you're eligible for Disney's Honeymoon Registry, a **free service** that allows your friends and family to contribute monetary gifts toward your honeymoon.

You select gifts for the registry from a long list of **experiences**, including tours, tickets, special events, meals, spa treatments, shore excursions, and merchandise. When a guest buys you an experience, the funds are credited to your special Disney Gift Card for Honeymoons, which can be used anywhere Disney gift cards are accepted. Note that certain experiences, including Walt Disney World tours, cannot be paid for with gift cards, so you would need to charge them to your room and then apply the gift card to your resort or stateroom bill.

Because the funds are **pooled** on the gift card, you are not limited to buying the specific experiences or items your guests gave you—if Aunt Edna buys you a $100 dinner at Jiko, you can choose to spend the money on 40 Mickey ice cream bars instead (although things may get tricky when Aunt Edna later asks how you enjoyed your African feast!).

You can even use the card to pay for your room-only **resort reservation** or a Magic Your Way Package (with the exception of reservations made through a consolidator like Expedia). If your card isn't funded until after you've paid for your room, you may call the Disney Reservations Center at 407-939-7776 to receive a credit in your original form of payment up to the amount available on your Disney Gift Card for Honeymoons.

If you wish to apply the funds to a **Disney Cruise**, you must use your card before or when you make your final payment. No credit is available after the cruise has been paid off, but you can use the funds for a variety of experiences onboard and ashore.

One thing you can't pay for with your Disney Gift Card for Honeymoons is the wedding itself—Disney's Fairy Tale Weddings cannot accept it as a form of payment.

All you need to sign up for Disney's Honeymoon Registry is your Disney resort reservation number, your Disney Vacation Club reservation number, or your Disney Cruise Line confirmation number. Visit http://www.disneyhoneymoonregistry.com at least 15 days before your trip to get started. The registry is managed entirely **online**, where you can add items, check the balance on your account, and see who has contributed. Guests can purchase experiences for you up until the last day of your honeymoon by going to the web site or by calling 407-566-7272 Monday-Friday from 9:00 am–5:00 pm EST.

Although guests will not be able to add money to the card after the last day of your honeymoon, the funds already on the card **never expire**.

VIP Experiences

Disney doesn't offer any special honeymoon packages for Walt Disney World, but you can create your own by choosing **top-of-the-line** accommodations and vacation packages like the ones listed below.

Club Level Concierge Service

When you reserve a room on the Club Level at a Deluxe Disney resort, you are eligible for a number of **concierge services**. The experience starts at check-in, when a dedicated cast member meets you in front of the resort or in the lobby

and escorts you to the Club Level to check you in to your room. The concierge team can then help you make reservations for dining, tours, transportation, and recreational activities, including golf tee times, during the length of your stay. Among the other perks of the Club Level are centrally located rooms on card-key accessed floors and an all-day buffet of snacks, desserts, and beverages in the Concierge Lounge.

Choosing Club Level accommodations will add at least **$100** to the nightly cost of a room. It is important to note that at some resorts, your Club Level room may not be in the main building or have the best view. And in most cases, the lobby-level concierge offers the same kinds of services and access to reservations that a Club Level concierge

Breakfast in the Concierge Lounge at the Grand Floridian

has. If you don't plan to spend much of your honeymoon in your room or at the Concierge Lounge, you may wish to save your money for another aspect of your trip. However, whether or not it is possible to quantify the benefits of Club Level accommodations, many guests swear the VIP experience alone is worth the price.

Magic Your Way Premium & Platinum Packages

The Walt Disney Travel Company offers five Magic Your Way **vacation packages** that combine accommodations at a Disney resort, admission to the theme parks, and, in some cases, all your meals. The price of each package depends on the time of year you plan to travel, the resort you choose, the length of your stay, and whether you want to add certain privileges, such as admission to the water parks, park-hopping privileges, or a no-expiration option for your tickets.

While most guests who take advantage of the Magic Your Way plan stick to the base package or add one of the Disney Dining Plans, Disney also offers two **high-end packages** that include a number of additional experiences and services that will make you feel like a VIP.

Disney's Magic Your Way **Premium Package** costs $169 per adult per day on top of the price of the base Magic Your Way Package for accommodations and park admission. In addition to hotel accommodations, park admission, three meals a day per person at any of 100+ participating restaurants, two snacks a day per person, and a refillable resort mug, the Premium Package includes complimentary access to numerous recreational activities that might appeal to honeymooners. Among your choices

The Premium Package includes mini-golf at Winter Summerland (above) and Fantasia Gardens

are golf, including lessons, greens fees, rental equipment, cart, balls, and shoes; miniature golf; water sports and watercraft rentals; guided fishing trips and cane pole fishing; horseback trail rides and pony rides; carriage and wagon rides; and bike rentals. The package also includes one admission per person to Cirque du Soleil's La Nouba, unlimited admission to certain theme park tours, access to a preferred fireworks viewing area at the Magic Kingdom and at Epcot, and a PhotoPass Resort Portrait Session and print package (photo CD not included). And, if you've brought along any children between the ages of 4 and 12, you can drop them off at Disney's Children's Activity Centers as often as you like at no charge.

For $229 per adult per day, Disney's Magic Your Way **Platinum Package** gives you all the amenities of the Premium Package plus personalized itinerary planning before you arrive, nightly turn-down service, private in-room child care, one spa treatment per person, one fireworks cruise during the Magic Kingdom's Wishes Nighttime Spectacular or Epcot's IllumiNations: Reflections of Earth, reserved seating at Disney's Hollywood Studios' Fantasmic!

The Platinum Package includes nightly turn-down service

show, a Richard Petty Ride-Along Experience, and a PhotoPass CD containing all the pictures you take with Disney's PhotoPass photographers at the four theme parks (but not the images from the PhotoPass Resort Portrait Session). The Platinum Package is also the only one that includes the option of dining at Victoria & Albert's at the Grand Floridian Resort & Spa.

These packages aren't cheap, and they aren't exactly a bargain if you tally up the number of options you'll actually use, but they do provide **one-stop shopping** for a memorable honeymoon experience!

Romantic Dining

Just about any meal can be a romantic one if the mood is right, but Walt Disney World offers many options for an **unforgettable** dining experience. In addition to gourmet food and romantic ambience, several table-service restaurants feature views of the fireworks at Epcot and the Magic Kingdom. If you call the restaurant directly a few weeks ahead, many can print a personalized menu with your names, the date, and even pictures you provide. And restaurants have been known to surprise honeymooners with confetti on the table or sometimes even a free dessert!

All About the Atmosphere

Many people consider **Victoria & Albert's** at Disney's Grand Floridian Resort & Spa to be the most romantic restaurant at Walt Disney World. In an opulent Victorian setting, a costumed pair of servers known as "Victoria" and "Albert" attends each table as a harpist plays in the background. Every couple is given personalized menus, and women receive a rose. The multi-course prix fixe menu changes nightly according to what's in season, and prices are $125/person or $185/person with wine pairings. For an

even more extravagant experience, you may reserve the Chef's Table in the kitchen, where you can watch the action and work with the chef to tailor a menu of up to 10 courses. The price is $200/person or $295/person with wine pairings. You can get the same menu at the same price in the four-table Queen Victoria's Room, which also offers French *gueridon* service—tableside preparation of certain dishes on a rolling cart.

Victoria & Albert's restaurant

Any of Disney's other **Signature Dining** restaurants would be a lovely setting for a honeymoon meal, but a few stand out as particularly romantic. Artist Point at Disney's Wilderness Lodge features Craftsman decor and views of Bay Lake. After an early dinner, you can walk down to the dock for a romantic boat ride to the Magic Kingdom in time for fireworks. Disney's Animal Kingdom Lodge is home to Jiko—The Cooking Place, where low lighting and plush booths create an intimate atmosphere and the entire staff may send out a signed card of congratulations on your special occasion. Before you call it a night, share a quiet moment in the rocking chairs surrounding the blaze at the resort's Arusha Rock fire pit. Citricos, at the Grand Floridian, offers a fresh combination of American and Mediterranean flavors and cozy contemporary decor, making it another good choice for a romantic meal. Although the restaurant does not have a water view, you can stroll down to the Grand Floridian's beach after dinner and watch the Electrical Water Pageant make its way around Seven Seas Lagoon.

Fantastic Fireworks

The only thing better than a romantic dinner is a romantic dinner within view of fireworks! The most popular place for this winning combination is **California Grill**, atop the Contemporary Resort. However, the dining room can become crowded and noisy as patrons rush to the windows to see the Magic Kingdom's Wishes fireworks show. For a more sedate dining experience, make your reservation for earlier in the evening and then adjourn to the restaurant's outdoor viewing platform a few minutes before the show. Even if you leave after your meal, you will be readmitted to watch the fireworks when you return later.

View of IllumiNations: Reflections of Earth from Bistro de Paris

The Grand Floridian's **Narcoossee's** is perched over Seven Seas Lagoon directly across from the Magic Kingdom, making it another popular spot for dining during the fireworks. Note that the outdoor viewing area runs under the lagoon-facing windows, which means it can sometimes be difficult to see around the diners who step outside when the show starts.

You can also see fireworks from inside **Ohana** at the Polynesian Resort, although this restaurant's boisterous atmosphere may disqualify it as a romantic dining spot for some honeymooners.

Epcot's **Bistro de Paris** is arguably the most romantic restaurant from which to view fireworks. This out-of-the-way spot on the second floor of the France Pavilion serves fine Continental cuisine in a classic setting and offers views of IllumiNations from many of its windows.

But for the ultimate fairy tale evening, try dinner at **Cinderella's Royal Table** inside the Magic Kingdom. Tables under the windows afford a unique view of the Wishes fireworks show—almost as if you were inside it!

View of Wishes fireworks from Cinderella's Royal Table

Private Dining

Sometimes the most romantic way to dine is **completely alone**–together! Whether it's a simple room service meal on the balcony of your hotel room or an elaborate lakeside affair attended by a butler, Disney can help you set up the ultimate intimate feast.

For an impromptu **in-room** celebration, Private Dining (a.k.a., room service) at your resort can help you arrange a meal in your room on a moment's notice or up to a day ahead. Full meal service is available at all of Disney's Deluxe resorts and at Disney's Coronado Springs Resort. The other Moderate resorts and the Value resorts only offer pizza delivery.

However, anyone staying on Disney property can arrange a **private meal** in a secluded public space at the Grand Floridian, the BoardWalk Inn, or any of the Deluxe resorts no matter which resort they call home.

To plan an intimate dinner on the **Grand Floridian**'s terrace or at the Marina within view of the Magic Kingdom's fireworks, contact Private Dining at the Grand Floridian (407-824-2474). Prices start at $85/person if you choose from the menus provided by Private Dining or customize them with specific dishes. For a 25% surcharge, you may order off the menu at Citricos or Narcoossee's. There is also a $75 fee for a private butler, who will meet you in the hotel lobby, guide you to your decorated table, and serve each course. The rain backup location is on the fifth floor breezeway under a wall of windows. It is recommended that you call to arrange your meal about 90 days in advance. Private Dining can also arrange a meal for you onboard the Grand 1 Yacht.

To book a private meal at any of the other **Deluxe resorts**, contact Disney'sCatered Events team (321-939-7278). Although they deal primarily with large groups and high food and beverage minimums, they will also work with individuals to tailor a less expensive affair for two (figure on at least $250 to start). When you call, you will be assigned to a Sales Lead at the Disney resort where you are staying, but you can plan your event for just about anywhere in the World—even inside Epcot during IllumiNations! Most events cannot be booked until 90 days out, but you may contact Disney's Catered Events ahead of time to discuss the options.

The patio of the St. James Room is one of several private-event locations at BoardWalk Inn

Romantic Enhancements

There are a number of ways you can enhance your romantic meal, including special desserts, gifts, and flower arrangements. The most popular enhancement is cake. If you wish to order a cake to be served at a restaurant, call Walt Disney World's **Cake Hotline** at 407-827-2253 at least 72 hours before you plan to dine. If you wish to pick up a custom cake, your only option is BoardWalk Bakery.

The smallest customizable cake is 6 inches and serves 4-6 people, with prices starting at $30; 8-inch cakes start at around $43, and 10-inch cakes start at $50. Fondant-covered cakes start at around $55 and only the Contemporary Resort, the Grand Floridian, the BoardWalk Resort, and the Yacht & Beach Club are equipped to create them. Note that certain resorts may require you to order an 8- or 10-inch cake in order to get fondant and fancy decorations. If you had a Disney's Fairy Tale Wedding and are dining at the Grand Floridian, the resort's bakery can access your BEO to make a 6-inch replica of the top tier of your wedding cake. The Grand Floridian Bakery is also the only one on property to offer **mini-wedding cakes with white chocolate castle toppers**. These single-serving cakes come in three flavors: chocolate cake with dark chocolate mousse, yellow cake with white chocolate mousse, or cheesecake. The price is $30, and the cake is available only to those who are staying or dining at the Grand Floridian. However, both the Grand Floridian and BoardWalk bakeries can create miniature two-tier wedding-style cakes for one or two people—call for details.

If you order a customized cake, be sure to remind the person at the restaurant podium and your server about the cake when you arrive. Payment is usually not due until you get to the restaurant, but in some cases you may be asked to pay when you place your order. Most restaurants offer a previously frozen **6-inch cake** that can be ordered for $21 when you check in for your reservation. These come in vanilla with vanilla filling or chocolate with chocolate filling. They can be personalized with a message but are not otherwise customizable.

The Cake Hotline is also the number to call for delivery of chocolate-covered strawberries, chocolate truffles, fruit and cheese baskets, and assorted other goodies; the selection varies by restaurant location. Additionally, the Cake Hotline handles requests for the chocolate **Cinderella slipper dessert**, which is only available at Cinderella's Royal Table and the restaurants at the Grand Floridian.

To order a cake for a Wishes **cruise**, call Private Dining at the Grand Floridian (407-824-1951). For an IllumiNations cruise, call the Cake Hotline or Private Dining at the Yacht & Beach Club.

If you will be dining at Cinderella's Royal Table, you may also preorder several romantic enhancements to your meal, including themed **champagne flutes** and a crystal Cinderella slipper engraved with a name, a date, and a message of up to 20 characters. For more information, call the restaurant's Special Event Line at (407) 824-4477 or e-mail wdwcrtspecialevents@email.disney.com.

To order a special **floral arrangement** for your meal, contact Walt Disney World Florist at 407-827-3505. They will work with the restaurant to deliver and set up the arrangement.

Romantic Transportation

With all the different transportation options at Walt Disney World, sometimes getting there really is half the fun! Probably the most romantic mode of transport is a **horse-drawn carriage**. Carriage rides are offered at Disney's Fort Wilderness Resort & Campground and Disney's Port Orleans Riverside Resort. The price is $45 for 45 minutes, and you can buy tickets directly from the driver using cash or your Disney resort room charge only—credit cards are not accepted.

Rides are held between the hours of 5:00 pm–10:00 pm nightly, weather permitting. Carriages depart from Crockett's Tavern at Fort Wilderness' Pioneer Hall and in front of Boatwright's Dining Hall at Port Orleans Riverside. You may reserve a ride up to 180 days in advance by calling 407-WDW-PLAY, but there is a $45 fee for no-shows or cancellations less than 24 hours in advance.

Carriage ride at Fort Wilderness

During the month of December, Disney's Wilderness Lodge Resort offers **sleigh rides** at a cost of $60 for a 25-minute ride. These depart every 30 minutes from 5:30 pm–9:30 pm nightly. Call 407-WDW-PLAY to book up to 180 days in advance.

Boats are another romantic mode of transport, and Walt Disney World gives you plenty of opportunity to get out on the water. In addition to the public ferryboats and Friendship Boats that take you between theme parks and resorts, there are numerous private watercraft for rent at Downtown Disney and at the Disney resorts that have marinas: Yacht & Beach Club Resorts, Caribbean Beach Resort, Contemporary Resort, Coronado Springs Resort, Port Orleans Resort, Grand Floridian Resort & Spa, Polynesian Resort, Wilderness Lodge, Fort Wilderness Resort & Campground, and Old Key West Resort.

Even something as simple as a Friendship Boat ride can be romantic

Take a pair of Sea Raycers out for some friendly competition on Disney's waterways

The smaller watercraft are perfect for a couple and include sailboats, pedal boats, canoes, kayaks, and Sea Raycers. Sailboat rental costs $21.30/hour, while pedal boats, kayaks, and canoes cost $6.93 for 30 minutes or $11.72 for 60 minutes. Motorized Sea Raycers cost $34.04 for up to 30 minutes, $42.60 for up to 45 minutes, and $47.93 for up to 60 minutes.

More adventurous couples may wish to try **tandem parasailing** at the Contemporary Resort Marina. The price is $170 for 8 to 10 minutes at 450 feet up and $195 for 10 to 12 minutes at 600 feet up.

Life jackets must be worn on all boats, and guests must present a Walt Disney World resort ID or valid driver's license to rent. You may book up to 180 days in advance by calling 407-WDW-PLAY.

For an extra-special boat ride, you may book a **cruise** on Seven Seas Lagoon during Wishes at the Magic Kingdom or under the International Gateway to see IllumiNations at Epcot. Check out Chapter 5: Additional Events for more information about booking fireworks cruises.

Tandem parasailing

The Magic Kingdom's **trains** can also be romantic even without private seating. Look for a spot in the back and settle in for the Grand Circle Tour.

Romantic Experiences

After the work of planning the wedding is done, the honeymoon provides couples the opportunity to relax and enjoy each other's company. For some, this may involve heavy-duty park touring, but for many, the honeymoon may be the first time they explore Walt Disney World's numerous **leisure** opportunities.

Resort Activities

Check out the activity schedule at your Disney resort and you may find enough to occupy you for a week without leaving the property. The list on the following page shows the kinds of activities found at Disney's Moderate and Deluxe resorts. You do not have to be staying on-site to participate in most of these activities, although **pool hopping** is among the exceptions. Potentially romantic activities are listed in bold!

- ❏ animal feeding
- ❏ arcades
- ❏ architectural tours
- ❏ basketball
- ❏ **beaches**
- ❏ bike rental
- ❏ **butterfly garden**
- ❏ **campfires**
- ❏ crafts
- ❏ croquet
- ❏ cultural tours
- ❏ DVD rental
- ❏ fishing excursions
- ❏ fitness centers
- ❏ games
- ❏ **horseback rides**

- ❏ horseshoes
- ❏ **Jacuzzis**
- ❏ **nature walks**
- ❏ **outdoor movie screenings**
- ❏ parasailing
- ❏ ping-pong
- ❏ **pool**
- ❏ salons
- ❏ shuffleboard
- ❏ **spas**
- ❏ tennis
- ❏ tetherball
- ❏ volleyball
- ❏ wakeboarding
- ❏ **watercraft rental**
- ❏ waterskiing

You might enjoy touring all the different resorts in one day. Or maybe your idea of the perfect honeymoon day is one spent entirely at your resort's pool! Why not stop in at the Polynesian after dinner and take in the Magic Kingdom's fireworks from a hammock on the beach? Or you could roast marshmallows around the campfire at Fort Wilderness, then watch a free Disney movie on the large outdoor screen.

For more ideas, check out the Disney for Romance sub forum on the PassPorter Boards (http://www.passporterboards.com/forums/disney-romance/).

Guided Tours

Although a backstage tour might not be the first thing that springs to mind when you think of romance, it does provide the opportunity to share a special experience—and some of the secrets behind Disney's magic—with your significant other. For instance, after you've been on Epcot's Behind the Seeds tour, whenever you ride Living With the Land, you'll **share the memory** of tasting some of the gorgeous produce that hangs just out of reach of boat-bound guests.

All the parks and many of the resorts offer guided tours. In this section we'll highlight some of the more popular ones, but you can find a complete list with details at http://www.wdwinfo.com/wdwinfo/tours.htm.

The 7-hour **Backstage Magic** tour will give you and your new spouse an insider's knowledge of what goes on behind the scenes at the Magic Kingdom, Epcot, and Disney's Hollywood Studios. The tour costs $224/person and includes lunch.

To see backstage at Disney's Animal Kingdom park, you can take the 3-hour **Backstage Safari** tour for $72/person.

Clocking in at just under 5 hours, the **Keys to the Kingdom** tour is a shorter, cheaper way to see backstage at the Magic Kingdom. The tour costs $74/person and includes lunch.

The previously mentioned **Behind the Seeds** tour at Epcot takes you into the working greenhouses of the Living with the Land ride in Future World to see where some of the park's restaurants get their produce and fish and to learn about Epcot's futuristic growing methods. The price is $16/person, and the tour lasts 1 hour.

View from the Behind the Seeds Tour at Epcot

If you want to get your feet wet, Epcot provides several tours that put you in the water inside the Living Seas Pavilion. The ultimate underwater experience is **Epcot DiveQuest**, a 3-hour tour that includes a 40-minute dive in the pavilion's huge tank. Proof of SCUBA certification is required. The price is $175/person.

Those who are not SCUBA certified may take Epcot's **Seas Aqua Tour**, a 2 1/2-hour excursion that includes 30 minutes in the tank. The price is $140/person, and bathing suits and the ability to swim are the only requirements.

For an up-close-and-personal experience with one of the tank's inhabitants, you can take the 3-hour **Dolphins in Depth** tour. The second half of the tour is spent in waist-deep water interacting with a dolphin, and no swimming or SCUBA diving is required. The price is $194/person and includes a photograph with the dolphin, refreshments, and a T-shirt.

Guided Tours (continued)

Landlubbers may be more interested in Walt Disney World's two Segway tours. The **Around the World at Epcot Segway Tour** will teach you to ride one of the two-wheeled vehicles and then send you on a tour of the World Showcase before it opens to the public. If you were married in the World Showcase, this tour could give you the rare opportunity to spend a few (almost) private moments at the site of your wedding before it opens to day guests! The price is $99/person.

For an off-road experience, there's the **Wilderness Back Trail Adventure Segway Tour**, which takes you on the trails of Fort Wilderness. The price is $85/person. Both Segway tours have a weight limit of 250 pounds.

Guests ride Segways on Epcot's French Island

To book, call 407-WDW-TOUR. There may be **discounts** available for Annual Pass and Disney Visa Card holders and for members of AAA, the Disney Vacation Club, and the military. Most tours require a good deal of walking, and some do not allow photography or videography.

Special-Occasion Photography

Disney offers several ways to **commemorate** your honeymoon at Walt Disney World in pictures. You can have your photo taken by Disney's in-park photographers on the spur of the moment or schedule a private photo shoot at a resort or in the parks using Disney's PhotoPass service, the professional photographers of Disney Event Group Photography, or a local photographer.

Disney's **PhotoPass** is an in-park and online service that allows you to view and buy photos taken by Disney photographers stationed at picturesque theme park locations like Cinderella Castle at the Magic Kingdom.

The first time you have your picture taken, the PhotoPass photographer will hand you a card with a Web address and an ID number. Hand that card to any PhotoPass photographer before he or she takes your picture, and all the images will be stored in the same account for you to view and purchase later. If you happen to end up with multiple cards from different photographers, the images can later be combined within the same account. Once your photos are uploaded, you can add **special effects** like borders, graphics, and characters and have the images printed on a variety of merchandise.

PhotoPass photographers can be found at landmarks like Spaceship Earth

There is **no charge** to have your picture taken by a PhotoPass photographer or to use the cards. Prices for the photos range from $12.95 for a 5x7-inch print to $99.95 for a 16x20-inch gallery-wrapped canvas on a frame, and you can order them from kiosks in the park or online within 30 days of your trip. For $149.95 you can purchase Disney's PhotoCD, containing every photo taken of you by PhotoPass photographers during your trip. Occasionally Disney offers the CD for $99.95 if you pre-order it— check http://www.disneyphotopass.com/previsitoffer.aspx before you leave home.

For more personal attention, you can schedule a 30-minute **private resort photography session** with a PhotoPass photographer at the Beach Club, Grand Floridian, Polynesian, Animal Kingdom Lodge, or Wilderness Lodge. The photo package costs $49.95, and you can choose one of three combinations of prints: two 8x10s and three 5x7s; two 5x7s and four sets of two 4x6s; or seven 5x7s. The $99.95 option gives you your choice of print package plus all images on a PhotoPass CD (anywhere from 40-70 images, depending on the pacing of the session). If you pre-order the PhotoPass CD

The Grand Floridian: popular for private photo shoots

online or purchase it in the parks, the cost of the portrait session is $70 with proof of purchase. Images from the session cannot be enhanced with borders, characters, etc. at the kiosks in the parks, but you can enhance them on the PhotoPass web site when you get home. You can book a private session up to 30 days before you arrive by calling 407-934-4004. Sessions are scheduled from 8:30 am until sunset.

For a private in-park or resort photo shoot, you may book a **Honeymoon or Anniversary Portrait Session** with a professional from Disney Event Group Photography, the department that provides photography for corporate events, and many Disney's Fairy Tale Weddings. The $310 Honeymoon Portrait Session may take place at any Walt Disney World resort or at Epcot, although admission to the park is not included in the price. You will receive a 6x6-inch, soft-cover photo book with 25 images, one 4x6-inch print of every image, and online posting of the images. For $65 you can upgrade to an 8x8-inch, hard-cover photo book. Casual attire is required (i.e., wedding dresses are not allowed) and comfortable walking shoes are recommended. To schedule a portrait session, call 407-827-5099.

Or, for the ultimate in-park photography experience, you may schedule a **Theme Park Bridal Portrait Session** in your wedding attire at Epcot, Disney's Hollywood Studios, or Disney's Animal Kingdom before the park opens. The cost is $650 for 12 5x7-inch prints in an album and a 4x6-inch print of every image. The same package is available at both of Disney's water parks, where it goes by the name "Trash the Dress." Expect to get wet!

If you're interested in a photojournalistic style of photography or more flexibility with package options, you may want to consider hiring your own photographer for a resort photo shoot. Many local **wedding photographers** offer relatively inexpensive engagement photo sessions that would also be perfect for couples celebrating their honeymoon or anniversary. To learn more about finding your own photographer, check out "How to Find Your Own Vendors" on page 122 of Chapter 3: Wishes Collection.

Spa Experiences

Visiting one of Walt Disney World's spas can be a great way to relax and indulge during your honeymoon. Although most spa services are designed for individuals, the Grand Floridian Spa and Saratoga Springs Spa offer two kinds of **couple's massages**. The Grand Floridian's Grand Romantic Couple's Massage includes aromatherapy and costs $275 for 50 minutes or $375 for 80 minutes. A 180-minute Couple's Instructional Massage gives you and your partner step-by-step instruction in massage techniques and costs $300. Saratoga Springs Spa offers a Couples Aromatherapy Massage at $270 for 50 minutes or $380 for 80 minutes, plus a Couples Relaxation Package for $400.

Both the Grand Floridian and Saratoga Springs offer **in-room** Swedish massage services, which would allow you to be together as one partner receives a massage. The price is $160 for 50 minutes or $210 for 80 minutes. Alternatively, you could book simultaneous individual treatments at the spa. Although men's and women's locker room areas are separate at these facilities, Saratoga Springs Spa and Mandara Spa at the Swan & Dolphin Resort have common waiting areas where couples can relax together.

The Grand Floridian Spa

To book, call the Grand Floridian Spa at 407-824-2332 or the Saratoga Springs Spa at 407-827-4455. You can view complete **treatment menus** for both spas at http://www.relaxedyet.com. More information on Mandara Spa is available at http://www.swandolphin.com/activities/spa.html.

The Grand Floridian Spa offers clothing and skin care products for sale in its lobby

Save a trip to the parks by ordering a gift basket with bride and groom mouse ears

Treats & Gifts

To have a cake, chocolate truffles, or other **sweet treat** delivered to your room, contact Private Dining at your Disney resort to see what they offer; the selection varies by resort. For resorts that do not offer full room service, you

An arrangement by Disney Floral & Gifts

may be able to arrange a cake through the food court kitchen—call Walt Disney World's Cake Hotline at 407-827-2253 to see if your resort is among those listed. Alternatively, you can special order a cake for pick-up at BoardWalk Bakery. Call the resort at (407) 939-5100 and ask to be transferred to the bakery.

Disney Floral & Gifts will deliver **floral arrangements** and gift baskets to your room after you've checked in. Among the offerings in the "Romance and Anniversary" category are a glass slipper and tiara on a pillow, a bottle of sparkling wine and bride and groom mouse ears, and a sprinkling of rose petals for the bed. Call 407-827-3505 or visit http://www.disneyflorist.com. You can also arrange for delivery by national services such as 1-800-FLOWERS, Teleflora, and Edible Arrangements—potentially at lower prices than Disney's.

Another option is Memories By Betsy (http://memoriesbybetsy.com), a local vendor who will deliver a range of standard and custom **gift baskets** to your resort.

And if you're having trouble coming up with ideas on your own, Presentations: Gifts of a Lifetime can provide **magical moments** ranging from decorating your hotel room to devising an elaborate treasure hunt through the theme parks. Their "pixies" will also make surprise deliveries of flowers or gifts on rides and arrange for a professional photographer to follow you around for the day so you don't have to worry about taking pictures. Check out http://giftsofalifetime.com for more information.

Honeymoon To Do List

❑

❑

❑

❑

❑

❑

❑

❑

❑

❑

❑

❑

❑

❑

❑

❑

❑

Chapter 9

Honeymoons & Anniversaries on the Disney Cruise Line

For many people, a cruise is the ideal honeymoon getaway—the **perfect combination** of comfort and convenience with sun, surf, and sand. Disney brings its own brand of magic to popular cruise itineraries, including the same world-class hospitality found at the Disney theme parks and resorts. And while the Disney Cruise Line is known for being kid-friendly, adults will find plenty of areas and experiences reserved exclusively for them.

Simply being on a cruise can be romantic, but in this chapter we've gathered suggestions for making your honeymoon or anniversary cruise extra special. Although the terminology is geared toward honeymoons, any of the ideas presented here would be a great addition to an **anniversary or engagement** trip.

First we'll take a look at the romance package offered by the Disney Cruise Line, along with **onboard amenities** geared toward adults.

This section will also cover romantic spa experiences and the options for having treats and gifts delivered to your stateroom.

Last, we'll highlight a few **shore excursions** at each port that offer a chance to spend quality time with your partner as you explore or just relax.

The Disney Magic visits St. Thomas

Onboard Amenities

Despite the Disney Cruise Line's reputation as catering exclusively to families, there are actually many onboard amenities reserved just for **adults**.

The **Quiet Cove Pool** is accessible only to those 18 and older. The pool area includes two whirlpool spas, a bar, and the adults-only coffeehouse Cove Café.

The equivalent of one of Walt Disney World's Signature restaurants, adults-only **Palo** offers fine Northern Italian cuisine and upscale atmosphere, making it the perfect spot for a romantic dinner, brunch, or high tea. There is a supplement of $15/person, and jeans, shorts, swimwear, and tank tops are prohibited.

Wine buffs may be interested in the **Stem to Stern Wine Tasting**, an hour-long seminar that features five wines and one sparkling wine or Champagne. The price is $12/person, and reservations can be made onboard at Guest Services.

Disney Magic Adult Pool

Both Disney cruise ships have an adults-only **entertainment district** on Deck 3: Beat Street on the Disney Magic, and Route 66 on the Disney Wonder. The Magic's Sessions and the Wonder's Cadillac Lounge offer drinks, hors d'oeuvres, and, in the evening, live piano music. Rockin' Bar D (Magic) and WaveBands (Wonder) become adults-only dance clubs after 9:00 pm that feature cabaret shows, karaoke, salsa lessons, and theme nights like the '60s Dance Party, the '70s Disco Night, and the '80s Time Warp Party.

Rockin' Bar D on the Disney Magic

Spa Experiences

The **adults-only** Vista Spa & Salon can be found on both ships and offers a variety of services, including massages, manicures, pedicures, facials, hair cuts and color, and body treatments. Appointments for most services can be pre-booked online at http://www.disneycruise.com.

The Swedish Massage for **couples** includes the use of aromatherapy oils and costs $242. Couples can also book a Cabana Massage on Castaway Cay for $294. The popular Exotic Rasul treatment lets you apply your own exfoliating mud treatment in a special room with sitting area, steam room, and shower. The price is $89 for 50 minutes.

You can also select from a variety of couples spa packages in your own **Spa Villa**. These private treatment rooms are designed for singles or couples and have their own verandahs, whirlpool tubs, open-air showers, and lounge beds. Every Spa Villa treatment package includes a tea ceremony, a bathing ritual, and a foot-cleansing ceremony, plus extra time alone before and after the treatments.

The $449 Romantic Hideaway package includes a 50-minute spa treatment of your choice and lasts 2 hours. For $475, the 130-minute Couples Choice package includes a 75-minute spa treatment.

Vista Spa's Tropical Rainforest

© Jennifer Marx

Among your **treatment choices** are Elemis Aroma Stone Therapy, the Elemis Exotic Lime & Ginger Salt Glow with half body massage, and the Exotic Frangipani Body Nourish Wrap with half body massage. The 150-minute Ultimate Indulgence package costs $589 and includes a facial and a deep tissue massage.

You may also purchase passes to use the spa's **Tropical Rainforest** of steam rooms, heated loungers, and scented showers. The price is $16 per day, or $9 on each day that you have also booked a "hands-on" spa service. Unlimited-use passes cost $42 for 3-night cruises, $59 for 4-night cruises, and $99 for 7-night cruises. Passes cannot be pre-booked online, but if you are having a Cruise Collection wedding or vow renewal, your Wedding Coordinator can book them for you in advance.

Treats & Gifts

As at Walt Disney World, you may arrange delivery of a number of **fun extras** aboard the Disney Cruise Line. These include floral arrangements, candy, gourmet food, wine and Champagne, gift baskets, party decorations, and even mini-Christmas trees! The full list can be found in the Planning Center section of the web site at http://disneycruise.disney.go.com/planning-center/gifts-and-amenities.

Orders must be placed **before sailing**—no inventory is kept onboard, so you will not be able to order these gifts once you are on the ship. Your order will be put in your stateroom on embarkation day. The cutoff times for ordering are listed below.

Champagne and chocolate-covered strawberries

Sailing Day	Order By
Sunday	Friday at noon
Thursday	Wednesday at noon
Saturday	Friday noon

Items may be ordered by **phone** (800-601-8455 or 407-566-7000) from 8:00 am-10:00 pm EST Monday-Friday, and from 9:00 am-8:00 pm EST Saturday and Sunday. You may also download the order form found on the web site and fax it to 407-938-4288. For e-mail inquiries, contact dclgifts@disneycruise.com. Sales tax is assessed at 6% when trips originate from Port Canaveral, and there is VAT for sailings from Barcelona and Dover. A 15% gratuity is added to the price of wine and Champagne.

You may also use approved outside vendor The Perfect Gift (http://www.theperfectgift.cc/) for delivery of floral arrangements and gift baskets. There is a $14/item delivery fee.

 What Happened to the Romantic Escape at Sea Package?
In years past the Disney Cruise Line has offered an add-on package that included turndown service, dinner at Palo, breakfast in bed, and passes to the Tropical Rain Forest—basically one-stop shopping for anyone looking to add a little romance to a cruise. However, at press time, this package was not available for 2011 sailings.

Shore Excursions

Each of the ports visited by the Disney Cruise Line offers myriad activities, including organized excursions available for a fee and free pastimes like shopping and exploring. Complete descriptions of every port and shore excursion are available in *PassPorter's Disney Cruise Line and Its Ports of Call*, so in this section we'll focus on those that offer the potential for romance, adventure, or just some quality time together.

Castaway Cay

Disney's private island features a beach just for adults, called **Serenity Bay**. You can relax on the sand, grab a drink at the Castaway Air Bar, have lunch at the Air Bar BBQ, or get a solo or couples massage in an open-air cabana.

If you're interested in something a little **more active**, check out the Walking & Kayak Nature Adventure. This three-hour excursion includes a 45-minute guided walk with a lesson on the history of the Bahamas, a one-hour kayak tour, and 30 minutes of swimming and relaxing on a secluded beach open only to your group. The price is $64/person.

Serenity Bay is open to adults only

For even more activity, try the self-guided Extreme Getaway Package, which includes snorkel equipment rental, one-hour bike rental, float or tube rental, and participation in Castaway Ray's Stingray Adventure, where you'll snorkel in Stingray Lagoon and **feed rays** by hand. The Extreme Getaway Package costs $54/person.

Boat rentals and parasailing are another fun way to get time alone on Castaway Cay. Thirty-minute rentals cost $15 for an Aqua Fin, $10 for a two-seat Sea Kayak, $18 for a Hobie Cat, $15 for an Aqua Trike, $8 for a two-seat Paddle Boat, and $20 for a Sun Kat. A two-seat Wave Runner costs $160 for a 45-minute ride. Parasailing costs $79/person for a 45-minute excursion, with five to seven minutes in the air at 600-1,000 feet. The weight limit is 375 pounds for solo and tandem flights, and you may be required by the captain to fly tandem.

Hobie Cats on the beach

Nassau

One of the most popular shore excursions at this port is the Blue Lagoon Island Dolphin Encounter. For $125/person you'll be transported by catamaran to Blue Lagoon Island for an 20-minute encounter with a Pacific Bottlenose **dolphin**. Use of a private beach is included in the price, and photos and videos of your encounter are available to purchase. For $295/person you can have a similar

dolphin encounter plus admission to the Atlantis resort's 141-acre water park on the Atlantis Dolphin Cay & Aquaventure shore excursion. A light lunch and access to the resort's private beaches, casino, and shopping village are included.

Swim with dolphins, shop, or dine at Atlantis

Foodies may prefer to spend the day on the Graycliff Hotel Wine and Cheese Pairing excursion. For $189/person, you'll taste four red and four white **wines** paired with cheeses from around the world, tour one of the largest private collections of fine and rare wines in the world, and receive a wine-themed souvenir. Afterward, you are welcome to stay for a meal for two at the colonial mansion's restaurant (at an additional cost).

You may also choose to explore Nassau on your own for free. Although they are located on the grounds of the One&Only Ocean Club resort, the **Versailles Gardens** and Cloisters are open to the public. Located on Paradise Island, about a 15-minute walk from Atlantis or a short taxi ride from the dock, the gardens boast statuary, fountains, waterfalls, and reflecting pools. The Greco-Gothic monastery was purchased by William Randolph Hearst in France and sold to A&P heir Huntington Hartford, who had the cloisters reassembled in the Versailles Gardens in 1962. There is no admission charge to visit the gardens or the cloisters.

St. Maarten/St. Martin

No matter how you spell it, the port of St. Maarten/St. Martin offers plenty for honeymooners to do. For $89/person, the Rhino Rider & Snorkeling Adventure sends you across Simpson Bay in an inflatable **boat for two**, followed by 30 minutes of swimming and snorkeling. Afterward you can relax on the beach with a complimentary beverage.

Nature lovers might enjoy the St. Maarten Island & Butterfly Farm Tour, a narrated bus tour of the island with a stop at the French Quarter's **Butterfly Farm**. The price is $38/person.

If money is no object, consider The Ultimate Charter Choice, a private **luxury yacht** available for up to 8 1/2 hours that includes lunch, snorkel equipment, and the services of a Captain and a First Mate. The price is $1,599 for up to 10 people.

St. Thomas/St. John

What could be more romantic than a Skyride to **Paradise Point**? For $18/person, you'll get a ride on the Paradise Point Tramway to see the island from 700 feet up. Before you descend, check out the scenic nature trail, the wedding gazebo, thrice-daily performances by exotic birds, or the shops.

If you prefer to remain at sea level, try the St. John **Eco Hike**, a guided 1 1/2-mile forest excursion with a stop for swimming at Honeymoon Beach and a tour of the historic Caneel Bay Plantation. The cost is $69/person for this five-hour experience.

And if you'd rather stick close to your floating home, the **Butterfly Anytime** excursion takes place just a three-minute walk from the pier, in the heart of St. Thomas. After an up-close-and-personal encounter with the Butterfly Farm's denizens, you can explore the grounds' tropical landscaping and water features. The cost is $15/person.

Key West

For a fun twist on the usual guided city tour, check out the **GPS Walking Tour** of Key West's most famous landmarks and hidden gems. You'll be given a GPS and instructions on how to use it before embarking on a designated path or one of your own choosing. The GPS map will play video with fun facts and further information at each featured destination. When you return to the starting point to turn in your GPS, you'll receive a complimentary beverage at Pat Croce's Rum Barrel. The price is $29/person.

If you've always wanted to **scuba dive** but don't have a certification, the Snuba Key West excursion will give you a feel for the experience. You'll breath through a scuba regulator attached to an air tank that floats on a raft at the surface, allowing you to explore as much as 20 feet underwater without wearing dive gear. The ratio of guests to dive master is 6-to-1, and you'll receive a complete safety briefing and practice time before you set off on your own. The cost is $109/person, and there are numerous health restrictions—check out the complete excursion description on http://www.disneycruise.com before you pre-book.

Grand Cayman

Like St. Maarten, Grand Cayman offers an $84/person **Aquaboat & Snorkel Adventure**, which is like the Rhino Rider & Snorkeling Adventure. For $39/person, you can snorkel around a shipwreck and explore a tropical reef.

The Dolphin Encounter & Turtle Farm excursion offers something you don't get at every port—a chance to see **sea turtles**! After a 30-minute encounter with a dolphin, you'll have 45 minutes to explore the Cayman Turtle Farm.

Or, if you just want to relax, try the Seven Mile Beach Break, which includes transportation to one of Grand Cayman's gorgeous beaches, a beverage, and a beach chair. The price is $36/person.

Cozumel

Adventure awaits active honeymooners in Cozumel. Gallop into the past on the Mayan Frontier **Horseback Riding** Tour, a four-hour excursion through small replicas of Mayan ruins and a visit to a working ranch. The price is $89/person, and the tour is restricted to those between the ages of 12 and 65.

For $88/person you can try the Speed Boat Beach Escape, which gives you and your partner a chance to cruise the waters off Barracuda Beach in a two-person **speedboat**. After your hour-long ride, you can relax on the beach or join a volleyball game before your 20-minute taxi ride back to the pier.

Or leave the navigating to someone else—Cozumel is another port where you can book a Luxury Yacht Charter. You'll enjoy a four-hour private tour of the coast and a stop at a secluded sand bar, where you'll have a 20-minute break for swimming before you continue on to one of Cozumel's finest beaches for snorkeling, more swimming, and sunbathing. The package includes the services of a captain and a guide aboard the 46-foot motor-powered **yacht**, use of two cabins with surround-sound stereos and bathrooms with showers, plus snacks, and open bar, and a lunch of fresh lobster. The price is $1,999 for up to 10 people.

Tortola

Like St. Croix, Tortola offers a number of activities similar to those at other ports. If you missed your chance to swim with **dolphins** ($159/person), enjoy an eco hike ($45/person), or take in a mountain-top view ($39/person) earlier in your trip, Tortola can help you make up for lost time. It's also the place to live in the lap of luxury, either on your own yacht or in a private villa for the day. For more information and pricing, e-mail dcl.shore.excursions@disney.com.

Meet a dolphin in Tortola

Chapter 10

Planning Pages

The worksheets on the following pages are customized for weddings, vow renewals, and commitment ceremonies at Walt Disney World and on the Disney Cruise Line. Planning pages specific to Escape, Cruise, and Wishes/Couture Collection events are grouped together, followed by a group of worksheets applicable to all events. Use them to track your plans, keep information organized and accessible, create to-do lists, and capture ideas as inspiration strikes.

This Book Is Evolving!

If you have suggestions for improving the functionality of these planning pages or an idea for an additional worksheet that would be helpful when planning an event, please send us an e-mail at weddingsandhoneymoons@passporter.com.

To Do

Tasks	To Do	Done

To Do

Tasks	To Do	Done

Escape Collection Event Overview

Wedding Consultant:_____

Phone:_____ E-mail:_____

Wedding Services Coordinator:_____

Phone:_____ E-mail:_____

Cell:_____ Best Time to Contact:_____

Disney Resort Reservation #:_____

Deposit
Amount:_____ Date Due:_____

Date Sent:_____ Date Received:_____

Final BEO
Date Received:_____ Date Due:_____

Date Sent:_____ Date Received:_____

Balance
Amount:_____ Date Due:_____

Date Sent:_____ Date Received:_____

Ceremony Location:_____

Date:_____ Time:_____ # of Guests:_____

Reception Location:_____

Time:_____ ADR #:_____

# of Guests:_____ Contact:_____

Phone:_____ E-mail:_____

Escape Collection Event Overview (continued)

Rehearsal Dinner/Welcome Party

Date:_____ Location:_____

Time:_____ ADR#:_____

# of Guests:_____ Contact:_____

Phone:_____ E-mail:_____

Dessert Party

Date:_____ Location:_____

Time:_____ # of Guests:_____ # of Viewing Fees:_____

Bridal Portrait Session

Date:_____ Time:_____

Pick-up Time:_____ Sunrise:_____

Contact:_____ Phone:_____

E-mail:_____

After-hours Contact:_____ Phone _____

Notes:

Escape Collection Budget

This budget is broken into two main sections, one for the charges paid to Disney's Fairy Tale Weddings and one for additional expenses. A third section adds up the grand totals of these two to show the overall cost of your event. Enter each item's cost in the Price column, multiply it by 6.5% tax (if applicable) and place the result in the Tax column. Food and beverages also receive a taxable service fee, so these have a fourth column in the row. The rate is 21% if paid to Disney's Fairy Tale Weddings and 18%-21% elsewhere. We've left blank rows so you can include additional expenses in each category.

Disney's Fairy Tale Weddings Expenses

Item	Price	Tax/Gratuity	
Escape Package Fee		n/a	
Extra Beverages			
Cake Upgrade			
Extra Floral			
Additional Transportation		n/a	
Additional Photography		n/a	
Entertainment		n/a	
Dessert Party			
Subtotals			
GRAND TOTAL			

Additional Expenses

Item	Price	Tax/Gratuity	
Meals:			
Reception			
Rehearsal Dinner			
Attire:			
Bridal Gown & Accessories			
Alterations			
Formalwear Rental			
Gown Steaming			

Item	Price	Tax/Gratuity
Outside Vendors:		
Photography		
Videography		
Floral		
Officiant		
Travel Expenses:		
Flight		
Accommodations		
Rental Car		
Meals		
Miscellaneous:		
Invitations & Postage		
Rings		
Cosmetology		
Welcome Bags		
Favors		
Attendants' Gifts		
Tips		
License		
Subtotals		
GRAND TOTAL		

Disney's Fairy Tale Weddings Expenses	
Additional Expenses	
TOTAL EVENT COST	

Escape/Cruise Collection Music

This chart will help you compile your song requests and note which ones require sheet music for the musician.

Event	Song(s)	Composer/Album	Sheet music?
Prelude/ Seating			
Family's Entrance			
Officiant & Groomsmen Entrance			
Groom's Entrance			
Bridesmaids' Entrance			
Bride's Entrance			
Unity Ceremony			
Recessional			
First Dance			
Father-Daughter Dance			
Mother-Son Dance			
Cake Cutting			

Cruise Collection Event Overview

Wedding Consultant: _____

Phone: _____ E-mail: _____

Cell : _____ Best Time to Contact: _____

Guest Services Groups Manager (onboard): _____

Phone: _____

Disney Cruise Confirmation #: _____

Deposit

Amount: _____ Date Due: _____

Date Sent: _____ Date Received: _____

Balance

Amount: _____ Date Due: _____

Date Sent: _____ Date Received: _____

DFTW Confirmation Letter received: _____

Ceremony Location: _____

Date: _____ Time: _____ # of Guests: _____

Palo Reservation

Date: _____ Time: _____

Walt Disney World Bridal Portrait Session

Date: _____ Time: _____

Pick-up Time: _____ Sunrise: _____

Contact: _____ Phone: _____

E-mail: _____

After-hours Contact: _____ Phone _____

Cruise Collection Budget

This budget is broken into two main sections, one for the charges paid to Disney's Fairy Tale Weddings and one for additional expenses. A third section adds up the grand totals of these two to show the overall cost of your event. Enter each item's cost in the Price column, multiply it by 7% tax (if applicable) and place the result in the Tax column. Food and beverages also receive a taxable service fee, so these have a fourth column in the row. The rate is 15% if paid to Disney's Fairy Tale Weddings. We've left blank rows so you can include additional expenses in each category.

Disney's Fairy Tale Weddings Expenses

Item	Price	Tax/Gratuity	
Cruise Collection Package Fee		n/a	
Extra Beverages			
Cake Upgrade			
Extra Floral			
Photography		n/a	
Entertainment		n/a	
Walt Disney World Bridal Portrait		n/a	
Additional Guest Fee		n/a	
Subtotals			
GRAND TOTAL			

Additional Expenses

Item	Price	Tax/Gratuity	
Meals:			
Additional Palo Guest Fees			
Attire:			
Bridal Gown & Accessories			
Alterations			
Formalwear Rental/Purchase			

Item	Price	Tax/Gratuity
Outside Vendors:		
Photography		
Videography		
Floral		
Travel Expenses:		
Flight		
Accommodations		
Rental Car		
Meals		
Miscellaneous:		
Invitations & Postage		
Rings		
Cosmetology		
Welcome Bags		
Favors		
Attendants' Gifts		
Tips		
Subtotals		
GRAND TOTAL		

Disney's Fairy Tale Weddings Expenses	
Additional Expenses	
TOTAL EVENT COST	

Cruise Guest Travel Information

Make as many copies of this worksheet as you need to keep track of all your guests' travel information, including their flight numbers and method of transportation to the ship.

Name:	
Confirmation #:	
Arrival Date:	
Time:	
Flight #:	
Transportation:	
Stateroom #:	
Departure Date:	
Time:	
Flight #:	
Transportation:	

Name:	
Confirmation #:	
Arrival Date:	
Time:	
Flight #:	
Transportation:	
Stateroom #:	
Departure Date:	
Time:	
Flight #:	
Transportation:	

Cruise Collection Guest Travel Information (continued)

Name:	
Confirmation #:	
Arrival Date:	
Time:	
Flight #:	
Transportation:	
Stateroom #:	
Departure Date:	
Time:	
Flight #:	
Transportation:	

Name:	
Confirmation #:	
Arrival Date:	
Time:	
Flight #:	
Transportation:	
Stateroom #:	
Departure Date:	
Time:	
Flight #:	
Transportation:	

Wishes/Couture Event Overview

Event Date: _____

Wedding Consultant: _____

Phone: _____ E-mail: _____

Wedding Event Planner: _____

Phone: _____ E-mail: _____

Cell : _____ Best Time to Contact: _____

Event Planner's Assistant: _____

Phone: _____ E-mail: _____

Deposit
Amount: _____ Date Due: _____

Date Sent: _____ Date Received: _____

Final BEO
Date Received: _____ Date Due: _____

Date Sent: _____ Date Received: _____

Balance
Amount: _____ Date Due: _____

Date Sent: _____ Date Received: _____

Ceremony
Location: _____ Time: _____

Pre-Reception
Location: _____ Time: _____

Reception
Location: _____ Time: _____

Wishes/Couture Event Overview (continued)

Dessert Party

Date: _____ Location: _____

Time: _____ # of Guests: _____ # of Viewing Fees: _____

Rehearsal Dinner/Welcome Party

Date: _____ Location: _____

Time: _____ ADR#: _____

# of Guests: _____ Contact: _____

Phone: _____ E-mail: _____

Bridal Tea

Date: _____ Location: _____

Time: _____ ADR#: _____

# of Guests: _____ Contact: _____

Phone: _____ E-mail: _____

Farewell Brunch

Date: _____ Location: _____

Time: _____ ADR#: _____

# of Guests: _____ Contact: _____

Phone: _____ E-mail: _____

Bridal Portrait Session

Date: _____ Time: _____

Pick-up Time: _____ Sunrise: _____

Contact: _____ Phone: _____

E-mail: _____

After-hours Contact: _____ Phone: _____

Room Block Worksheet

Use this worksheet to compile the information you need to fill in the Room Block form sent by your Wedding Consultant. He or she can tell you the minimum number of room nights you are required to fill.

Room-Night Minimum: _____

Resort & Room Type	Date	Day of the Week	# of Rooms
Resort:			
Room Type:			
Resort:			
Room Type:			
Resort:			
Room Type:			
Resort:			
Room Type:			
Total # Room Nights			

Complimentary Room Night

Resort: _____ Date: _____

Site Visit Worksheet

Date: _____ Time: _____ Contact: _____

Phone: _____ Meeting Place: _____

Venue:

Min. Capacity: Max. Capacity:

Venue Rental Fee:

Food & Beverage Minimum:

Buffet or Plated Menu?

# of Tables and Sizes:

Dance Floor?

Restroom Location:

Parking Location:

Notes:

Venue:

Min. Capacity: Max. Capacity:

Venue Rental Fee:

Food & Beverage Minimum:

Buffet or Plated Menu?

# of Tables and Sizes:

Dance Floor?

Restroom Location:

Parking Location:

Notes:

Planning Session Checklist

Date:	Time:

Items to Bring	✔

Questions to Ask	✔

Important Wedding Dates and Information

At your planning session, your Wedding Event Planner will print out an Important Wedding Dates and Information sheet listing the vital statistics of your event and the deadlines for making certain decisions or returning information. You can transfer that information to this worksheet to keep everything in one place.

Wedding Name _____

Wedding Event Manager _____

Wedding Date _____

GMR # _____

Contracted Minimum Room Nights _____

Room Block Cut-off Date _____

Comp. Room Location _____

Dining Reservations Available Beginning _____

Minimum Expenditure Payment Due Date _____

Entertainment Changes Deadline _____

Floral Changes Deadline _____

Wedding Cake Style Deadline _____

Wedding Cake Guest Count Deadline _____

Table Assignments (if using escort cards) _____

Food/Beverage Guest Count Deadline _____

Minimum Expenditure Payment Due Date _____

Final Payment Due Date _____

Wishes/Couture Collection Budget

Enter each item's cost in the Price column and (if applicable) the 21% gratuity amount will appear in the Service Fee column. Calculate Orange County sales tax of 6.5% on the total price including service fee (except for Disney audiovisual services, which receive no tax on the service fee) and place it in the Tax column. If an item provided by Disney on the day of your event counts toward your overall minimum expenditure, it is shaded pink and will be tallied in the minimum expenditure box at the end.

Item	Price	Service Fee	Tax	Total
Attire:				
Bridal Gown				
Alterations				
Accessories				
Groom's Formalwear				
Gown Steaming				
Cosmetology:				
Hair				
Makeup				
Trial				
Bridal Portrait Hair & Makeup				
Transportation:				
Bridal Couple				
Bridal Party & Family				
Guests				
Specialty Transportation				
Ceremony:				
Venue Rental Fee				
Ceremony Audio Package				
Entertainment				

Item	Price	Service Fee	Tax	Total
Reception:				
Venue Rental Fee		███		
Wedding Cake				
Groom's Cake/Sheet Cake				
Pre-Reception Menu (___ @ $____ each)				
Bar Package/BOC				
Soft Drink & Water Package/BOC (___ @ $____ each)				
Bartender Fee		███		
Reception Meal (___ @ $____ each)				
Kids Meal (___ @ $____ each)				
Champagne/Cider Toast (___ @ $____ each)				
Specialty Dessert (___ @ $____ each)				
Vendor Meal (___ @ $____ each)				
DJ/Band/iPod Audio Package				
Outside Vendor DJ/Band Staging Fee		███	███	
Entertainment		███	███	
Personal Floral:				
Bridal Bouquet		███		
Groom's Boutonniere		███		
Bridesmaids Bouquets (___ @ $____ each)		███		
Groomsmen/Family Boutonnieres (___ @ $____ each)		███		
Family Corsages (___ @ $____ each)		███		
Flower Girl Basket/Petals/Wand		███		
		███		

Item	Price	Service Fee	Tax	Total
Ceremony Floral & Decor:				
Altar Arrangement				
Pew/Aisle Decor (___ @ $____ each)				
Aisle Runner				
Aisle Petals				
Toss Petals				
Vase/Column/etc. Rental				
Unity Candle/Sand Ceremony				
Presentation Floral (___ @ $____ each)				
Chuppah				
Chuppah Decor				
Chair Covers (___ @ $____ each)				
Specialty Chairs (___ @ $____ each)				
Specialty Chair Delivery Fee				
Reception Floral & Decor:				
Ceremony Floral Move Fee				
Sweetheart/Head Table Floral				
Guest Book Table Floral				
Cake Table Floral				
Cake Floral				
Centerpieces (___ @ $____ each)				
Toss bouquet				
Upgraded Place Settings (___ @ $____ each)				
Upgraded Linens (___ @ $____ each)				
Table Overlays (___ @ $____ each)				
Chair Covers (___ @ $____ each)				
Specialty Chairs (___ @ $____ each)				
Specialty Chair Delivery Fee				

Item	Price	Service Fee	Tax	Total
Landscaping Package				
Gobos (___ @ $____ each)				
Vase/Column/etc. Rental				
Favors (___ @ $____ each)				
Guest Book				
Place Cards (___ @ $____ each)				
Menus (___ @ $____ each)				
Misc. Floral:				
Bridal Portrait Floral Refresh				
Floral Preservation				
Photography: (tax=$0 unless photos are delivered in Florida)				
Package				
High-Res Disc				
In-Park Bridal Portrait Session				
Videography: (tax=$0 unless video is delivered in Florida)				
Package				
Dessert Party:				
Venue Rental Fee				
Viewing Fees (___ @ $____ each)				
Dessert Menu (___ @ $____ each)				
Beverage Package/BOC (___ @ $____ each)				
Set-up Fee				
Event Guide				
Floral & Decor				
Photography				
Guest Transportation				
Bridal Couple Transportation				

Item	Price	Service Fee	Tax	Total
Welcome/Rehearsal Dinner:				
Dinner Menu (___ @ $___ each)				
Beverage Package/BOC (___ @ $___ each)				
Floral & Decor				
Floral Delivery Fee				
Bridal Tea:				
Menu (___ @ $___ each)				
Beverage Package/BOC (___ @ $___ each)				
Cake				
Entertainment				
Floral & Decor				
Miscellaneous:				
Invitations				
Postage				
Marriage License				
Officiant Fee				
Rings				
Welcome Bags				
Attendants' Gifts				
Tips				

Disney's Fairy Tale Weddings Minimum Expenditure	
Tax & Service Fee on Minimum Expenditure Items	
All Other Expenses	
TOTAL EVENT COST	

Transportation Schedules

Bridal Couple			
Ceremony			
Bride Pick-up Location	Time	Groom Pick-up Location	Time
Photos			
Pick-up Location		Time	
Reception			
Pick-up Location		Time	

Bridal Party			
Ceremony			
Bridesmaids Pick-up Location	Time	Groomsmen Pick-up Location	Time
Family Pick-up Location	Time	Family Pick-up Location	Time
Reception			
Pick-up Location		Time	

Guests			
Ceremony			
Resort Pick-up Location	Time	Resort Pick-up Location	Time
Resort Pick-up Location	Time	Resort Pick-up Location	Time
Reception			
Pick-up Location		Time	

Ceremony Music Selections

This chart will help you compile your song selections. There is space to note whether you will need to provide sheet music for the musician(s) or a recording so the song may be played on a sound system.

Event	Song(s)	Composer/Album	Music/ Disc?
Prelude/Seating			
Family's Entrance			
Officiant & Groomsmen Entrance			
Groom's Entrance			
Bridesmaids' Entrance			
Bride's Entrance			
Unity Ceremony			
Recessional			
Postlude			

Menu Information

Type of Meal:	
Number of adults:	Cost per adult:
Number of children:	Cost per child:

Pre-reception Menu Name:

Appetizers:

Reception Menu Name:

Appetizers:

Salad:

Soup:

Sorbet Course:

Entrée(s)/Action Stations:

Desserts:

Kids' Menu:

Beverage Information

Package Bar

Package	# of Guests	Length of Service	Cost per Person

Bill on Consumption

To estimate the cost per person, use Disney's formula of two drinks for the first hour and one for each subsequent hour. Do not include guests under age 21 when calculating the cost of alcoholic beverages.

Drink	Price	Length of Service	Cost per Person

By the Bottle

Drink	Price per Bottle	# of Bottles	Total

Bring Your Own

The service fee is 21% of what Disney would charge for each beverage you bring.

Drink	Corkage Fee	# of Cans/ Bottles	Service Fee	Total

Cake Information

Cake Style Name:	
Number of Guests:	
Price Per Person:	
Topper/Fresh Floral Price:	
Service Charge/Handling Fee:	
Total Cost:	

	Cake Flavor	Filling
Layer 1 (top)		
Layer 2		
Layer 3		
Layer 4		
Layer 5		
Special Instructions:		

Sheet Cake/Groom's Cake

Size	Cake Flavor	Filling
Special Instructions:		

Reception Table Assignments

Table #/Name	Guest Name	Meal Preference
	1.	
	2.	
	3.	
	4.	
	5.	
	6.	
	7.	
	8.	
	9.	
	10.	
	1.	
	2.	
	3.	
	4.	
	5.	
	6.	
	7.	
	8.	
	9.	
	10.	
	1.	
	2.	
	3.	
	4.	
	5.	
	6.	
	7.	
	8.	
	9.	
	10.	

Reception Table Assignments (continued)

Table #/Name	Guest Name	Meal Preference
	1.	
	2.	
	3.	
	4.	
	5.	
	6.	
	7.	
	8.	
	9.	
	10.	
	1.	
	2.	
	3.	
	4.	
	5.	
	6.	
	7.	
	8.	
	9.	
	10.	
	1.	
	2.	
	3.	
	4.	
	5.	
	6.	
	7.	
	8.	
	9.	
	10.	

DJ Information

Reception Location:
Room Name:
Reception Start/End Times:
Number of Guests:
Photographer's Name:
Videographer's Name:
DJ to Introduce Wedding Party?   Yes ☐   No ☐
Wedding Party Names (spelled phonetically)
Bridesmaid #1:
Groomsman #1:
Bridesmaid #2:
Groomsman #2:
Bridesmaid #3:
Groomsman #3:
Bridesmaid #4:
Groomsman #4:
Bridesmaid #5:
Groomsman #5:
Flower Girl:
Ring Bearer:
Maid of Honor:
Best Man:
Bride:
Groom:
First Dance Song Title and Artist:
Who Will Give the Toast?
Who Will Give the Blessing?
Preferred Style of Background Music for Meal:
Bride-Father Dance Song Title and Artist:
Groom-Mother Dance Song Title and Artist:
Cake-cutting Song Title and Artist:
Last Dance Song Title and Artist:

DJ Information Sheet (continued)

DJ Style (i.e., subdued/traditional/wild & crazy):

Must-Play Song List:

Do-Not-Play Song List:

May the DJ Accept Requests?

Important Phone Numbers

Below are phone numbers you may find useful as you are planning your wedding, honeymoon, or anniversary at Walt Disney World or on the Disney Cruise Line. Space has been left for you to add your own important phone numbers.

Disney's Fairy Tale Weddings	321-566-6474
Walt Disney World Reservations	407-934-7639
Walt Disney World Dining	407-939-3463
Walt Disney World Group Dining	407-939-7700
Disney's Catered Events	321-939-7278
Walt Disney World Florist	407-827-3505
Walt Disney World Information	407-824-4321
Walt Disney World Merchandise Gift Services	407-363-6200
Walt Disney World Tours	407-939-7529
Cinderella's Royal Table Special Event Line	407-824-4477
Disney Cruise Line	800-511-1333
Disney Cruise Gifts and Amenities	800-511-1333
Disney's Honeymoon Registry	407-566-7272
Disney's Magical Express	866-599-0951
Disney Event Group Photography	407-827-5099
Disney's PhotoPass	407-934-4004
Disney Cake Hotline	407-827-2253
Grand Gatherings	407-939-6244
Orange County Courthouse	407-836-2067
Osceola County Courthouse	407-742-3530
Brevard County Clerk	321-637-5413

Contact List

Use the list below to keep all your most important phone numbers in one place. Certain contacts may need to know your resort room number on the day of your event, including vendors and members of the bridal party. Use the "Room #" column to check them off as you contact them.

Contact	Phone	Room #

Guest List

Name	Invitation Sent	Accept	Decline	Gift Description	Thank-you Note Sent

Guest List

Name	Invitation Sent	Accept	Decline	Gift Description	Thank-you Note Sent

Guest Travel Information

Make as many copies of this worksheet as you need to keep track of all your guests' travel information, including their flight numbers and method of transportation to and from Walt Disney World.

Name:	
Arrival Date:	
Time:	
Flight #:	
Transportation:	
Resort:	
Resort phone:	
Confirmation #:	
Room #:	
Departure Date:	
Time:	
Flight #:	
Transportation:	

Name:	
Arrival Date:	
Time:	
Flight #:	
Transportation:	
Resort:	
Resort phone:	
Confirmation #:	
Room #:	
Departure Date:	
Time:	
Flight #:	
Transportation:	

Event Time Line

Enter your own times and events for the big day.

Time	Event	Location	Notes

Pocket Schedules

These pocket schedules can be given to vendors, wedding party members, and anyone who needs a cheat sheet on the events of the ceremony, the reception, or the entire day. For example, you can give your videographer an overview of when important events like the first look, the sand ceremony, and cake cutting will occur. Fold along the red dotted line to make two double-sided schedules, or cut them into four single-sided schedules.

_____ Time Line

Time	Event

_____ Time Line

Time	Event

_____ Time Line

Time	Event

_____ Time Line

Time	Event

Cosmetology Information

You can print one or more copies of this page to use when comparing cosmetologists and to record your cosmetology appointment(s) for your event.

Name:	
Phone:	E-mail:
Event Date:	Arrival Time:
Rate for Bride Hair:	Makeup: Trial:
Rate for Attendants Hair:	Makeup:
Rate for Family Hair:	Makeup:
After-hours/Travel Fee:	
Trial Date:	
Deposit:	Due Date:
Balance:	Due Date:

Name:	
Phone:	E-mail:
Event Date:	Arrival Time:
Rate for Bride Hair:	Makeup: Trial:
Rate for Attendants Hair:	Makeup:
Rate for Family Hair:	Makeup:
After-hours/Travel Fee:	
Trial Date:	
Deposit:	Due Date:
Balance:	Due Date:

Photography Information

Use this as a questionnaire when interviewing photographers and to record the information for the photographer you choose.

Photographer:
Phone:
E-mail:
Years of experience:
Disney wedding experience:
Who will actually shoot event?
Will there be an assistant?
Type of equipment:
Liability insurance?
Ratio of candid to posed:
Retouching included/available?
Packages and prices:
Cost of additional hours:
Cost of digital rights:
Cost of reprints:
Payment policy:
Cancellation policy:
Proof delivery date:
Album delivery date:

Videography Information

Use this as a questionnaire when interviewing videographers and to record the information for the videographer you choose.

Videographer:
Phone:
E-mail:
Years of experience:
Disney wedding experience:
Liability insurance?
Who will actually shoot event?
When do you arrive at site?
How many manned/unmanned cameras?
Type of camera(s) and editing equipment:
Packages and prices:
A la carte services:
Cost of additional shooting/editing hours:
Finished product format (DVD, Blu-Ray, MiniDV, **etc.**):

Cost of raw footage:	Format:

Cost of additional copies:
Payment policy:
Cancellation policy:
Delivery date:

Women's Formalwear Information

Bridal Gown	
Date Ordered:	
Store/Web Site:	
Contact:	
Phone:	
Address:	
Web site:	
Designer:	
Style Number:	
Color:	
Size:	
Price:	
Arrival Date:	
First Fitting:	
Second Fitting:	

Gown	
Slip	
Crinoline/Hoop	
Lingerie	
Stockings	
Garter	
Veil/Headpiece	
Gloves	
Purse	
Shoes	
Jewelry	
Something old	
Something new	
Something borrowed	
Something blue	

	Maid/Matron of Honor	Bridesmaid	Bridesmaid
Date Ordered:			
Store/Web site:			
Contact:			
Phone:			
Address:			
Web site:			
Designer:			
Style Number:			
Color:			
Size:			
Price:			
Arrival Date:			
Fitting Date:			

Men's Formalwear Information

If you will be renting formalwear, this worksheet will help you keep track of fitting and event dates, along with everyone's sizes and styles.

Fitting Date: _____ Time: _____ Location: _____

Event Date: _____ Delivery Time: _____ Location: _____

Measurements

	Groom	Best Man	Groomsman	Groomsman
Name:				
Height:				
Weight:				
Chest:				
Coat Size:				
Waist:				
Outseam:				
Neck:				
Sleeve:				
Shoe Size:				

Style Numbers & Prices

	Groom	Groomsmen
Coat Style:		
Trouser Style:		
Shirt Style:		
Vest/Cummerbund:		
Neckwear:		
Jewelry Style:		
Shoe Style:		
Outfit Price:		

Vendor Payment Information

BRIDAL SHOP	Paid in Full ☐
Deposit:	Date Paid:
Balance:	Date Due:
COSMETOLOGIST	Paid in Full ☐
Deposit:	Date Due:
Date Sent:	Date Received:
Balance:	Date Due:
FLORIST	Paid in Full ☐
Deposit:	Date Due:
Date Sent:	Date Received:
Balance:	Date Due:
Date Sent:	Date Received:
FORMALWEAR DEALER	Paid in Full ☐
Deposit:	Date Due:
Date Sent:	Date Received:
Balance:	Date Due:
Date Sent:	Date Received:
GOWN STEAMER	Paid in Full ☐
Fee:	Date Due/Paid:
OFFICIANT	Paid in Full ☐
Fee:	Date Due:
Date Sent:	Date Received:
PHOTOGRAPHER	Paid in Full ☐
Deposit:	Date Due:
Date Sent:	Date Received:
Balance:	Date Due:
Date Sent:	Date Received:
VIDEOGRAPHER	Paid in Full ☐
Deposit:	Date Due:
Date Sent:	Date Received:
Balance:	Date Due:
Date Sent:	Date Received:

Tips Budget Worksheet

Use this chart to anticipate the tips you expect to offer to the various vendors who assist you on the day of your event. Make note of minimum and maximum amounts you plan to tip before you go (your budget) and the actual tip amounts paid by your designated tipper (your expense record). Note that business owners and officiants who charge a fee are not usually tipped.

	Minimum	Maximum	Actual Tips
Cosmetology:			
DJ & Musicians:			
Gown Steaming:			
Officiant:			
Photo Assistant:			
Transportation:			
Video Assistant:			
Others:			
Total Amounts:			

Welcome Bag Worksheet

If you will be making welcome bags for your guests, this page will help you gather ideas for their contents and check items off as you acquire them. If you plan to leave the bags at the front desk of each guest's resort, be sure to include the following information on each bag: name on the reservation, arrival date, and reservation number.

# of Adult Bags:	# of Kids' Bags:
Adult Bag Items	**Kids' Bag Items**

Packing/Shipping Worksheet

For each category, fill in the wedding-related items you want to pack or ship (put the quantity of each item in the **#** column). Put a check mark in the **$** column for any items that need to be purchased. As you pack the item, put a check mark in the **✔**column and note the bag or box you packed it in.

Items to Pack	#	$	✔	Bag

Items to Ship	#	$	✔	Box

DFTW Contract Items To Do

Tasks	To Do	Done

Travel Planning To Do

Tasks	To Do	Done

Attire To Do

Tasks	To Do	Done

Music To Do

Tasks	To Do	Done

License/Officiant To Do

Tasks	To Do	Done

Photography/Videography To Do

Tasks	To Do	Done

Ceremony To Do

Tasks	To Do	Done

Cocktail Hour & Reception To Do

Tasks	To Do	Done

Dessert Party To Do

Tasks	To Do	Done

Favors/Gifts To Do

Tasks	To Do	Done

Miscellaneous To Do

Tasks	To Do	Done

Miscellaneous To Do

Tasks	To Do	Done

One Month or More Before I Leave

Tasks	To Do	Done

One Week Before I Leave

Tasks	To Do	Done

One Day Before I Leave

Tasks	To Do	Done

Just Before I Leave

Tasks	To Do	Done

❧Ideas❧

❧Inspiration❧

30% Discount Coupon

Save 30% off <u>any</u> PassPorter guidebook (*see below for title list*) when you order direct from the publisher!

How to order a PassPorter at your 30% discount:
1. Visit http://www.passporterstore.com/store to view our guidebooks and place an order (type in this discount code during checkout: speedplanner).
2. Call us toll-free at <u>877-WAYFARER</u> (that's 1-877-929-3273) and mention the "weddings" code when placing your order.

This offer valid only for direct book sales through PassPorter Travel Press, an imprint of MediaMarx, Inc. Offer not valid in bookstores. Cannot be combined with other discounts. Discount code: weddings

Partial PassPorter Title List

All of the following titles are eligible for your 30% discount!

PassPorter's Walt Disney World—The unique travel guide, planner, organizer, journal, and keepsake! (spiral, deluxe starter kit, and refill kit)

PassPorter's Disney 500—A tried-and-true collection of more than 500 tips for Walt Disney World trips (paperback)

PassPorter's Disney Vacation Club—Tips for members and members-to-be, filled with practial information! (paperback)

PassPorter's Open Mouse for Walt Disney World—Easy-Access Trips for Travelers With Extra Challenges. Covers virtually every special challenge! (paperback)

PassPorter's Disney Cruise Line and Its Ports of Call—The take-along travel guide and planner. The most comprehensive guide to Disney cruising! (paperback)

PassPorter's Disney Cruise Clues—A tried-and-true collection of more than 250 tips for Disney Cruise Line vacations. (paperback)

PassPorter's Disneyland Resort and Southern California Attractions—The unique travel guide, planner, organizer, journal, and keepsake! (spiral, deluxe starter kit, and refill kit)

PassPorter's Treasure Hunts at Walt Disney World—Discover what everyone else is missing with more than 100+ hunts for a variety of ages and skills (paperback)

More information about PassPorter's innovative guidebooks and descriptions of each of the above titles are on the following pages.

PassPorter's Club

Do you want more help planning your Disney vacation? Join the PassPorter's Club and get all these benefits:

✔ "All-you-can-read" access to EVERY e-book we publish (12 titles at press time). PassPorter's Club passholders also get early access to these e-books before the general public. New e-books are added on a regular basis, too.

✔ Interactive, customizable "e-worksheets" to help make your trip planning easier, faster, and smoother. These are the electronic, interactive worksheets we've been mentioning throughout this book. The worksheets are in PDF format and can be printed for a truly personalized approach! We have more than 50 worksheets, with more on the way. You can see a sample e-worksheet to the right.

✔ Access to super-sized "e-photos" in the PassPorter Photo Archives—photos can be zoomed in up to 25 times larger than standard web photos. You can use these e-photos to see detail as if you're actually standing there—or use them for desktop wallpaper, scrapbooking, whatever!

✔ Our best discount on print guidebooks ... 35% off!

There's more features, too! For a full list of features and current e-books, e-worksheets, and e-photos, visit http://www.passporter.com/club. You can also take a peek inside the Club's Gallery at http://www.passporterboards.com/forums/passporters-club-gallery. The Gallery is open to everyone—it contains two FREE interactive e-worksheets to try out!

Price: A PassPorter's Club pass is currently $4.95/month, or the cost of just one e-book!

How to Get Your Pass to the PassPorter's Club

Step 1. Get a free community account. Register simply and quickly at http://www.passporterboards.com/forums/register.php.

Step 2. Log in at http://www.passporterboards.com/forums/login.php using the Member Name and password you created in step 1.

Step 3. Get your pass. Select the type of pass you'd like and follow the directions to activate it immediately. We currently offer monthly and annual passes. (Annual passes save 25% and get extra perks!)

Questions? Assistance? We're here to help! Please send e-mail to club@passporter.com.

You may also find many of your questions answered in our FAQ (Frequently Asked Questions) in the Gallery forum (see link above).

What Is PassPorter?

PassPorters are unique, all-in-one travel guides that offer comprehensive, expert advice and innovative planning systems. Many of our guidebooks feature built-in worksheets and organizer "PassPockets." The PassPockets help you organize your vacation by building trip itineraries on the front before you go, storing maps, passes, and receipts inside while you're there, recording memories and expenses on the back to enjoy when you return.

PassPorter Walt Disney World Resort

It all started with Walt Disney World (and a mouse)! Our general Walt Disney World guidebook covers everything you need to plan a practically perfect vacation, including fold-out park maps; full-color photos and charts; resort room layout diagrams; KidTips; descriptions, reviews, and ratings for the resorts, parks, attractions, and restaurants; and much more!

This edition also includes 14 organizer pockets you can use to plan your trip before you go, hold papers while you're there, and record your memories for when you return. The PassPockets are our readers' #1 favorite feature because they make planning, organizing, and capturing your vacation very easy.

Learn more and order at http://www.passporter.com, or get a copy at your favorite bookstore. Our Walt Disney World guide is available in a spiral-bound edition, and a Deluxe Edition in a ring binder with interior pockets is also available—see the next page.

Don't take our word for it—ask others what they think of PassPorter. Here's a letter we recently received (printed with permission). If we show it in small type, does that mean we aren't tooting our horn so loudly? Sorry, we're really shameless promoters!

Listen, I'm not well organized. OK, that's an understatement. I'm a mess. I don't plan either. I'm more fly by the seat of my pants. However, 6 years ago on my honeymoon, my husband and I wandered aimlessly around Disney World and didn't get to see half the stuff we wanted and didn't even know about the other half.

So, my first trip with my daughter would have to be different. I found the boards at http://www.disboards.com and asked what book I needed to buy. Most everyone suggested yours. "What would I do with pockets?" I asked myself.

Through the planning stages, I found myself furiously writing different phone numbers, confirmation numbers, and other important information into my Passporter. I stuffed all kinds of information and plans into those pockets.

When we got to Disney, my husband could not believe how organized I was. Check-ins were a breeze. I had all the information I needed at my fingertips. I think his mouth was hanging open at one point.

He'd say, "What's on the agenda for today?" And I'd whip out my book and tell him.

I had touring plans so we knew exactly where to go when. The lady at the Rainforest Café could not believe I had all my info right there for her. I think she thought I am always that organized. (Can you make a Passporter for my regular life?)

My vacation could not have gone any smoother and I owe it all to you!

Thanks so much,
Sydonie Davis

More PassPorters

You've asked for more PassPorters—we've listened! We have four PassPorter print books and ten e-books (and growing), all designed to make your Disney vacation the best it can be. And if you've wished for a PassPorter with all the flexibility and features of a daily planner, check out our Deluxe Editions (described below). To learn more about the new PassPorters and get release dates, please visit us at http://www.passporter.com.

PassPorter's Walt Disney World Deluxe Edition

Design first-class vacations with this loose-leaf ring binder edition. The Deluxe Edition features the same great content as *PassPorter's Walt Disney World* spiral guide. Special features of the Deluxe Edition include ten interior storage slots in the binder to hold guidemaps, ID cards, and a pen (we even include a pen). The Deluxe PassPorter binder makes it really easy to add, remove, and rearrange pages ... you can even download, print, and add in updates, feature articles, and supplemental pages from our web site, and refills are available for purchase. Learn more at http://www.passporter.com/wdw/deluxe. htm. The Deluxe Edition is available through bookstores by special order—the ISBN is 978-1-58771-083-4 (2011 Deluxe Edition), or search for the latest edition.

PassPorter's Disney Cruise Line and its Ports of Call
Updated annually! Get your cruise plans in shipshape with our updated, award-winning field guide ... includes details on all new ports and the new ships to come!

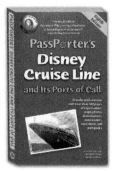

Authors Jennifer and Dave Marx cover the Disney Cruise Line in incredible detail, including deck plans, stateroom floor plans, original photos, menus, entertainment guides, port/shore excursion details, and plenty of worksheets to help you budget, plan, and record your information. We also include reader tips, photos, and magial memories! In its ninth edition in 2011, this is the original and most comprehensive guidebook devoted to the Disney Cruise Line! Learn more and order your copy at http://www.passporter.com/dcl or get a copy at your favorite bookstore. ISBN for the eighth edition paperback, no PassPockets is 978-1-58771-079-7. Also available in a Deluxe Edition with organizer PassPockets (ISBN: 978-1-58771-080-3).

Even More PassPorters

PassPorter's Disneyland Resort and Southern California Attractions— Second Edition

PassPorter tours the park that started it all in this updated book! California's Disneyland, Disney's California Adventure, and Downtown Disney get PassPorter's expert treatment, and we throw in Hollywood and Downtown Los Angeles, San Diego, SeaWorld, the San Diego Zoo and Wild Animal Park, LEGOLAND, and Six Flags Magic Mountain. All this, and PassPorter's famous PassPockets and planning features. Our second edition follows the same format as the 2010 edition of PassPorter's Walt Disney World, complete with glossy, full-color pages, tons of photos from your authors and fellow readers, and plenty of brand-new pages! We een include the special photo supplement at the end to get you in the mood for our California

vacation. Whether you're making the pilgrimage to Disneyland for a big celebration or planning a classic Southern California family vacation, you can't miss. Learn more at http://www.passporter.com/dl, or pick it up at your favorite bookstore (ISBN: 978-1-58771-042-1). This guidebook is also available as a Deluxe Edition in a padded, six-ring binder (ISBN: 978-1-58771-043-8).

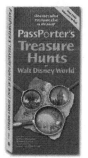

PassPorter's Treasure Hunts at Walt Disney World

Have even more fun at Walt Disney World! Jennifer and Dave's treasure hunts have long been a favorite part of PassPorter reader gatherings at Walt Disney World, and now you can join in the fun. Gain a whole new appreciation of Disney's fabulous attention to detail as you search through the parks and resorts for the little (and big) things that you may never have noticed before. Great for individuals, families, and groups, with hunts for people of all ages and levels of Disney knowledge. Special, "secure" answer pages make sure nobody can cheat. Learn more, see sample hunts, and order your copy at http://www.passporter.com/hunts or get a copy at your favorite bookstore (ISBN: 978-1-58771-026-1).

PassPorter E-Books

We have many e-books that cover narrower topics in delightful depth! See all the details at http://www.passporterstore.com/store/ebooks.aspx. And watch for select e-books to make it into print in the near future.

PassPorter E-Books

Looking for more in-depth coverage on specific topics? Look no further than PassPorter E-Books! Our e-books are inexpensive (from $5.95–$8.95) and available immediately as a download on your computer (Adobe PDF format). If you prefer your books printed, we have options for that, too! And unlike most e-books, ours are fully formatted just like a regular PassPorter print book. A PassPorter e-book will even fit into a Deluxe PassPorter Binder, if you have one. We offer 12 e-books, at press time, and have plans for many, many more!

PassPorter's Disney 500: *Fast Tips for Walt Disney World Trips*
Our most popular e-book has more than 500 time-tested Walt Disney World tips—all categorized and coded! We chose the best of our reader-submitted tips over a six-year period for this e-book and each has been edited by author Jennifer Marx. For more details, a list of tips, and a sample page, visit http://www.passporter.com/wdw/disney500.asp.

PassPorter's Cruise Clues: *First-Class Tips for Disney Cruise Trips*
Get the best tips for the Disney Cruise Line—all categorized and coded—as well as cruise line comparisons, a teen perspective, and ultimate packing lists! This popular e-book is packed with 250 cruiser-tested tips—all edited by award-winning author Jennifer Marx. Visit http://www.passporter.com/dcl/cruiseclues.asp.

PassPorter's Disney Character Yearbook
A 268-page compendium of all the live Disney characters you can find at Walt Disney World, Disneyland, and on the Disney Cruise Line. Also includes tips on finding, meeting, photographing, and getting autographs, plus a customizable autograph book to print! Visit http://www.passporter.com/disney-character-yearbook.asp.

PassPorter's Disney Speed Planner: *The Easy Ten-Step Program*
A fast, easy method for planning practically perfect vacations—great for busy people or those who don't have lots of time to plan. Follow this simple, ten-step plan to help you get your vacation planned in short order so you can get on with your life. It's like a having an experienced friend show you the ropes—and have fun doing it! Visit http://www.passporter.com/wdw/speedplanner.asp.

PassPorter's Free-Book
A Guide to Free and Low-Cost Activities at Walt Disney World
It's hard to believe anything is free at Walt Disney World, but there are actually a number of things you can get or do for little to no cost. This e-book documents more than 150 free or cheap things to do before you go and after you arrive. Visit http://www.passporter.com/wdw/free-book.asp.

PassPorter's Sidekick for the Walt Disney World Guidebook
An interactive collection of worksheets, journal pages, and charts
This is a customizable companion to our general Walt Disney World guidebook—you can personalize worksheets, journals, luggage tags, and charts, plus click links to all the URLs in the guidebook and get transportation pages for all points within Walt Disney World! Details at http://www.passporter.com/wdw/sidekick.asp.

PassPorter's Festivals and Celebrations
at Walt Disney World
Get in on all the fun in this updated 78-page overview of all the wonderful and magical festivals, celebrations, parties, and holidays at Walt Disney World. Included are beautiful color photos and tips on maximizing your experience at the festivals and celebrations. Read more and see a sample page at http://www. passporter.com/wdw/festivals-celebrations.asp. Placeholder text.

PassPorter's Answer Book
Get answers to the most popular topics asked about Walt Disney World, Disneyland, Disney Cruise Line, and general travel. You've asked it, we've answered it! The e-book's questions and answers are sorted geographically and topically. The e-book is authored by our amazing PassPorter Guide Team, who have heaps of experience at answering your questions! Details at http://www.passporter. com/answer-book.asp.

PassPorter's Disney Weddings & Honeymoons
This is both a guidebook and a bridal organizer tailored to the unique requirements of planning a wedding, vow renewal, or commitment ceremony at Walt Disney World or on the Disney Cruise Line. It will take you through the entire process, outline your options, offer valuable tips, organize your information, and help you plan your event down to the last detail! Details at http://www. passporter.com/weddings.asp.

PassPorter's Disney Vacation Club Guide
A 170-page in-depth guide to all aspects of the Disney Vacation Club, from deciding whether to join to deciding where and when to use your points. Included are beautiful color photos and tips on maximizing your experience. If you've ever wondered what the club is all about or wanted to learn more, this is the perfect introduction. Visit http://www.passporter.com/disney-vacation-club.asp.

Learn more about these and other titles and order e-books at:
http://www.passporterstore.com/store/ebooks.aspx

Register Your PassPorter

We are <u>very</u> interested to learn how your vacation went and what you think of the PassPorter, how it worked (or didn't work) for you, and your opinion on how we could improve it! We encourage you to register your copy of PassPorter with us—in return for your feedback, we'll send you **two valuable coupons** good for discounts on PassPorters and PassHolder pouches when purchased directly from us. You can register your copy of PassPorter at http://www.passporter.com/register.asp, or you can send us a postcard or letter to P.O. Box 3880, Ann Arbor, Michigan 48106.

Report a Correction or Change

Keeping up with the changes at Walt Disney World is virtually impossible without your help. When you notice something is different than what is printed in PassPorter, or you just come across something you'd like to see us cover, please let us know! You can report your news, updates, changes, corrections, and even rumors (everything helps!) at http://www.passporter.com/report.asp.

Contribute to the Next Edition

You can become an important part of future editions of PassPorter! The easiest way is to rate the resorts, rides, and/or eateries at http://www.passporter.com/wdw/rate.htm. Your ratings and comments become part of our reader ratings throughout the book and help future readers make travel decisions. Want to get more involved? Send us a vacation tip or magical memory—if we use it in a future edition of PassPorter, we'll credit you by name in the guidebook and send you a free copy of the edition!

Get Your Questions Answered

We love to hear from you! Alas, due to the thousands of e-mails and hundreds of phone calls we receive each week we cannot offer personalized advice to all our readers. But there's a great way to get your questions answered: ask your fellow readers! Visit our message boards at http://www.passporterboards.com, join for free, and post your question. In most cases, fellow readers and Disney fans will offer their ideas and experiences! Our message boards also function as an ultimate list of frequently asked questions. Just browsing through to see the answers to other readers questions will reap untold benefit! This is also a great way to make friends and have fun while planning your vacation. But be careful—our message boards can be addictive!

PassPorter Online

A wonderful way to get the most from your PassPorter is to visit our active web site at http://www.passporter.com. We serve up valuable PassPorter updates, plus useful Walt Disney World information and advice we couldn't jam into our book. You can swap tales (that's t-a-l-e-s, Mickey!) with fellow Disney fans, play contests and games, find links to other sites, get plenty of details, and ask us questions. You can also order PassPorters and shop for PassPorter accessories and travel gear! The latest information on new PassPorters to other destinations is available on our web site as well.

PassPorter Web Sites	Address (URL)
Main Page: PassPorter Online	http://www.passporter.com
Walt Disney World Forum	http://www.passporter.com/wdw
PassPorter Posts Message Boards	http://www.passporterboards.com
Book Updates	http://www.passporter.com/customs/bookupdates.htm
Rate the Rides, Resorts, Restaurants	http://www.passporter.com/wdw/rate.htm
Register Your PassPorter	http://www.passporter.com/register.asp
PassPorter Deluxe Edition Information	http://www.passporter.com/wdw/deluxe.htm

About The PassPorter Series

PassPorter guidebooks are **independently published** by a family-owned and family-run small business. As journalists, we strive to present accurate information with a fair and balanced viewpoint. Our books are "unofficial," meaning we can call it as we see it.

We travel as our readers do. Although we enlist the help of local experts who live and breathe our destinations, we fly or drive long distances from our home bases, and stay in the hotels, giving us a perspective that no "local" can possess. We make all our own reservations and arrangements, sometimes with the help of a travel agent, but mostly we "shop direct." We pay our own way, so we're always looking for the best deal. We buy our own admission, pay for all our excursions, tours, and add-ons. We make our reservations through normal channels—no VIP treatment, no media discounts or freebies. We need to know that our experience will be like yours and hasn't been enhanced for the sake of a better review. While we may be invited to visit a hotel, restaurant, or attraction as members of the media, we do not use those visits to evaluate matters like quality of service or level of amenities offered, as regular guests may not receive quite the same treatment.

PassPorter guidebooks are truly a community effort. Through our PassPorter.com web site, message board community, PassPorter News weekly e-newsletter, and many face-to-face encounters, we interact with you, our readers, year-round. Whether or not we join a particular discussion, we're always watching the message boards to see what's important to you, and we're thinking of how we can better address those issues in our books. You contribute in so many ways! These pages are filled with your tips and photos, and your suggestions and questions over the years have led to improvements large and small. Your reports on our message board make you our field researchers, witnessing and experiencing far more than we could ever manage on our own. Dozens of you, as Peer Reviewers, pore over each manuscript, and each manages to uncover items to be updated, clarified, or fixed that nobody else has managed to find. Few publishers, in any field, subject their manuscripts to this level of scrutiny. Unlike many travel books, which, once printed, are set aside until it's time to produce the next edition, we're immersed in our topic 365 days a year, following the news and rumors, and keeping in constant touch with you.

All of this makes PassPorter a uniquely interactive guidebook. Together, we've created what we like to think of as "book 2.0" and we're proud to be innovators of a new generation of guidebooks that encourage collaboration. Here are some of the special interactive features in this edition:

PassPorter Photos: We truly believe that a picture tells a thousand words, and we include photos in the book whenever we can! The majority of these photos were contributed by our amazing readers, as we feel a wider range of perspective makes a better guidebook. All of the photos were hand-picked from our vast collections and the online PassPorter Photo Archive. The photos do not appear to their best advantage in black and white, as they are printed in this guidebook, however. We encourage you to go online to http://www.passporter.com/photos to view tens of thousands of photos in glorious color.

PassPorter Articles: You just can't fit everything in a guidebook, so when we have more to tell you, we lead you to a web address or article online. You'll find many more PassPorter articles at http://www.passporter.com/articles.